Resistance and Transitional Justice

Despite a more reflective concern over the past 20 years with marginalised voices, justice from below, power relations and the legitimacy of mechanisms and processes, scholarship on transitional justice has remained relatively silent on the question of 'resistance'. In response, this book asks what can be learnt by engaging with resistance to transitional justice not just as a problem of process, but as a necessary element of transitional justice. Drawing on literatures about resistance from geography and anthropology, it is the social act of labelling resistance, along with its subjective nature, that is addressed here as part of the political, economic, social and cultural contexts in which transitional justice processes unfold. Working through three cases – Côte d'Ivoire, Burundi and Cambodia – each chapter of the book addresses a different form or meaning of resistance, from the vantage point of multiple actors. As such, each chapter adds a different element to an overall argument that disrupts the norm/deviancy dichotomy that has so far characterised the limited work on resistance and transitional justice. Together, the chapters of the book develop cross-cutting themes that elaborate an overall argument for considering resistance to transitional justice as a subjective element of a political process, rather than as a problem of implementation.

Briony Jones is an Assistant Professor in the Politics and International Studies department of the University of Warwick, UK, and a Senior Researcher at swisspeace, an associate research institute of the University of Basel, Switzerland.

Julie Bernath is a Senior Researcher and Programme Officer in the Dealing with the Past Program at swisspeace, an associate research institute of the University of Basel, Switzerland.

Transitional Justice
Series Editor: Kieran McEvoy
Queen's University Belfast

The study of justice in transition has emerged as one of the most diverse and intellectually exciting developments in the social sciences. From its origins in human rights activism and comparative political science, the field is increasingly characterised by its geographic and disciplinary breadth. This series aims to publish the most innovative scholarship from a range of disciplines working on transitional justice-related topics, including law, sociology, criminology, psychology, anthropology, political science, development studies and international relations.

Titles in this series:

Violence, Law and the Impossibility of Transitional Justice
Catherine Turner

Transitional Justice and the Politics of Inscription
Memory, Space and Narrative in Northern Ireland
Joseph Robinson

Resistance and Transitional Justice
Edited by Briony Jones and Julie Bernath

The Reparative Effects of Human Rights Trials
Lessons from Argentina
Rosario Figari Layus

Amnesties, Pardons and Transitional Justice
Spain's Pact of Forgetting
Roldán Jimeno

Rape, Sexual Violence and Transitional Justice Challenges
Lessons from Bosnia-Herzegovina
Janine Natalya Clark

Resistance and Transitional Justice

Edited by
Briony Jones and Julie Bernath

Routledge
Taylor & Francis Group
LONDON AND NEW YORK

First published 2018
by Routledge

2 Park Square, Milton Park, Abingdon, Oxfordshire OX14 4RN
52 Vanderbilt Avenue, New York, NY 10017

Routledge is an imprint of the Taylor & Francis Group, an Informa business

First issued in paperback 2019

British Library Cataloguing in Publication Data
A catalogue record for this book is available from the British Library

Library of Congress Cataloging in Publication Data
Names: Jones, Briony, editor. | Bernath, Julie, editor.
Title: Resistance and transitional justice / edited by Dr. Briony Jones and Dr. Julie Bernath.
Description: First edition. | Abingdon, Oxon [UK] ; New York : Routledge, 2017. | Series: Transitional justice | Includes index.
Identifiers: LCCN 2017002079 | ISBN 9780415785044 (hbk) | ISBN 9781315228341 (ebk)
Subjects: LCSH: Transitional justice. | Reparation (Criminal justice) | Genocide. | Reparations for historical injustices.
Classification: LCC K5250. R47 2017 | DDC 340/.115—dc23
LC record available at https://lccn.loc.gov/2017002079

ISBN: 978-0-415-78504-4 (hbk)
ISBN: 978-0-367-23223-8 (pbk)

Typeset in Baskerville
by Keystroke, Neville Lodge, Tettenhall, Wolverhampton

Contents

Acknowledgements

This book is the outcome of an exchange between scholars working in the global south and the global north on critical approaches to transitional justice. It is based on the research project 'Resistance to transitional justice? Alternative visions of peace and justice' carried out at swisspeace, an associate institute of the University of Basel, from 2012 to 2015, with a focus on the three case studies of Côte d'Ivoire, Burundi and Cambodia. This research project was generously funded by the Swiss National Science Foundation.

We warmly thank all authors of this edited volume for their contributions and for their work through several rounds of reviews. We extend our thanks to the editorial team at Routledge for their kind and helpful assistance in the process of preparing this book for publication. We also thank the two anonymous reviewers at Routledge for their constructive comments on the initial book proposal and manuscript.

Finally, we are greatly indebted to all respondents who took their valuable time to meet us during our research and who shared their insights, experiences and perspectives, thereby making this publication possible.

Briony Jones and Julie Bernath

Contributors

Julie Bernath is a senior researcher and programme officer in the Dealing with the Past Program at swisspeace, an associate research institute of the University of Basel. Her research specialisms include the politics of transitional justice, victim participation in transitional justice processes and dealing with the past in Cambodia. She has written her PhD thesis on resistances to transitional justice at the Extraordinary Chambers in the Courts of Cambodia (ECCC). Before joining swisspeace in 2012, she worked in the Public Affairs Section of the ECCC. She holds a PhD in political science from the University of Basel, Switzerland, and a MA in political science from the Institut d'Études Politiques in Paris, France (2011).

Gérard Birantamije holds a PhD in political and social sciences from the Université Libre de Bruxelles. From 2014 to 2016, he was a lecturer and Quality Assurance Director at Université du Lac Tanganyika in Burundi. Birantamije's research focuses on issues of security sector reform, governance and peacebuilding policies in the Great Lakes Region. He has recently published several chapters in books, including 'The University of Burundi and student organizations: Governance system, political development and student representation' in *Student Politics in Africa: Representation and Activism* (edited by Thierry M Luescher, Manja Klemenčič and James Otieno Jowi, 2016), as well as articles in scholarly journals such as 'Sending peacekeepers abroad, sharing power at home: Burundi in Somalia' (with Nina Wilén and David Ambrosetti) in the *Journal of Eastern African Studies* (2015). He is currently a post-doctoral research fellow at Université Saint Louis-Brussels in Belgium.

Adou Djané Dit Fatogoma obtained his PhD in sociology from the University of Abidjan Cocody, Côte d'Ivoire in 2013. His research expertise mainly includes governance; transitional justice; statehood; peacebuilding; humanitarian actions studies; politics of environment; and health. He has conducted fieldwork on Côte d'Ivoire for the research project 'Resistance to Transitional Justice?' financed by the Swiss National Science Foundation and carried out by swisspeace (2014–2015). He has also conducted field research on the dynamics of humanitarian action in Côte d'Ivoire for the French Red Cross and the

Institute of Research on Development (2014–2015); and on the interlinkages between large-scale development investments and local peacebuilding in western Côte d'Ivoire with the Institute of Development Studies of the University of Sussex (2015). He was a Swiss Government Excellence Postdoctoral scholarship holder (2015–2016). He is currently a research associate at the Swiss Centre of Scientific Research, Côte d'Ivoire and swisspeace, Switzerland.

Briony Jones is an assistant professor in the Politics and International Studies department of the University of Warwick and a senior researcher at swisspeace, an associate research institute of the University of Basel. She has previously held positions at the University of Manchester and the University of East London and has been specialising in transitional justice since 2003. Her research specialisms also include citizenship, the politics of intervention in transition contexts, education, peacebuilding and qualitative methodologies. She was a founding member of Oxford Transitional Justice Research and is currently leading a three-year research project on the politics of knowledge production in transitional justice funded by the Swiss National Science Foundation and the Swiss Agency for Development and Cooperation.

Kosal Path is an assistant professor of political science at Brooklyn College, The City University of New York. He was a researcher at Yale University's Cambodian Genocide Program from 1995 to 1997. He served as deputy director of the Documentation Center of Cambodia from 1997 to 2000. During this period, he was involved in documenting the atrocities committed by the Khmer Rouge regime between 1975 and 1979.

Sandra Rubli is an independent researcher. She graduated in political science with a master's degree from the University of Bern and with a PhD from the University of Basel. Between 2006 and 2014 she worked for swisspeace as a researcher and programme officer in the conflict early warning programme (FAST), the competency centre for peacebuilding (KOFF) and the Dealing with the Past department. Her research focuses on transitional justice and state-formation issues in Burundi. Since 2014, she has been working for the Civil Peace Service, a programme of GIZ Burundi, as a technical adviser on transitional justice.

Chapter 1

Introduction: resistance and transitional justice

Briony Jones and Julie Bernath

From a narrow focus on individual criminal accountability in the aftermath of the Second World War, the field of transitional justice has expanded to encompass increasingly diverse processes and mechanisms, aiming at achieving ambitious goals such as reconciliation, healing, justice, peace and democracy. Today, transitional justice has become established as a policy response designed to address human rights violations of the past in the aftermath of civil war, authoritarian regimes or occupation, whilst it is also mobilised in contexts that are not undergoing political transitions.

Along with the expansion and institutionalisation of the field of transitional justice, critical scholarship has increasingly highlighted the ways in which transitional justice processes are inherently political. Transitional justice can be analysed as a political process of negotiation between a set of diverse actors, including conflict parties, mediators, newly constituted governments, donor countries, intergovernmental organisations, civil society and victim groups. Transitional justice processes are the manifestation of the ability of these actors to determine the way in which dealing with a past of mass human rights violations becomes conceived, designed and enacted in a specific context. As such, transitional justice is never neutral or simply refers to a set of technical measures but, rather, necessarily prioritises certain practices, discourses and actors over others.

If we take this conceptual starting point that transitional justice is a political process, we can then expect resistance to be an inherent part of the empirical unfolding of transitional justice processes. And indeed, over the past two decades, critical scholarship on transitional justice has suggested the lines along which disagreements over the terms of transitional justice processes might emerge. In works on the everyday, for instance, scholars have highlighted the existing frictions between the local, national and global spheres that include 'the possibility of embracing and reworking transitional justice processes but also of avoiding, protesting against or rejecting them' (Riaño Alcalá and Baines 2012: 385; see also Kent 2011).

Disagreements might then surface as a result of the disconnectedness between internationally driven transitional justice processes and local realities (Shaw and Waldorf 2010; McEvoy and McGregor 2008; Pouligny 2005). It may also result from the embeddedness of transitional justice policies in the undemocratic status quo of world governance (Kagoro 2012; An-Na'im 2013) or in unequal power relations between different social and political groups at the national level (see e.g. Robins 2012). Finally, contestations may also stem from the ways in which transitional justice interventions lack transformative effects and do not address the root causes of conflicts (Mani 2008; Nagy 2013) or embody compromises and regulated politics in the context of failed revolutionary movements (Mullin and Patel 2016).

However, despite this more reflective scholarship in the last 20 years concerned with marginalised voices, justice from below, power relations and the legitimacy of mechanisms and processes, transitional justice scholarship has not often explicitly mobilised resistance as a concept. This is surprising since critical peace scholarship, which has been driven by a similar concern with the legitimacy of international peacebuilding interventions and their interactions with local contexts, actors and perceptions, has engaged with the idea of resistance (see e.g. Richmond 2010; Distler and Riese 2013). Resistance in particular features as an integral component of typologies of the hybrid peace (MacGinty 2011).

There are also only a few works specifically dedicated to analysing the empirical manifestations of resistance to transitional justice, i.e. analysing what resistance means for those who resist, why they might resist and what happens when they do. When resistance has actually been part of the academic discussions, it has come with a series of assumptions, which we will turn to in more detail in the next section. Whilst there are important exceptions (Thomson 2011; Brudholm and Rosoux 2009; Hamber and Wilson 2002) resistance often remains mainly associated with powerful spoilers who have something to lose in the transitional justice process. As such, resistance becomes cast as necessarily problematic and as something which has to be addressed in order for transitional justice processes to function smoothly and effectively. These assumptions, we argue, do not account for the political nature of transitional justice processes nor the empirical breadth of resistances to these processes.

This is a missed opportunity because researching resistance to transitional justice is key to understanding the legitimacy of these processes, the agency of the different actors involved and the diversity in systems of belief and imageries of peace, justice and political order. The study of resistance can enrich our understanding of the politics of transitional justice processes. This edited volume aims to address this limited conceptual and empirical understanding of resistance to transitional justice. It is based on the Swiss National Science Foundation funded research project 'Resistance to Transitional Justice? Alternative Visions of Peace and Justice' carried out at swisspeace, an associate institute of the University of Basel, from 2012 to 2015, with a focus on the three case studies of Côte d'Ivoire, Burundi and Cambodia.

Specifically, this book asks what we can learn if we engage with resistance to transitional justice not as a problem of process but as a necessary element in the empirical unfolding of transitional justice. This volume develops a unique approach to resistance to transitional justice. Resistance is defined by the subjective position of the actor who is resisting or labelling an act as resistance. Moreover, rather than departing from the norm of transitional justice in order to measure and explain resistance, the authors in this volume always take resistance as the conceptual and empirical starting point of their analysis. This allows us to engage with the multiple meanings with which transitional justice processes are endowed by diverse actors and to understand how these processes are embedded in longer-term political struggles and ongoing contestations over the nature and values of societies following periods of massive human rights violations.

In the next section of this introductory chapter, we review the existing literature on resistance to transitional justice. We then present in more detail our approach to resistance, before introducing the cases and methodology of this volume and providing an outline of the following chapters.

Resistance and transitional justice

Whilst the field of transitional justice has not yet comprehensively engaged with the subject of resistance, the limited scholarship that exists on resistance and transitional justice casts resistance in a particular light and assumes a certain set of motivations, objects and actors of resistance. This scholarship, we argue, tends to be concerned with the 'spoilerism' or 'deviancy' of those unwilling to accept transitional justice processes. This stems from the assumption that transitional justice is a moral 'good', i.e. that transitional justice is inherently positive and in the pursuit of unquestionable normative goals, such as justice, peace and democracy. It attributes a specific set of agency and normative values to the international and local actors involved in transitional justice processes, portraying on the one hand international actors as apolitical actors who are dedicated to 'doing good' and, on the other hand, local actors who might engage with transitional justice because of external pressures but will either try to subvert and block it or will remain unsatisfied by it. From this perspective, resistance then mainly becomes a question of implementation rather than politics.

Resistance is primarily associated with a first set of specific actors: those who have something to lose in the transition. This refers to the former political elite or the 'old-regime loyalists' (Subotić 2014: 135) who were involved in massive human rights violations, but also the direct perpetrators of violence, especially those who enjoy access to power and resources in the new government. The assumption is that these actors will oppose transitional justice processes out of fear of prosecution and in order to maintain their positions of power, legitimacy and access to resources. Resistance is then located beyond visible acts of blockages. It is assumed to take invisible forms and to be enacted behind closed doors through various stratagems during the negotiations not only for the establishment of transitional justice processes but also for their implementation. Thus, resistance becomes something static; it is assumed to be planned, strategic and seemingly enacted by a homogeneous group of actors.

Resistance is further associated with those social groups who benefited from a regime involved in serious human rights violations. Researching reconciliation in Australia, Jacobs (1997: 218, 208) has for instance shown how the projects of the Council for Aboriginal Reconciliation led parts of the 'most powerful sections of societies' to claim that they were the ones whose rights were being denied, since

'Aborigines now have too much – too much of the nation's history, too much land, too many special rights and services'. Some scholars also identify the traditional providers of justice, including state actors, as potentially resisting transitional justice processes. Since transitional justice corresponds to extensive interventions that deploy external actors in what is cast as an 'extraordinary' provision of justice in the aftermath of mass human rights violations, the usual justice providers may perceive transitional justice processes as 'incursions upon their sources of legitimacy, income and power' (Sriram 2012: 63).

The motivation ascribed to these actors for their resistance is thus again the fear that the transitional justice processes might rearrange power to their detriment and proceed to their delegitimisation in the new political order. The success of transitional justice processes and, in particular, international criminal justice, is thus perceived to be mainly dependent on the extent to which 'spoiler' resistance may be overcome. This is, for instance, what Hansen argues in the case of Kenya (2014: 119): 'the success of international justice may ultimately depend on whether the [International Criminal] Court itself and members of the international community adopt strategies that can circumvent the resistance in the national political leadership'.

In addition to this first set of actors, there is a sense in transitional justice scholarship that resistance is also staged by those who are not ready to compromise in times of transition and to accept that the justice achieved in these contexts does not correspond to one's ideal of justice but, rather symptomatically, reflects the context of transition in which it takes place. This type of resistance is most starkly associated with those victims who remain relentless in their demands for justice and unsatisfied by the transitional justice process. This can be seen in how transitional justice discourses 'project a distinction between the "good" (undamaged) and "bad" (unreconciled or recalcitrant) members of the victimised groups' (Meister 2002: 96). Reflecting on the case of South Africa, Madlingozi (2007: 112) tells us that such differentiations are pervasive in post-conflict societies and even more present in those contexts 'where the oppressed did not win the struggle through military force, but where an elite compromise was reached which ensures that previous material and social privileges are maintained'.

This specific framing of resistance to transitional justice can be well illustrated with the widely researched case of the Argentinean *Madres de la Plaza de Mayo*. Indeed, according to Hamber and Wilson (2002: 45), 'over the years, they have changed from being the "Mothers of the Nation" to *Las Locas* or the "Crazy Little Old Ladies" … The recalcitrant *Madres* were demonised as they no longer embodied the state's vision of a reconciled nation.' This group has continuously refused the closure expected from them, including diverse measures promoted as supporting this process of closure, such as exhumations and DNA investigations, indemnities, reparations or public tributes to their disappeared children (Lefranc 2002: 114). They thereby defy claims that such procedures, some of which have become defined internationally as constitutive of the 'right to truth', are fundamental to victims in their process of healing.

If we pay attention to their perspectives, we might learn that their resistance stems from the refusal of a symbolic closure of the past and the framing of the future as a continuation of revolutionary struggles (Lefranc 2002: 115). However, their resistance is most often boiled down to one of 'resentment'. As 'recalcitrant victims', they are portrayed as 'traumatised, self-preoccupied, resentful, and vindictive', i.e. affected by emotions that are all dismissed for being negative (Brudholm 2008: 2), unsocial or unacceptable (Chakravarti 2011). Rather than being perceived as the affirmation of a constructive position and counter-values, these emotions are indeed seen to be in simple opposition to the demands for certainty, closure and unity of transitional justice processes.

Whilst there is little detailed engagement in the field of transitional justice with the subject of resistance, the existing understandings of resistance disqualify it as an illegitimate object of enquiry. Resistance is identified in behaviour deemed to be deviant vis-à-vis the predefined goals and activities of transitional justice processes. This is not to say that resistance might not indeed be staged by powerful actors who have been involved in gross human rights violations and are motivated by self-preservation in times of transition rather than 'any desire to defend the rights and claims of the local population' (Sriram 2012: 69).

However, we argue that resistance should not be dismissed as only or even primarily the act of spoilers as this does not fully reflect the empirical story of transitional justice processes. Since transitional justice is inherently political and contested, resistance is necessarily present in multiple forms in the empirical unfolding of transitional justice. Moreover, we argue that there is analytical value in understanding how and why resistance comes to be enacted and how it is framed and perceived by different actors, even if it is by powerful 'spoilers' or relentless victims, as it can help us to better understand the politics of the empirical unfolding of transitional justice.

Our approach

Given that the field of transitional justice has not yet, with some important exceptions, engaged in depth with the subject of resistance, it would have been possible to contribute to the literature in a number of different ways. The approach we decided upon for this volume has been directly informed by what we understand as the possibilities and limitations of the work on the subject thus far. A tendency to take transitional justice as the starting point means that resistance to it is framed and analysed as a counterpoint to the values and purposes that advocates ascribe to transitional justice processes.

Seen through this lens, resistance is cast primarily as a response to transitional justice and cannot be understood as informed, shaped or motivated by other processes or contexts relevant to actors of the transitional society. We argue that such a lens has the potential to limit our analyses of a potentially wide range of motivations that actors ascribe to acts labelled as resistance and to render resistance as static and one-dimensional. This is important, because we miss valuable opportunities to learn more about subjects which currently rightly occupy the work of many transitional justice scholars; subjects such as legitimacy, power and politics.

The conceptual foundations on which this volume are based are drawn from both within the transitional justice field and from disciplines that have a long history of engaging with resistance such as sociology, anthropology and geography. A multidisciplinary approach is required in order to engage with the subject in the most fruitful way possible, particularly in light of the points raised in the previous sections of this chapter. An immediate point of contrast between studies of resistance and of some of the transitional justice literature on resistance is that of the assumed motivations of actors. Studies of resistance have been accused of 'romanticising' resistance owing to a conceptual approach that entirely attributes acts of resistance to less powerful actors and projects of emancipatory change (Abu-Lughod 1990: 41–42).

Prior to the 1980s studies of resistance were focused on specific types of group action that were open and organised, selfless, principled, openly defying state policies and with revolutionary consequences (Scott 1985: 292; Fletcher 2001: 44). This approach was challenged by a new perspective developed in agrarian and subaltern studies, most notably by Scott and Guha. They focused on 'everyday' acts of resistance seen as the preserve of those actors 'not afforded the luxury' of resistance, having to 'clothe their resistance in the public language of conformity' (Scott 1985: 289–90). A concern with the subtle, everyday and hidden coincided with the development of resistance studies as a boom industry (Moore 1998: 348). This field was further influenced by Foucault and Certeau's work, which 'led the search for new forms of less obvious resistance in the "practice of everyday life" and "marginal subjectivities"' (Fletcher 2001: 45). This work differs from much of that in the transitional justice literature, which as discussed above is often preoccupied with acts of 'spoilers' and 'deviants' labelled as such because they are seen to be refusing to accept the terms of either the justice process or the new social contract. These are usually once, or still, powerful actors who supposedly wish to maintain their positions.

Whilst studies of resistance are many and varied, what is useful for our work in the context of transitional justice is what we can learn from the literature which develops a more subjective and dynamic approach to resistance than that which currently exists in much of the transitional justice discussion. Bearing in mind the post-1980s shift in studies of resistance from organised and open acts to a concern with multiple and complex sites of resistance, which illuminate cracks in systems of dominance (Seymour 2006: 303), we draw more specifically on conceptualisations of resistance as subjective, i.e. a focus on the social act of labelling resistance. Sociology tells us that the transgression of established norms – transitional justice in the case of this project – through acts of resistance results in the social labelling of certain acts and actors as 'deviant' (see e.g. Paugam 2010; Becker 1963). We can certainly see this in the literature on 'spoilers' of transitional justice processes discussed in the previous section. But what we can learn when we focus on the process and outcome of labelling, rather than starting from the point of the act itself, is something about the relationships between actors and how and why such labelling becomes possible.

Referring to the case of Colombia, Díaz (2008) tells us that particular non-governmental organisations oppose some transitional justice measures such as paramilitary demobilisation, not because they oppose transitional justice but to advocate for a more radical approach including political transformation. We cannot know this unless we take a subjective approach to resistance, which would highlight how and why such actors are considered to be 'deviant' and prompt us to look further than the assumptions about the act itself as solely a 'for' or 'against' reaction to the transitional justice that is on the table. We might instead be able to imagine alternatives.

The process and outcomes of social labelling can therefore tell us something significant about the power relationships present in the society in which the labelling is taking place, as this requires the dominance of certain perspectives and actors over others. Geography, with its particular focus on context, further encourages us to think beyond innate political subjectivities and in terms of resistance arising from local power relations and from received and intended meanings (Pile 1997). In any given moment and in any given context one cannot pin down one objective form of resistance; rather, this will shift depending on the actor's positionality. As Keith (1997) argues, resistance can then be said to be defined through the creation of subjectivities, leading us to think of resistance not in terms of absolute deviancy from a norm, but 'as various valid ways of conceiving the world' (Rajagopal 2003: 11).

In reference to Sudan's state response to the International Criminal Court's indictment of President Omar al-Bashir, Sriram writes that: 'He and his government have also engaged in what might be termed acts of resistance, albeit quite cynical ones' (2012). Her reference to 'what might be termed acts of resistance' gets to the heart of the matter of our argument in this volume. We need to know how such an act comes to be understood as resistance, from which vantage point, and with what effect. This will then tell us about the relations between different actors, their mutual perceptions of legitimacy and the differences in their normative positions and visions for peace and justice. As we learn from scholars such as Keith and Pile, the positionality of the actor who names resistance is key.

This borrowing from multiple disciplines in which we can find studies of resistance provides us with a conceptual foundation for the volume, which includes (a) the process and outcome of labelling resistance and the relationships between actors which make this possible and (b) a view of resistance not as absolute deviancy but as a product of intended and received meanings, which can only make sense when analysed in a series of local contexts. Finding this subjective conceptualisation of resistance most helpful for speaking to the current concerns of transitional justice scholarship, the research project that has produced this volume and the contents of the volume chapters are not concerned with developing a typology of resistance. Rather, we aim to render visible and to analyse the many different ways in which resistance comes to be understood as such in transitional justice contexts.

Our approach defines an act of labelling of resistance as the identification of *a purposeful act intended by the actor to work against, prevent or disrupt the intended or implemented formal transitional justice process.* It can be organised or unorganised, an act of an individual or group, an act of the powerful or powerless, and is a subjective concept that is perceived differently from different vantage points. The key aspect is that it is purposeful, i.e. that there is perceived intentionality and thus not all acts of contestation and negotiation will necessarily be resistance. In the case study chapters that follow, we will see how this definition illuminates empirically some of the questions that are most pressing for transitional justice scholarship such as the perceived legitimacy of processes, the power relations that are produced by processes, and different understandings of justice, which are part of the political, economic, social and cultural contexts in which transitional justice processes unfold.

Our approach thus begins with resistance itself, assuming that the labelling of an act of resistance to transitional justice is potentially more than an act of deviance directed only at the transitional justice norm. Given the transitional justice literature, which is focused on the politics of the process in its many different forms, we have good reason to believe that the contexts in which transitional justice processes are embedded – social, political, cultural, economic and historical – will come to bear in shaping the intended and received meanings that determine a subjective act of labelling of resistance. This is not to suggest that transitional justice is a mere smokescreen for other, detached issues of relevance to the resistances we discuss here, but rather that resistance to transitional justice may take many different forms and have many different objects, including but not limited to transitional justice itself. In this way, we continue the work of other scholars in seeking to understand the practices and impacts of transitional justice in terms of the contexts in which it is embedded, to root it in societies, histories and particularities.

Cases, methodology and synopsis

The volume is organised around three case studies but is not designed to be a comparative project. Rather, the purpose is to provide depth and breadth through multiple case studies, each of which is able to illuminate a different process, understanding of resistance, or element of the subjectivity so central to the conceptual foundations outlined in this chapter.

The three case studies of Côte d'Ivoire, Burundi and Cambodia were chosen for a series of reasons. First, in each country there is a state-sanctioned transitional justice process, which is to say an established norm of transitional justice that has been afforded a certain level of legitimacy by the state. This provides a clear object of resistance. Secondly, they were each at a different stage of the process at the time of selection in 2012. Côte d'Ivoire was at the start of a process and thus the terms of transitional justice were being debated; Burundi had an agreed framework for a transitional justice process but had yet to implement any mechanism owing to debates over issues such as mandates and terms; and Cambodia was at the end of a process and thus debates over legacy and impact were relevant. Thirdly, in each of the cases there was a different type of dominant discourse concerning the local power relationships and intended and received meanings relevant for a subjective conceptualisation of resistance.

In Côte d'Ivoire the transitional justice process to be implemented by President Alassane Outtara and his government has been systematically accused of being a victor's justice. Indeed, neither the national courts nor the International Criminal Court have as yet tried a member of the 'winner's camp'. In Burundi, the government has been accused of stalling on its transitional justice obligations, being apparently more concerned with power plays between individuals and parties than with implementing the process agreed upon in the Arusha Peace Accords. In Cambodia, the transitional justice process has been popularly understood as limited by extensive political interference of a government that wishes to consolidate its position of power and to avoid extensive accountability for human rights violations of the past. This means that, fourthly, the kinds of contestations that we could expect to be part of transitional justice, given its political nature, are visible and clearly present in each of the cases.

Taking the case studies at face value, we can identify the 'usual suspects' of resistance to transitional justice. Actors such as supporters of the former President Laurent Gbagbo in the case of Côte d'Ivoire, self-serving politicians in the case of Burundi, and a powerful government concerned with self-protection in the case of Cambodia. In each of these cases it is easy to see the multiple potential forms of resistance, such as interference in the proceedings of a trial or protests against the ICC, as concerned solely with a counter-position to that articulated by advocates of transitional justice: those actors do not wish to implement justice; they prioritise their own particular interests over the universal values of human rights or the collective need to forge a sustainable democratic peace.

As we will read in the following chapters, such a framing of acts identified as resistance can only tell us part of the story of the empirical unfolding of transitional justice in these societies. This is because such analysis begins with the transitional justice intervention and looks outwards to judge how actors and acts can be understood in response to its values and objectives. The moral framing of transitional justice as a necessary 'good', as we described earlier in this chapter, makes this possible. This creates important blind spots, not least in terms of relevant contexts and additional motivations of actors perceived to be resisting.

At this stage, it is important to state clearly our own normative position in terms of the cases and analysis presented in the volume as a whole. The purpose of this research on resistance and transitional justice is not either to support or to deny the legitimacy of any act labelled as resistance in any of the case studies. We do not believe this to be an attempt to avoid acknowledgement of our own positionality as researchers; nor do we believe this to be a way of side-stepping the important moral and ethical questions that research on massive human rights violations of the past are unavoidably a part of. Whilst we do not take a moral or legal position on either the crimes committed or the acts of resistance, it is not our intention to imply that this is not important or necessary as a society decides how it will acknowledge and relate to its own 'pasts' over time. Rather, we are wary of the moral framing of transitional justice, and alert to what Meister highlights as 'the cost of achieving a moral consensus that the past was evil is to reach a political consensus that the evil is past' (2002: 96).

For reasons we elaborate here and in the rest of the volume, we have observed that a preoccupation with reaching a moral consensus that the evil is past, and that transitional justice is a necessary 'good' in the move towards a peaceful future, is not capable of seeing or understanding the empirical unfolding of transitional justice. Such an empirical unfolding can only be appreciated in its fullness if we step outside of the logic of transitional justice and start from the point of the actors and the acts of resistance themselves, alert to the possibility that they can tell us more than who is deviant at any given moment. They can tell us something significant about how legitimacy of the process is understood, the relevance of broader contexts or differing perceptions of what justice and peace could and should look like in a given society.

Each author has conducted qualitative fieldwork over a period of between two and twelve months in and on each case study country. The original project team of Briony Jones, Julie Bernath and Sandra Rubli began operationalising the research focus on subjective resistance with a series of two detailed case study maps. The first mapped the three state-sanctioned transitional justice processes in terms of genealogy, mechanisms and actors. The second mapped potential points of contestation or where we might expect to find acts labelled as resistance, based on our knowledge of the case studies. Fieldwork then took place using methods of elite interviews, semi-structured interviews, unstructured interviews and observation. Operationalising our theoretical approach meant a methodology which sought to identify how actors ascribed or did not ascribe the label of 'resistance' to acts or other actors. As stated above, this was not to develop a typology of different forms of resistance in a transitional justice context, but to explore how fruitful the entry point of resistance could be in contributing to our understanding of the empirical unfolding of transitional justice.

This of course raised a series of interesting methodological issues, some of which we will return to again in the concluding chapter. Of particular note was the question of how to identify an act of labelling of resistance given that not only were different languages involved but also that actors may understand resistance differently. Our focus on intentionality and the definition presented earlier in the chapter meant that we identified acts of labelling as resistance both through the decision of the interviewees themselves and our decision as researchers. This co-production of knowledge is an 'imperfect' process as all research is but we hope to have avoided some of the pitfalls of either romanticising resistance or of seeing it everywhere, by ascribing both agency to the interviewees in defining what counts as resistance and by working with a particular definition of resistance as researchers. Importantly, this is a definition that was informed by our perspective of the possibilities and limitations of current literature on the subject and by our belief in the analytical value of a subjective understanding of resistance.

Having completed the fieldwork, we decided to present the findings from the research project in the format of a broader exchange between scholars working in the global North and the global South. In addition to the introductory and concluding chapters written by the editors, there are two chapters for each case study, one of which is written by a member of the original Swiss research team and one of which is written by a national of that country. Whilst the cases are not analysed as part of a comparative study, each case is important as a unique instance of the phenomenon under study, aiming at depth and breadth for this thus far under-researched topic. In line with this volume's overall approach, each chapter included in the volume addresses a different form or meaning of resistance from the vantage point of multiple actors. As such, each chapter adds a different element to the overall argument of the volume, both in terms of the current gap in transitional justice scholarship and in terms of the benefits of a subjective approach to resistance.

In Chapter 2 on Côte d'Ivoire, Adou Djané Dit Fatogoma sets up a contrast between resistance by supporters of the former president as understood as mere spoilerism of the new regime, and a longer history of colonial resistance and the importance of ongoing political violence for providing a context in which current resistance to transitional justice must be understood. In Chapter 3 on Côte d'Ivoire, Briony Jones' analysis complements that of Fatogoma with an in-depth discussion of the discursive strategies employed by actors who self-identify as 'resistors'. Connecting the historical context and continuum of political violence in Chapter 2 with the discursive strategies of actors in Chapter 3, the case for resistance beyond spoilerism is made.

In Chapter 4 Sandra Rubli focuses on a specific set of actors: Burundian politicians often accused of blocking the transitional justice process. Her analysis, however, shows that their ambivalent position vis-à-vis transitional justice is not only a case of resisting its implementation per se but can be explained by changing perceptions of the legitimacy of the process over time, and of the shifting power relations between the different politicians and political parties. In Chapter 5 Gérard Birantamije looks at a different set of actors, those of civil society, to unpick the ways in which their participation in the making of the transitional justice process can also be understood as forms of resistance to the activities of the Burundian government. In both chapters on Burundi we learn that there is no clear dividing line between those actors who resist and those actors who do not. Understandings of resistance will change over time and be shaped by the broader context in which transitional justice is taking place. Moreover, we learn that resistance cannot be identified as mere self-exclusion from a process but may be understood as taking form through different channels of participation.

In Chapter 6 Julie Bernath continues to work on the theme of resistance through participation and analyses the actions of the civil parties to the ECCC in terms of how they are perceived by transitional justice entrepreneurs whose labelling of certain behaviours as resistance illuminates the complex negotiations over victim subject positions. In Chapter 7 Kosal Path looks beyond the usual accusations of resistance by the Cambodian government to the work of the ECCC, to analyse grassroots behaviour by former Khmer Rouge cadres who construct narratives of heroisation in resistance to constructions of innocence/guilt during the trials. In both chapters on Cambodia we are prompted by the authors to read resistance as part of a larger story of contestations over identities, subject positions and categorisations so present in transitional justice processes.

Although one of the strengths of this collection of case studies and chapters is their variety, breadth and empirical depth, it is of course a potentially complicated mosaic of analyses, which need to be brought together as a coherent whole. A consistent concern with resistance as subjective and with what we can learn if we read resistance to transitional justice in less common ways binds the chapters together in a common research cause. However, as becomes clear, each chapter engages with a different object of resistance and different actors, and is concerned with a different element that takes us beyond the transitional justice entry point and helps us to think more broadly about what motivates and informs perceptions of resistance.

The two chapters on Côte d'Ivoire focus first on the powerful 'usual suspects' of resistance and, secondly, on the disenfranchised 'spoilers', both of which the literature tells us to expect as part of the difficulty of securing transitional justice 'buy in' following experiences of violence and political change. However, in the first chapter the burden of interpretation of acts of labelling of resistance falls primarily to the researcher, whereas in the second chapter it is the actors themselves who self-identify as resistors. In each chapter the motivations and objects of resistance differ from the power to define Ivoirian democracy, to continued political violence. In both the chapters on Burundi there is a contrast between a focus on the powerful 'usual suspects' and those actors expected to participate in and support the transitional justice process. In the first case, the objects of resistance are framed around 'moments' of transitional justice, whereas in the second case it is a gradual and more subtle form of resistance that is possible when the actors are engaged in participatory spaces. In the two chapters on Cambodia, we see a similar set of differences from the disenfranchised but formerly powerful 'usual suspects' to the participants with something to gain from their participation in the process. The objects of resistance are less material and more discursive, symbolic and abstract.

By taking resistance as the starting point for their analyses, rather than the transitional justice process itself, the chapters each contribute to the common aim of disrupting the norm/deviancy dichotomy, which has thus far defined the limited work on resistance and transitional justice. Each chapter positions resistance at the centre, as a legitimate object of enquiry, and asks how it is subjectively defined in a given case. Together, they develop cross-cutting themes that support the overall argument of the volume that it is illuminating to think of resistance to transitional justice as a subjective element of a political process, rather than as a problem of implementation. By taking resistance as its focus each chapter in its own way argues that resistance to transitional justice cannot be dismissed as an act of a spoiler but is a necessary element in the empirical unfolding of a transitional justice process. It is to these cross-cutting themes that we return in the concluding chapter.

Bibliography

Abu-Lughod, Lila. 1990. 'The Romance of Resistance: Tracing Transformations of Power Through Bedouin Women'. *American Ethnologist* 17(1): 41–55.

An-Na'im, Abdullahi A. 2013. 'Editorial Note: From the Neocolonial "Transitional" to Indigenous Formations of Justice'. *International Journal of Transitional Justice* 7(2): 197–204.

Becker, Howard. 1963. *The Outsiders: Studies in the Sociology of Deviance*. New York: The Free Press.

Brudholm, Thomas. 2008. *Resentment's Virtue: Jean Améry and the Refusal to Forgive*. Philadelphia: Temple University Press.

Brudholm, Thomas and Valérie Rosoux. 2009. 'The Unforgiving: Reflections on Resistance to Forgiveness After Atrocity'. *Law and Contemporary Problems* 72: 33–49.

Chakravarti, Sonali. 2011. 'Agonism and Victim Testimony'. In *Theorizing Post-Conflict Reconciliation: Agonism, Restitution and Repair.*, edited by Alexander K. Hirsch, 11–26. New York: Routledge.

Díaz, Catalina. 2008. 'Challenging Impunity from Below: the Contested Ownership of Transitional Justice in Colombia'. In *Transitional Justice from Below: Grassroots Activism and the Struggle for Change*, edited by Kieran McEvoy and Laura McGregor. Oxford, Portland: Hart Publishing.

Distler, Werner and Sarah Riese. 2013. 'The Other Side of the Coin: Intervention and Resistance in Bosnia-Herzegovina and Kosovo'. *Zeitschrift für Friedens- und Konfliktforschung* 2: 177–208.

Fletcher, Robert. 2001. 'What Are We Fighting For? Rethinking Resistance in a Pewenche Community in Chile'. *Journal of Peasant Studies* 28(3): 37–66.

Hamber, Brandon and Richard Wilson. 2002. 'Symbolic Closure Through Memory, Reparation and Revenge in Post-Conflict Societies'. *Journal of Human Rights* 1(1): 35–53.

Hansen, Thomas O. 2014. 'The Vertical and Horizontal Expansion of Transitional Justice: Explanations and Implications for a Contested Field'. In Buckley-Zistel, Susanne, Teresa Koloma Beck, Christian Braun, and Friederike Mieth, eds. 2014. *Transitional Justice Theories*. New York: Routledge, 105–24.

Jacobs, Jane M. 1997. 'Resisting Reconciliation: The Secret Geographies of (Post) Colonial Australia'. In Pile and Keith 1997, 203–18.

Kagoro, Brian. 2012. 'The Paradox of Alien Knowledge, Narrative and Praxis: Transitional Justice and the Politics of Agenda Setting in Africa'. In *Where Law Meets Reality: Forging African Transitional Justice*, edited by Moses C Okello and others, 4–52. Cape Town: Pambazuka Press.

Keith, Michael. 1997. 'Conclusion'. In Pile, Steve, and Michael Keith, eds. 1997. *Geographies of Resistance*. London, New York: Routledge, 277–86.

Kent, Lia. 2011. 'Local Memory Practices in East Timor: Disrupting Transitional Justice Narratives'. *International Journal of Transitional Justice* 5(3): 434–55.

Lefranc, Sandrine. 2002. *Politiques du Pardon*. Paris: Presses Universitaires de France.

MacGinty, Roger. 2011. *International Peacebuilding and Local Resistance*. Basingstoke: Palgrave Macmillan.

Madlingozi, Tshepo. 2007. 'Good Victim, Bad Victim: Apartheid's Beneficiaries, Victims and the Struggle for Social Justice'. In *Law, Memory and the Legacy of Apartheid: Ten Years After Azapo V President of South Africa*, edited by Wessel Le Roux and Karin van Marle, 107–26. Pretoria: Pretoria University Law Press.

Mani, Rama. 2008. 'Editorial. Dilemmas of Expanding Transitional Justice, or Forging the Nexus Between Transitional Justice and Development'. *International Journal of Transitional Justice* 2(3): 253–65.

McEvoy, Kieran and Laura McGregor, eds. 2008. *Transitional Justice from Below: Grassroots Activism and the Struggle for Change*. Oxford, Portland: Hart Publishing.

Meister, Robert. 2002. 'Human Rights and the Politics of Victimhood'. *Ethics and International Affairs* 16(2): 91–108.

Moore, Donald S. 1998. 'Subaltern Struggles and the Politics of Place: Remapping Resistance in Zimbabwe's Eastern Highlands'. *Cultural Anthropology* 13(3): 344–81.

Mullin, Corinna and Ian Patel. 2016. 'Contesting Transitional Justice as Liberal Governance in Revolutionary Tunisia'. In *Resistance to Transitional Justice*, edited by Briony Jones and Thomas Brudholm. Special issue, *Conflict and Society: Advances in Research* 2: 104–24.

Nagy, Rosemary. 2013. 'Scope and Bounds of Transitional Justice and the Canadian Truth and Reconciliation Commission'. *International Journal of Transitional Justice* 7(1).

Paugam, Serge, ed. 2010. *Les 100 mots de la sociologie*. Paris: Presses Universitaires de France.

Pile, Steve. 1997. 'Introduction: Opposition, Political Identities and Spaces of Resistance'. In Pile and Keith 1997, 1–32.

Pile, Steve and Michael Keith, eds. 1997. *Geographies of Resistance*. London, New York: Routledge.

Pouligny, Béatrice. 2005. 'The Forgotten Dimension of "Transitional Justice" Mechanisms: Cultural Meanings and Imperatives for Survivors of Violent Conflicts'. International Conference on Global Justice, Local Legitimacy, Amsterdam, 2005.

Rajagopal, Balakrishnan. 2003. *International Law from Below: Development, Social Movements and Third World Resistance*. Cambridge: Cambridge University Press.

Riaño Alcalá, Pilar and Erin Baines. 2012. 'Editorial Note. Transitional Justice and the Everyday'. *International Journal of Transitional Justice* 6(3): 385–93.

Richmond, Oliver. 2010. 'Resistance and the Post-Liberal Peace'. *Millenium: Journal of International Studies* 38(3): 665–92.

Robins, Simon. 2012. 'Transitional Justice as an Elite Discourse: Human Rights Practice Where the Global Meets the Local in Post-Conflict Nepal'. *Critical Asian Studies* 44(1): 3–30.

Scott, James. 1985. *Weapons of the Weak: Everyday Forms of Peasant Resistance*. New Haven/London: Yale University Press.

Seymour, Susan. 2006. 'Resistance'. *Anthropological Theory* 6(3): 303–21.

Shaw, Rosalind and Lars Waldorf, eds. 2010. *Localizing Transitional Justice: Interventions and Priorities After Mass Violence*. With the assistance of P. Hazan. Stanford, California: Stanford University Press.

Sriram, Chandra. 2012. 'Post-Conflict Justice and Hybridity in Peacebuilding: Resistance or Cooptation?' In *Hybrid Forms of Peace: from Everyday Agency to Post-Liberalism*, edited by Oliver Richmond and Audra Mitchell. Hampshire, England: Palgrave Macmillan.

Subotić, Jelena. 2014. 'Bargaining Justice: A Theory of Transitional Justice Compliance'. In *Transitional Justice Theories*, edited by Susanne Buckley-Zistel and others, 128–43. New York: Routledge.

Thomson, Susan. 2011. 'Whispering Truth to Power: the Everyday Resistance of Rwandan Peasants to Post-Genocide Reconciliation'. *African Affairs* 110(440): 439–56.

Section introduction: Côte d'Ivoire

www.defap.fr/images/cartes-pays/carte-de-la-cote-divoire/image_view_fullscreen (last accessed 30 March 2017).

7 August 1960: Independence of Côte d'Ivoire, which was proclaimed a French colony in 1893.

1961: France and Côte d'Ivoire sign a defence agreement, protecting the power of Houphouët Boigny against *coups* and political instability.

April 1963: Arrests of many elites falsely accused of plotting against the state.

1970: Repression of an uprising in the Bete ethnic group in western Côte d'Ivoire, led by Kragbé Gnagbé, founder of an opposition party, who is arrested and disappears.

1982: Closure of the University of Côte d'Ivoire after student protests led by Laurent Gbagbo, which lay the foundations of the Ivorian Popular Front. Gbagbo goes into exile in France.

1990: Return to multiparty system and formalisation of 14 political parties. First open presidential election, with Houphouët-Boigny declared the winner against Gbagbo. Alassane Ouattara becomes prime minister.

7 December 1993: Death of Houphouët-Boigny. Henri Konan Bédié, constitutional successor, takes power and establishes an ethno-nationalist ideology with the concept of 'Ivoirité' to ostracise Ouattara.

October 1995: Boycott of the presidential election by Gbagbo and Ouattara. Bédié is elected president.

23 December 1999: *Coup* and overthrow of Henri Konan Bédié by General Robert Guei.

22 October 2000: Guei runs for the presidency with Gbagbo as only real challenger and Bédié and Ouattara barred from the elections. Gbagbo comes to power following a violent post-election crisis.

19 September 2002: An attempted *coup* turns into a rebellion and divides the country in two until 2010.

15–26 January 2003: Negotiations and signing of the Marcoussis Agreement in France.

29 March 2007: Signing of the Ouagadougou Agreement between the government and the rebels after several unimplemented agreements and military attacks from both sides. Guillaume Soro is appointed prime minister to conduct general elections to end the crisis.

28 November 2010–11 April 2011: Post-election crisis, following incumbent President Gbagbo's refusal to concede defeat in the second round of elections to his opponent, Ouattara, who is backed by the international community.

11 April 2011: Arrest of Gbagbo, following military operations conducted by forces loyal to Ouattara, and troops from France and the United Nations Operation in Côte d'Ivoire.

28 September 2011: Setting up of a Commission of Dialogue, Truth and Reconciliation by Ouattara; other transitional justice mechanisms follow.

29 November 2011: Gbagbo is transferred to the International Criminal Court in The Hague.

Chapter 2

Resistance to transitional justice in the context of political violence in Côte d'Ivoire

Adou Djané Dit Fatogoma

Introduction

> The time of the CDVR's[1] hearings of victims in Facobly coincided with the operation for the population and environment census which was boycotted by the FPI.[2] When we arrived in the villages, the people said to us to go elsewhere, it was the same thing in other places, we are not involved, that does not concern us. The pro-Gbagbo victims did not come out to go before the hearings.[3]

This quote provides an idea of the complexity of the Ivorian transitional justice process and the extent to which it is anchored in the ongoing political contestation in Côte d'Ivoire. The theoretical position of this chapter is to read resistance to transitional justice in Côte d'Ivoire through the continuity of violence that characterises its political system (see e.g. Bayart and others 1999; Banégas 2006; Besly and Persson 2011). In so doing, acts of resistance can be seen as a continual doubting of the political and social contract to which the current transitional justice process has been appended. This analysis differs from prevalent approaches, which seek to analyse the political situation as an opposition between pro-Ouattara and pro-Gbagbo camps (Koné 2014, 2015). However, as we explore in this chapter, such a reading is incomplete and misses the importance of the historical and contemporary contexts (Biershenk 2010) in which transitional justice takes place.

In addition, the arguments of this chapter contrast with the existing scholarship, which explicitly links resistance and transitional justice. Such work examines resistance to transitional justice in a segmented fashion either by period or by stakeholder, and often takes a normative stance, which reads resistance as standing

1 Dialogue, Truth and Reconciliation Commission.

2 Ivorian Popular Front: The main opposition party and that of former President Laurent Gbagbo. Gbagbo was removed from power when he refused to step down following the declaration of Alassane Ouattara as winner of the election.

3 Interview with a former agent at the CDVR hearing, 3 March 2015 in Duékoué in the West of Côte d'Ivoire. By boycotting the census operation, understood as a mass integration strategy for 'foreign' persons, some westerners boycotted the CDVR's work at the same time.

in opposition to the normative goals of transitional justice (see e.g. Hazan 2006; Subotic´ 2009; Thomson 2013). In this regard, resistance appears as the consequence of strategic relations between the state undergoing transitional justice and international institutions in the implementation of dictates (Subotic´ 2009). Broadly speaking, the analysis emphasises the conflict between international dictates and their strategic reinvestment by the elite within the current regime. According to Subotic´ (2009), this is the case in Serbia, Cambodia and Uganda, where the current regimes develop strategies to circumvent the dual symbolic and coercive pressure of the international community and adopt cosmetic measures that tend speedily to meet some demands of this pressure. Such avoidance of the pressure applied under the framework of certain norms of the international community can be either active, when the apparatus is consciously used as means of circumvention of transitional mechanisms, or passive, in the case of technical failings in the implementation of international tools and their adaptations on the ground (Stromzeth 2009; Bueger 2011).

Another characteristic of this literature on resistance to transitional justice is the placement of 'the strong', i.e. those who control the apparatus of the state, in opposition to 'the weak', i.e. those who remain on the margins of state power (Scott 1990; Thomson 2013; Clark 2014). Thomson, in particular, examined how ordinary rural Rwandans experience everyday resistance to national unity and reconciliation and how by 'whispering truth to power' they challenge the conventional wisdom on post genocide Rwanda (Thomson 2013). Many of the poorest Rwandans disturb the local officials charged with implementing the state programme. Their everyday resistance is 'subtle, indirect, and non-confrontational acts that those subject to power enact to show their anger, opposition, or indignation vis-à-vis what they perceive as unfair or unjust actions against them' (ibid: 129).

The consequence of such a binary is the rigid categorisation of actors. For example, it becomes possible to identify those involved in the previous regime and implicated in human rights violations as 'the strong' and the victims as 'the weak' with limited acknowledgement of the variations within categories and the potentially shifting relationships of power over time. Moreover, transitional justice is presented as a form of resilience, which breaks from the violent past and aims at establishing a new political democratic order, and thus implies a segmented timeframe, which separates periods before the conflict, during the conflict and after the conflict. This additional rigidity of analysis interacts with categories of actors with the effect of decontextualizing transitional justice and responses to it.

In sum, it is argued here that these approaches, whilst making important contributions to opening up the question of resistance to transitional justice, cannot fully capture the ways in which changing socio-political relations (Ellis 2004; Davenport 2007; Mémier and Luntumbue 2012) shape resistance to transitional justice. Such an analysis requires a longer-term perspective on the contexts in which transitional justice processes operate, and a more detailed theoretical approach to resistance in such contexts. In order to address this gap, this chapter asks what the relationship is between the continuum of political violence in Côte d'Ivoire and resistance to transitional justice of the kinds alluded to in the quote that this chapter began with. In doing so it argues that we cannot understand resistance to transitional justice without understanding or acknowledging the continuum of political violence. Before moving on to the main part of the analysis we first need to outline the two main components of the theoretical approach: a working definition of resistance; and a working definition of political violence.

Resistance here concerns the ways of doing things, of thinking about, of taking actions, which disturb the transitional process in Côte d'Ivoire. It is based on Scott's conception of resistance from his theory of voice under domination (Scott 1990: 137). This includes both the forms of disclosed or declared resistance, such as boycotts and protests, and disguised or low profile resistance, such as tales of revenge or acts by actors who disguise themselves. Specifically, it involves in this context of political violence, the boycott of the transitional justice process, the strategies of exclusions and self-exclusions from it, the withdrawal from the process and the use of the transitional mechanisms for self-serving political ends. To turn to political violence, the approach taken here is based on Nieburg's concept of political violence as an

> Act of disorganisation, destruction, and injury, the object of which, the choice of targets or of victims, the circumstances, the execution, and/or the effects, take on a political meaning, i.e. they tend to modify the behaviour of others in a bargaining situation which has consequences on the social system.
>
> (cited by Braud 2006: 4)

This definition includes acts that the perpetrators can present as non-violent, and emphasises the meaning the act acquires.

This theoretical framework allows us to understand the continuity of key features relating to political violence in/and the Ivorian political system, which is vital in order to understand the resistance of the stakeholders of transitional justice in Côte d'Ivoire, a process too often understood as pro-Gbagbo victims setting up obstacles to a victor's justice. In particular, it illuminates the context in which transitional justice is carried out, such as the armed actions both from the official or parallel army, the civil acts of sabotage or counter reaction and the virulence of the rhetoric from all stakeholders that have a political meaning.

From a methodological point of view, this is a qualitative study that combines different methods. The primary fieldwork was carried out between January and December 2014,[4] complemented by additional data collection in the first half of 2015. More precisely, 30 individual semi-structured interviews were carried out with respondents from ten state institutions, five international representatives, including the United Nations system in Côte d'Ivoire, five political parties, five civil society organisations and five independent experts on transitional justice. In addition, focus groups with ten participants each were held, with four groups

4 This fieldwork was generously funded by the Swiss National Science Foundation.

representing major positions in the process. Further, a two-day workshop with 30 experts and stakeholders was held from 4–5 November 2014. A collection of press articles from ten printed media organisations, as well as monitoring of radio and television appearances of stakeholders in the Ivorian transitional process complements the primary sources used. Visits and observations of sites of large-scale violations of human rights were carried out in Abidjan and in the country's interior, in particular in the west of Côte d'Ivoire, as well as in two Ivorian refugee camps in Ghana, namely in Elubo and Accra.

The argumentation has two main parts. First, this chapter presents transitional justice and the militia violence as a background to show how the continuum of political violence plays out in the Ivorian context. It explains how different actors manoeuvre themselves with respect to transitional justice and this political violence in the background, shaping their actions and perspectives. The second part then analyses how transitional justice is caught between irreconcilable approaches (Leebaw 2008),[5] which results in different forms of resistances to transitional justice that are absolutely connected to a rejection of the current political situation, and how the truth commission is at the core of political tensions.

Transitional justice and militia violence

Political competition in Côte d'Ivoire has existed in a very noticeable environment of violence and counter-violence since the return of the multiparty system in 1990. Vidal (2003: 45) highlights the fact that: '[t]he violence which now pervades daily life in Côte d'Ivoire does not date from 2002, nor even from 1999. The brutalisation of political power relations commenced, or more precisely recommenced, at the beginning of the 1990s'. This situation was accentuated in the immediate post-conflict period, i.e. from 2011 to 2014, and the current transitional process is being implemented in a tense political and military context. The result of which is that transitional justice policy-making and debates unfold through the prism of the continued political violence in Côte d'Ivoire and must be understood with this context in mind. As the following analysis will illustrate, transitional justice may be both less important than and at the same time entangled with political and military concerns for elites in the country.

5 For Leebaw (2008), the promotion of transitional justice to support national reconciliation is puzzling. Indeed, since truth commissions and criminal tribunals investigate extremely divisive and violent histories, they have often been viewed as obstacles to reconciliation and charged with 'opening old wounds', generating political instability and interfering with forward-looking political change (96–97). In the case of Côte d'Ivoire, these irreconcilable approaches are characterised by strong opposite options proposed by the different stakeholders. On the one hand, the pro-Gbagbo stakeholders propose amnesty, 'general estates of the republic' and forgiveness, and focus the entire debate on the question of the true winner of the 2010 presidential elections, which is the starting point of the post-elections violence and has led to the delegitimisation of institutions in charge of the process. On the other hand, the government and its supporters claim the need for the fight against impunity and involve national and international courts.

Several bodies were simultaneously set up or reactivated after Ouattara's investiture as president on 21 May 2011. Regarding the judicial dimension of the process, the Special Inquiry and Investigation Unit (CSEI) on the post-electoral crisis was set up, the Rome Statute was ratified, the International Criminal Court (ICC) began its proceedings and the national courts were activated, in particular the Military Tribunal and the courts of Assize. Regarding the non-judicial process of transitional justice, many institutions were established, including the *Commission de Dialogue, Vérité et Réconciliation* (CDVR), the Ministry of Solidarity, Family, Women and Children (MSFFE) and its war victims' department, and the National Programme for Social Cohesion (PNCS). As regards the right to the guarantee of non-recurrence, institutional reforms have been announced, notably that of the judicial system, as well as Security Sector Reform (SSR) and the reinstatement of the National Security Council. These bodies were set up almost simultaneously after 11 April 2011, at the end of the post-electoral crisis.

The government and its international partners were confronted with militia violence in the implementation and functioning of these official transitional justice mechanisms. This form of violence should be situated within the general context of political violence that has reigned in the country for several years. These acts of militia violence do not primarily target transitional justice institutions, but rather happen in parallel to the transitional justice process. They illustrate how the ongoing political violence is designed to target the political transition itself, i.e. the current regime and state, which forms the very basis of any transitional justice process.

In 2012, during the first year of operation of most of the formal institutions of transitional justice, the country faced around ten pockets of military violence, with armed attacks targeting the positions of the armed forces. One of the symbols of military violence in the post-conflict period is the Carrefour Saho attack of 7 June 2012 in the sub-prefecture of Taï, near the border with Liberia. According to the government and the Operation of the United Nations in Côte d'Ivoire (UNOCI), this attack resulted in ten deaths, seven of which were troop members from the UN's peacekeeping operations in Côte d'Ivoire. In 2013 and 2014, several attacks of the same type took place against the Ivorian Republican Forces of Côte d'Ivoire (FRCI) or populations judged to be close to Alassane Ouattara, especially in the west of Côte d'Ivoire.

On the pro-Gbagbo side, several targets were also subject to violent attacks and destruction. Several violent clashes between the FRCI or militia on both sides in known pro-Gbagbo areas, notably in the south of the department of Agboville, in the department of Dabou, and at the border with Liberia in the west are also known to have taken place. One of the symbols of the victimisation of Gbagbo supporters is the attack on the Nahibly refugee camp in Duékoué in the west of Côte d'Ivoire, during the night of 19–20 July 2012. The Nahibly camp was built after the post-electoral crisis of December 2010 to April 2011, to house displaced people, mainly from the Guéré ethnicity, who were considered fervent supporters of Laurent Gbagbo and were subject to pro-Ouattara reprisals. This area was a hotbed of resentment between the two conflicting parties, with the underlying issue being one of land control. Following this attack, a mass grave was discovered at Toguéi a few months later. The frustrations of Gbagbo's supporters are even greater, given that the attack was not the subject of any inquiries on the part of the Ivorian justice system. The case was put on hold because neither the exhumation to identify the bodies nor the legal proceedings have started yet. The mass grave and the wells thought to contain bodies have been placed under the supervision of UNOCI troops for potential future inquiries.

These attacks have been reinterpreted by the parties in conflict in order to legitimise their positions in the transitional process and to delegitimise the opposite side, in a context dominated by security imperatives (see e.g. MacGinty and Richmond 2013). For the current leadership, they were acts of destabilisation of the state committed by supporters of the ex-President Laurent Gbagbo. For their part, Laurent Gbagbo's supporters claim that the current leadership conceived the strategy to discredit the other side, and thus justify the use of force and the silencing of the opposition. The minister of security, who is a main pillar of the current regime, consistently articulates the official interpretation of these attacks and the alleged perpetrators. He systematically blames actors in the pro Gbagbo camp:

> I can tell you, these are terrorist attacks because the aim is to sow terror, to frighten people, instil panic ... We are going to be very determined in facing up to this situation, which in fact is sabotage. It is a question of sapping the morale of Ivorians, of discouraging investors, of putting a brake on our return to normality.[6]
>
> The interrogations gave some clues. What I can say at this stage of the inquiry, is that these are people from the sphere of pro-Gbagbo militia and ex-FDS[7] troops nostalgic for the Gbagbo regime ... There is collusion, and I also think that everything is being coordinated from Ghana by pro-Gbagbo ex-FDS troops. This period has been identified as one of harassment ...[8]

This is how Blé Goudé, the leader of the young patriots close to Laurent Gbagbo, who had sought refuge in Ghana after the post-electoral war, was arrested in Accra and transferred to Abidjan on 17 January 2013. The attacks helped to legitimise the arrest of persons accused or suspected of being involved in their planning and execution. In fact, this militia violence is one facet among many others of the ongoing political violence, and reflects the working of the political system from many years. This background is very important to understand how different actors manoeuvre themselves with respect to transitional justice, shaping their actions and perspectives. It is key to understanding how the context shapes the actors'

6 Speech by the Minister of Security, 8pm news (5 August 2012) RTI (Radiodiffusion Télévision Ivoirienne).

7 Former security and defence forces, the name of the army and the security forces during Gbagbo's rule.

8 Interview with the Minister of Security (7 October 2012) RFI (Radio France Internationale (International French Radio)).

resistances to transitional justice. In addition to this militia violence, several other types of violence can be observed in the course of the transitional process in Côte d'Ivoire, which are manifestly not armed forms of violence, but they converge to influence the course of the transitional process.

Transitional justice caught between irreconcilable approaches

As described above, the history of the Ivorian political system has been one of 'exclusion': either exclusion of the opposition by the regime in power, or self-exclusion by opposing powers who refuse to participate. Since the introduction of multiparty politics in the 1990s, this dynamic has continued and indeed shapes the political landscape of transitional justice today. The mechanisms of transitional justice in Côte d'Ivoire, set up by the Ouattara Government, do not escape this reality and different forms of resistance take shape in this context. The following sections will focus on different forms of resistance in order to argue that resistance to transitional justice itself is a result of the ongoing political violence. These forms of resistance include the delegitimation of the ongoing process by promoting other mechanisms, the use of boycotts, the fixation on certain symbols of the conflict to determine the 'true victims', the withdrawal strategy or staying on the sidelines of the process.

The 'Estates-General of the Republic'[9] and 'general amnesty' as a resistance against 'victors' justice'

The context of political violence as presented above leads to a reinterpretation, or circumvention, of the process by several actors, notably by the opposition party, which has proposed alternatives to settle the political conflict. For the head of the FPI, the process ought to be based on the 'Estates-General of the Republic' in order to put aside the successive electoral conflicts and lay a consensual path for the political future of Côte d'Ivoire. As such, the format proposed by Alassane Ouattara is under attack by Gbagbo's party and allies, who judge it to be part of a unitarian plan to keep hold of power and eliminate political opposition.[10]

9 This concept in French involves the assessment of a situation or a policy in order to reach a consensus on the actions that are to be taken as a priority to reach the expected results. According to Scott (1990: 145), before the Revolution, the king summoned the Estates-General for the first time since 1614 and initiated the compiling of complaints. The people were then invited not only to elect their representatives but also to draw up the *cahiers de doléances*: the king wished to hear the true voice of his people so that he might know their sufferings, their needs and their desires, presumably so that he could redress all wrongs (ibid: 146).

10 The contents of the proposal supported by the FPI were solemnly presented at the 2014 New Year greetings ceremony, after the release from prison of Affi N'Guessan, the president of the FPI. *Notre voie* (Thursday 9 January) 2–5.

After coming out of prison, following the post-electoral crisis of 2010–2011, the president of Gbagbo's party declared before his militants that:

> Today, there are two Côte d'Ivoires. The Côte d'Ivoire of the defeated and that of the victors. And as long as we do not complete reconciliation, it is deluded to think that the defeated who have been thrown in prison, who have had their accounts frozen and their homes occupied, who have to go into exile, will join in the initiatives of the victors. The defeated suffer in silence.[11]

The Estates-General requested by the FPI are based around six commissions: (i) the truth, justice and damage reparations commission; (ii) the constitutional, institutional and electoral reform commission, (iii) the rule of law, freedoms and democracy commission; (iv) the secularism, republican ethics, social cohesion and national consciousness commission; (v) the security sector reform commission; and (vi) the territorial administration and decentralisation commission. According to this proposal from the FPI, three categories of stakeholders should take part in the Estates-General of the Republic. The first category includes representatives of the government and institutions of the Republic, of political parties, of civil society, representatives of regions, communities and traditional authorities, religions, union and employer organisations, representatives of the diaspora, representatives of youth and women's movements, representatives of constitutional bodies (justice, the army, the police, the *gendarmerie*, the public administration etc). The second category includes national and international experts, in order for them to share their experiences and shed light on the issues debated. The third category is made up of what the FPI calls the 'stakeholders of the crisis'. These are the leaders of the three main political parties involved in the quest for power (Laurent Gbagbo, Alassane Ouattara and Henri Konan Bédié), the presumed perpetrators of the crimes and human rights violations, victims of socio-political events, and witnesses of the events.

In this approach, the Estates-General of the Republic would be run by a committee, which could be the CDVR, but with changes to its composition, organisation and functioning. The Estates-General would use the results of all inquiries and reports, and all documentation relating to the events at issue. The board would analyse the reports of all previous experiences of reconciliation and political regeneration, the *Commission consultative constitutionnelle et électorale* (Consultative Constitutional and Electoral Commission of 2000), the *Forum de la Réconciliation nationale* (Forum of National Reconciliation of 2001), and previous political agreements for the resolution of the crisis caused by the armed rebellion (Lomé, Marcoussis, Accra, Pretoria, Ouagadougou).

In addition to the emphasis placed on the 'Estates-General of the Republic' or general amnesty, and confronted with the different responses of those in power, an

11 *Notre voie* (Thursday 9 January) 2–5.

additional tactic of the boycott constitutes one of the forms of resistance to the process of exiting the crisis of which the opposition is making use.

Boycott as resistance against the 'enforcers'

Another strategy used by the main opposition party as a form of resistance to the current transitional process is to boycott the government's actions in general. The boycott of the CDVR's work, of political dialogue, and of the general census of population and environment (RGPH) in 2013–2014 are a few examples. For supporters of the FPI, the CDVR was set up at a time when the party was in complete decay because of the current regime. Indeed, when this commission was set up, ex-President Laurent Gbagbo and his wife were detained, the main leaders of the FPI were either in prison or in exile, and their property and other goods were confiscated. This context, combined with the composition and mandate of the CDVR, which they judge to have been set unilaterally by Ouattara's regime, serve to support them in their disqualification of and their resistance to the transitional process.

For the FPI leaders, the CDVR is disqualified to lead the transitional justice process because, according to FPI leaders:

> While it was expected that the CDVR would associate the true protagonists of the crisis, the political parties, civil society and the victims, in the process of national reconciliation, this party chose to work alone, without the knowledge of the people nor the warring factions ... Who leads the operation on the ground? Who testifies? How, when and where do they testify? Even though there are only pilot sessions, they are premature, given the climate of distrust and permanent insecurity that still reigns across the country and which can in all evidence constitute an obstacle to free expression of the victims, who come from different political and ethnic groups, and a large number of whom currently still reside abroad.[12]

The strategies implemented by those in power in order to get around the opposition boycott converge to maintain this climate of violence and the feeling of normalisation without reconciliation.[13] Seemingly, the main institutions of the state are in place and function as they would after the election crisis of 2010–2011. The official rhetoric of the government presents the country as being in a period of normality, with a united army (former rebels and Gbagbo supporters back FDS), the restoration of state authority and the deployment throughout the country of

12 FPI speech of 18 March 2014 on the CDVR's methodology, in particular the hearings of the victims www.linfodrome.com/vie-politique/15088 (last accessed 30 March 2017).

13 At the inaugural speech at the workshop on 4 November 2014 on 'taking stock of the place of transitional justice in Côte d'Ivoire three years after the post-electoral crisis' at the Centre Suisse de Recherches Scientifiques in Abidjan, Francis Akindès remarked on the feeling of normalisation without reconciliation that prevails in the country.

state administration, the gradual return of displaced people, refugees and other international organisations. However, at the same time there are many 'political' prisoners (despite the denial of this status by the government) who are still in prison and awaiting their trials after at least two years, many parallel army groups continue to exist, the politics of the regime are boycotted and relations between the regime and the opposition remain strained. The strained relations between the regime and the opposition that influence the transitional process are illustrated in the following statement of the general secretary of the FPI:

> [I]s it politically correct, morally decent and technically serious to wish to unilaterally, ill preparedly and hurriedly undertake a census worthy of its name? Is it normal to undertake such an important development operation in a traumatised, divided country occupied by militia from all over the place and in the service of a segregationist regime, incapable of reconciling its population and which advocates for ethnic adjustment? Is it just to carry out a census which ignores the absence of thousands of nationals who have been displaced by war or are in exile, who are going to find themselves robbed of their belongings and their lands to benefit millions of self-proclaimed stateless people once the operation has been completed?[14]

The idea advocated here by Gbagbo's camp is that all protagonists of the Ivorian crisis must be present and free in order to initiate genuine dialogue to achieve a 'true reconciliation'. The transitional justice process is caught between irreconcilable approaches in a context of brutal and strained relations between the government and the opposition. In this context, the proposal of the Estates-General of the Republic or general amnesty appears to be resistance against a victors' justice. Another form of resistance is the boycott of government politics in general, which involves also the transitional justice process and activities. One of the characteristics of the antagonists to the implementation of the transitional process lies in the way in which certain elements of the crisis are brought to bear in order to legitimise or disqualify the different positions.

Fixation on certain symbolic representatives of the conflict to the exclusion of the 'true victims'

The CDVR's activities span the period from 1990 to 2011. Several violent political acts have marked this period and produced a variety of victims whose cases are

14 Speech of the secretary general and spokesman of the FPI on 9 May 2014, after the summons before the attorney general of the main leaders of the FPI, President Pascal Affi N'Guessan, the Vice-Presidents Marie-Odette Lorougnon and Kodjo Richard, as well as the president of the party, Pascal Affi N'Guessan. See http://news.abidjan.net/h/496960.html (last accessed 30 March 2017).

brought by different political parties. In this way, each camp works to put the spotlight on their victims, and pushes those who could be considered responsible to the sidelines, with the sensation of hijacking the question of who is a victim for political ends (Taylor 2014). In this way, the normative discourses on who constitutes the true or legitimate victims informs resistance to transitional justice.

In Gbagbo's camp, the victims' symbols remain, above all, the failed coup d'état of 19 September 2002, the emblematic figure of which is Boga Doudou (Ministry of the Interior and Security at the time, who was killed during the attempted coup), the death of gendarmes and the summary executions of their prisoners during the attempted retaking of the town of Bouake from the rebels by forces loyal to Gbagbo. In addition to that are the deaths of 'patriots' protesting against the action of the French forces in Operation Dignity in front of the Hôtel Ivoire in 2004, the massacres of indigenous Guérés in Duékoué when the city was taken in March 2011 by pro-Ouattara forces, and later the massacres in the Nahibly refugee camp.

In general, the indigenous Guéré villagers near Duékoué consider that the failed coup of 2002 is the cause of the challenges they are facing today:

> There is no electricity in this village, it was when the country was attacked in 2002 and the rebels destroyed everything, they removed the cables and the transformers, etc. They even dug up the utility poles. Look at all the villages around Duékoué like Guitrozon, Toa Zéo, when you go towards Bagouoho, etc. In 2011, it was the Guérés only who were in the refugee camps, for example thousands of people at the Catholic mission. Look at the mass graves in Carrefour etc.[15]

Indeed, at the height of the 2011 electoral crisis, and when Ouattara's forces gained the upper hand over Gbagbo's, there was a mass displacement of indigenous Guéré people who were considered fervent supporters of Gbagbo. For around two weeks, over 35,000 internally displaced people were assembled at the Catholic mission in Duékoué following the massacres (of over 800 people, according to the national inquiry commission) in the Carrefour area and the neighbouring villages (Commission Nationale d'Enquête 2012). The indigenous Guérés, who consider themselves to be the 'true victims', say that they are overlooked in favour of the perpetrators' supporters, as in the following statement of a village chief:

> The people at the CDVR, when they came, you know we are the ones who are really victims of war. I did not have a house or a home. You have no money, they move you around and around. And it is the Dioula and the Baoulé who have been very much taken into account. For two million Baoulés there are perhaps 200 Guérés. Yet really we are the victims.[16]

15 Interview with a resident of Carrefour on 26 February 2015. Man of 45 years, Duékoué, Côte d'Ivoire.

16 Interview with a Guéré village chief in Toa Zéo on 28 February 2015. Man of 67 years.

On the pro-Ouattara side, it is an issue of emphasising the deaths during the violence following the 2000 elections, with the discovery of a mass grave in Yopougon, the victims of the post-electoral crisis, in particular the massacres of women in Abobo and the summary executions of their supporters by the pro-Gbagbo militia in Yopougon. In addition to the physical victims, pro-Ouattara supporters consider that they were victims of the denial of Ivorian nationality during the *ivoirité* policy implemented by Bédié to disqualify Ouattara from the electoral race in Côte d'Ivoire.

As regards the inversion of symbolic references of the conflict and subsequent victims, each party judges the actions of the CDVR based on whether the victims on its own side feel that they have been taken care of. In the opinion of the Gbagbo camp, the CDVR has been subject to a takeover in terms of its members and its mandate. The conditions of trust for victims' hearings have not been met, and the CDVR's victims are virtual. For the FPI, the collapse of the CDVR is clear and its illustration can be found in the tiny number of people heard at Duékoué in the pilot phase of hearings for victims of the crisis. This position is defended by the FPI's leaders in the speech of its general secretary to disqualify the CDVR'S methodology, in particular the hearings of the victims, on 18 March 2014:

> They tell us that, for the pilot phase in Duékoué, there were 200 people. But, in this city, in a single day, there were 800 deaths. Then after that there were the events in Nahibly. But, before that, there were Guitrozon and Petit Duékoué. In such an area, if the conditions are met and the process is inclusive, there would not be just 200 people![17]

This sentiment is even more marked, given that the different stakeholders do not know how the choice of victims was made. One feature of the reproaches made against the CDVR's actions by several stakeholders remains the incomprehension of the criteria for the identification and selection of victims. Although the CDVR has finished identifying victims and hearing its 800 emblematic cases, the law on the identification of victims has not yet been adopted. The bill being drafted covers victims of the 2002–2007 war, and those of the post-electoral war from October 2010 to 31 December 2011. Each political camp has its victims, as does each part of the state apparatus in the transitional space.

The fixation on certain symbolic representatives of the conflict leads every camp to deny the quality of being a true victim to others. This position follows the contestation of the power and legitimacy of the actors in the political area. As highlighted above, the political system in Côte d'Ivoire is marked by a succession of exclusion strategies of opponents by those in power (*ivoirité, réfondation, rattrapage*) and self-exclusion (xenophobia, boycott of the election, delegitimisation of the judiciary system, etc) of the opponents from the election race and other government

17 See www.infodrome.com/vie.politique (last accessed 30 March 2017).

politics. In this way, the normative discourses on who constitutes the true or legitimate victims informs resistance to transitional justice. These representations are part of explicit discursive strategies of resistance to transitional justice, which move the transitional justice debate from legal definitions of victims to normative claims on victimhood and truth. Therefore, a number of those who consider themselves as 'true' victims withdraw from the process, and this also constitutes a strategy of survival.

Withdrawal as resistance and a survival strategy of the 'true victims'

In the discourse of the concerned parties and other social stakeholders there is a strategic withdrawal, either because of a sense of resignation or to avoid the violence which openly stating their position could incite. In the areas known to be pro-Gbagbo, in the south and the west, the same discourse that describes this withdrawal is widespread, as expressed here by an indigenous village chief in Duékoué in the west:

> It is as if we were helpless. So to survive we must accept it. Otherwise, one morning you disappear and they say they are investigating. Investigations that come to nothing, then? It is because we are afraid of dying on our own lands, in our own homes, that we give in. But otherwise, the law does not normally say that![18]

This situation of political violence was explicitly recognised by the president of the CDVR himself, when he was receiving a delegation of traditional leaders of Agboville, a well known pro Gbagbo area:

> Côte d'Ivoire is facing a serious problem of reconciliation. But Ivorians do not have a choice, they must move towards reconciliation. The Ivorian people want peace and their will is strong. But certain selfish and egocentric political interests act against this common will to move towards peace ... peace is not a slogan but a behaviour, a series of acts. Peace is also, it is said, the right to difference, the freedom of expression, security for all, trust and mutual respect, which leads to development.[19]

This concern of populations considered to be pro-Gbagbo can be seen in the way they hold back from the process or commit acts of sabotage. The spokesman

18 Interview with indigenous Guérés in Toa Zéo on 28 February 2015 in the sous-préfecture of Duékoué, Côte d'Ivoire.

19 The head of CDVR during a meeting with the delegation of the leadership of Agboville, a known pro-Gbagbo area.

of the traditional leaders of Agboville, during their reception by the president of CDVR on Wednesday 17 October 2012, for instance, expressed publicly the concern of those considered to be pro-Gbagbo:

> Today it is difficult to give opinions contrary to those of the current leadership, without taking risks. The frustration which stems from this can become an obstacle when the opposition has no means of expression, that is frustration. And that is dangerous. The leadership has to create the conditions for the opposition to express itself freely. Some of us cannot go to our villages because there is a price on our heads for having participated in his [Gbagbo's] campaign ...[20]

The mechanisms of transitional justice are experiencing the repercussions of the continuing unresolved political tensions that structure the social arena in Côte d'Ivoire, and which present themselves as resources for obtaining, controlling and keeping state power. The form of resistance developed here to deal with what the pro-Gbagbo consider as the brutality of the regime, is to stay outside of the process of transitional justice. This also constitutes a strategy of survival and goes beyond the transitional justice process itself. Finally, the transitional justice mechanisms such as the other elements of the state apparatus are used as resources by politicians for accessing or reinstating their power and enjoying greater legitimacy. This conception of the state apparatus puts the transitional mechanisms in a situation of fragility and opens the debate on the legitimacy of those institutions to lead the process.

From the CDVR to the National Reconciliation and Victims' Compensation Commission (CONARIV): the transition with the test of political tensions

The functioning of the Ivorian party system is based on the idea that only mastery of the apparatus of the state and of civil society and religious bodies allows one to keep political power, or to win it (back). This control reflex (Herbst 2000) of all types of power is reflected in the implementation of the mechanisms of transitional justice, and in particular the workings of the CDVR or the CONARIV. All parties (the government, the opposition, victims, and others) disqualified the CDVR, largely because it is considered to be so central to the fight for power. The president of the truth commission, Charles Konan Banny, was himself involved in the presidential election contest in 2015.[21] In this way, the truth commission faces

20 Spokesperson of the traditional leaders of Agboville, during a meeting with the delegation of the leadership of Agboville, a known pro-Gbagbo area, on Wednesday 17 October 2012 with Charles Konan Banny.

21 The election took place in October 2015 and the incumbent president was re-elected.

resistance from all sides. A facet of this resistance is the underlying contentious relationship between the president of the CDVR and the leadership in general, and the president of the Republic in particular.

Looking forward to the 2015 presidential elections, the presidential camp was suspecting the president of the CDVR of using this body as a trampoline for his own candidacy for the presidency. An air of suspicion has crept in between him and the president's camp. As such, boycotts are constantly being proposed to contain the political ambition of Charles Konan Banny. Ivorian television also blacked out the public hearings of emblematic cases in September 2014, arguing that the CDVR had worked alone and wanted to impose images selected in these conditions. However, it was especially the suspicion that this was an attempt by Banny to use these images to discredit the regime and to position himself as a credible alternative that led to this power struggle. A newspaper close to the ruling party explicitly accused the president of the CDVR of using the institution for his own political ends, on 14 October 2014:

> He finally showed his hand. The back of Banny the swimmer, broad and damp, is now clearly visible and glistening from a thousand leagues away … Because everyone knows that Charles Konan Banny used the institution charged with leading the process of reconciling the Ivorian people for his own political ends. On the contrary, it has become more pronounced over time. He has made use of his nomination as President of the CDVR to constitute a solid electorate for himself.[22]

Suspicions that Banny[23] was making strategic use of the CDVR as a springboard to position himself in the political arena and capture the sympathies of the Ivorian electorate were confirmed at the official end of his mandate as head of this body. The same mechanisms of political violence were implemented to counteract this. This included, for example, the arrest of members of his pre-campaign staff for alleged embezzlement. Nor does the setup of the CONARIV to 'complete' the work of the CDVR escape this context of exacerbated political tension. The CONARIV is torn between seeking legitimacy and acting as a strategy to aid its bid to gain control through power. It seeks legitimacy by placing a clergyman at its head, and control of the apparatus by entrusting the real power to the National Programme for Social Cohesion (PNCS). The president of the Republic then approves these decisions and lists of victims to be compensated in the final instance.

22 M'bah Aboubakar, '2015 presidential elections, how Banny has used the CDVR' *L'Expression* no 1543 (Friday 14 October 2014) 2.

23 After the election campaign, Banny in fact took himself out of the race two days before the day of the vote, citing irregularities and lack of trust in the process.

Conclusion

This chapter has focused on the resistances to transitional justice in Côte d'Ivoire through a political violence continuum context. The transitional justice mechanisms put in place by the state and its international partners after the end of 2011's post-electoral crisis are working in a brutal environment of competition between different political forces. Resistance here concerns the ways of doing things, of thinking about, of taking actions, which disturb the transitional justice process in Côte d'Ivoire. Specifically, it involves in this context of political violence the boycott of the transitional process, the strategies of exclusions and self-exclusions from it, the withdrawal from the process and the use of the transitional mechanisms for self-serving political ends. The resistances are analysed through the use of the repressive apparatus of the state, counter-violence or the use of militia violence. The chapter has highlighted the violent political context that generates the conditions for acts of resistance. Transitional justice is paying the price for the way in which the political system works in Côte d'Ivoire, independently of the current stakeholders.

This approach goes beyond the scholarship explicitly linking resistance and transitional justice, which examines resistance to transitional justice in a segmented fashion either by period or by stakeholder, and takes a normative stance since it identifies resistance according to predetermined norms (Hazan 2006; Subotić 2009) or to the silent avoidance of the process by the weak in face of state power (Thomson 2013). By going beyond the conflict between international dictates and their strategic reinvestment by the elite within the current regime, or the relationship between strong and weak, this theoretical framework allows us to understand the continuity of key features relating to political violence in/and the Ivorian political system, which is vital in order to understand the resistance of the stakeholders of transitional justice in Côte d'Ivoire, a process too often understood as pro-Gbagbo victims setting up obstacles to a victor's justice.

This is important for those implementing transitional justice and for researchers. It changes the model of analysis, practice and ethics of transitional justice. It is not resistance to transitional justice directly, but rather the product of the continuum of political violence. Whilst this theoretical framework remains to be proven by the situation in other countries going through a transitional justice process, it has allowed us to revisit the theory of voice under domination of Scott (1990) through the main concepts of declared and disguised resistances. However, resistance does not only refer to the visible and invisible resistances from the powerless, but also concerns the resistance of the power holders through their strategies of mastering the political space.

The resistance to the transitional justice process in Côte d'Ivoire joins many points of Thomson's whispering resistance (2013) observed in the case of Rwanda, but goes beyond the resistance of the powerless against the state power holders. Whilst our analysis of resistance has not taken the international actors as a focus, unlike Lambourne (2014) who focuses on the UN and observes in Burundi the lack of civil party participation, we nonetheless find that the implementation of transitional justice remains firmly in the hands of the government, which is comprised of former rebel leaders who understandably resist being held accountable for the past.

Bibliography

Banégas, Richard. 2006. 'Côte d'Ivoire: Patriotism, Ethnonationalism and Other Modes of Self-Writing'. *African Affairs* 105(421): 535–52.

Bayart, Jean-François, Stephen Ellis, and Béatrice Hibou. 1999. *The Criminalization of the State in Africa*. Oxford: Indiana University Press.

Besley, Timothy and Torsten Persson. 2011. 'The logic of political violence'. *The Quarterly Journal of Economics* 126(3): 1411–45.

Biershenk, Thomas. 2010. 'States at Work in West Africa: Sedimentation, Fragmentation and Normative Binds'. Working Paper No 113, Department of Anthropology and African Studies. Mainz: Johannes-Gutenberg- Universität.

Braud, Philippe. 2006. 'La violence politique: repères et problèmes'. *Cultures & Conflits 09–10*. http://conflits.revues.org/406 (last accessed 30 March 2017).

Bueger, Christian. 2011. 'The clash of practice: political controversy and the United Nations Peacebuilding Commission'. *Evidence & Policy* 7(2): 171–91.

Clark, Phil. 2014. *The Gacaca Courts, Post Genocide Justice and Reconciliation in Rwanda. Justice Without Lawyers*. Cambridge: Cambridge University Press.

Commission Nationale d'Enquête. 2012. 'Rapport d'enquête sur les violations des droits de l'homme et du droit international humanitaire survenues dans la période du 31 octobre 2010 au 15 mai 2011'. http://news.abidjan.net/documents/docs/Crimes_post_electoraux.pdf (last accessed 30 March 2017).

Davenport, Christian. 2007. 'State Repression and Political Order'. *Annual Review of Political Science* 10: 1–23.

Ellis, S. 2004. 'Interpreting Violence: Reflections on West African Wars'. In Whitehead, N. L. (ed.), *Violence*, Oxford, James Currey: 107–24.

Hazan, Pierre. 2006. 'Mesurer l'impact des politiques de châtiment et de pardon: plaidoyer pour l'évaluation de la justice transitionnelle'. *International Review of the Red Cross* 8: 343–65.

Herbst, Jeffrey. 2000. *States and Power in Africa: Comparative Lessons in Authority and Control*. Princeton NJ: Princeton University Press.

Koné, Gnangadjomon. 2014. 'De la violence post-électorale de 2011 à Duékoué'. *Fraternité matin* (16 July 2014).

Koné, Gnangadjomon. 2015. *Les 'jeunes patriotes' ou la revanche des 'porteurs de chaises' en Côte d'Ivoire*. Abidjan: Les classiques ivoiriens.

Lambourne, Wendy. 2014. 'What Are the Pillars of Transitional Justice? The United Nations, Civil Society and The Justice Cascade in Burundi'. *Macquarie Law Journal* 3: 41–60.

Leebaw, Bronwyn Anne. 2008. 'The Irreconcilable Goals of Transitional Justice'. *Human Rights Quarterly* 30: 95–118

MacGinty, Roger and Oliver P. Richmond. 2013. 'The Local Turn in Peacebuilding: A Critical Agenda for Peace'. *Third World Quarterly* 34(5): 763–83.

Mémier, Marc and Michel Luntumbue. 2012. 'La Côte d'Ivoire dans la dynamique d'instabilité ouest-africaine. Les racines de la crise postélectorale 2010 – 2011'. Note d'analyse, Groupe de Recherche et d'Information sur la Paix et la Sécurité (GRIP), Bruxelles.

Scott, James C. 1990. *Domination and Arts of Resistance, Hidden Transcripts.* London: Yale University Press.

Stromzeth, Jane E. 2009. 'Justice on the Ground: Can International Criminal Courts Strengthen Domestic Rule of Law in Post-conflict Societies?' *Hague Journal on the Rule of Law* 1: 87–97. Cambridge University Press.

Subotić, Jelena. 2009. 'The Paradox of International Justice Compliance'. *International Journal of Transitional Justice* 3: 362–83.

Taylor, David. 2014. 'Victim Participation in Transitional Justice Mechanisms: Real Power or Empty Ritual?' Discussion paper 12, *Impunity Watch.*

Thomson, Susan. 2013. *Whispering Truth to Power. Everyday Resistance to Reconciliation in Postgenocide Rwanda.* The University of Wisconsin Press.

Vidal, Claudine. 2003. 'La brutalisation du champ politique ivoirien, 1990–2003'. *Revue africaine de sociologie* 7(2): 45–57.

United Nations. 2011. 'Rapport de la commission d'enquête internationale sur la Côte d'Ivoire' presented to the seventeenth session of the Human Rights Commission, New York (1 July 2011).

Chapter 3

Seeking a 'just justice': discursive strategies of resistance to transitional justice in Côte d'Ivoire

Briony Jones

Introduction

> What we are doing is resistance, and if there is any better word that is stronger than resistance, it is a fight ... It is resistance to the order that has been imposed on Ivory Coast; resistance to the involvement of France in the internal affairs of the country; resistance to the ways in which the current regime in the Ivory Coast has been managing the development of the country in terms of justice ...'[1]

This quote is taken from an interview with a representative of a coalition of Ivorian diaspora in the United States of America; a coalition that self-identifies as resisting the formal transitional justice process in Côte d'Ivoire, a process that was put in place following the post-election violence of 2010/11.[2] Despite the brevity of the quote, one can already understand that for this interviewee theirs is a just cause of those who have been oppressed on two counts: by a transitional justice process imposed by a former colonial power; and by a transitional justice process which is biased and partial and therefore not in fact just. As part of their resistance the coalition refused to take part in the diaspora consultation platform of the *Commission de Dialogue, Vérité et Réconciliation* (CDVR)[3] and continue to lobby for the release of former President Laurent Gbagbo from the International Criminal Court (ICC) in The Hague, a man they believe to have rightfully won the 2010 election, but who was ousted following a declaration by the United Nations (UN) that his competitor Alassane Ouattara had won. Laurent Gbagbo now faces charges of crimes against humanity, charges that have been confirmed by the ICC and the trial opened on 28 January 2016.[4]

1 Interview conducted by phone on 29 May 2014.
2 A working definition of transitional justice will be provided later in the chapter.
3 Dialogue, Truth and Reconciliation Commission.
4 This trial has been joined with that of Blé Goudé; see www.icc-cpi.int/EN_Menus/icc/situations%20and%20cases/situations/icc0211/related%20cases/icc-02_11-01_15/Pages/default.aspx (last accessed 30 March 2017).

The interviewee quoted above used to speak regularly on behalf of Ivorian diaspora in the United States, but since the 2010 elections and the start of the transitional justice process his experience is that 'all those doors are shut'.[5] His voice and the voices he represents are, in his understanding, no longer invited into the public space in order to engage legitimately in the ongoing discussion about what justice and peace should look like in Côte d'Ivoire in the present and in the future.

This opening story provides multiple entry points into the main topic of this chapter: resistance to transitional justice in contemporary Côte d'Ivoire. Recent scholarship on transitional justice has engaged with debates over local viewpoints and ownership (see eg Shaw and Waldorf 2010), with the possibilities of a universal understanding of transitional justice vis-à-vis other approaches such as an African transitional justice (see eg Bennett and others 2012), and with the dominance of certain actors in defining the type of processes and mechanisms put in place (see eg Kagoro 2012). There is thus an understandable concern with who defines the terms of transitional justice and what the politics of the process means for how those who are the subjects of such initiatives will respond. We might refer to this as seeking a 'just justice'. It is therefore striking that there has been no systematic engagement with 'resistance' either as an empirical phenomenon or as the subject of a body of theoretical work, which has the potential to contribute to transitional justice scholarship.

Whilst some work has been done connecting resistance and transitional justice (see below) this chapter speaks to the gap that remains through an analysis of resistance to transitional justice in Côte d'Ivoire following the 2010/11 post-election violence. In particular, it focuses on discursive strategies of resistance, following the work of Jansen to mean discursive practices that are deployed by different actors in different contexts as a way of exploiting the 'oppositional location of discourses in relation to a more influential discourse or institution' (2000: 394).

The working assumptions of this chapter are threefold. First, the author contends that it is a useful exercise to bring together work on resistance and work on transitional justice. It is hoped that such an exercise will enhance the current debates relevant for transitional justice, which have been summarised here as a search for a 'just justice'. In addition, by drawing on an established and theoretically rich area of literature such as that on resistance this chapter also speaks to concerns over the limited role and presence of theory in transitional justice scholarship (see eg Buckley-Zistel and others 2014).

Secondly, this chapter is written from a starting point of assuming that the subjects of transitional justice are agents who should be treated as such and that transitional justice will therefore meet with a variety of responses, including resistance. Such an assumption is informed by critical approaches to transitional

5 Interview conducted by phone on 29 May 2014.

justice, which highlight its necessarily contested nature (McEvoy and McGregor 2008), given its attempt to support a particular type of social and political order (Iliff 2012). If contestation is present then we may reasonably expect resistance[6] to be present, which renders it a valuable object of study.

Thirdly, it is assumed that resistance itself does not necessarily denote deviancy from the broader aims of justice, but might in fact highlight different ways in which justice is understood in the society in question. Following from the second point we can assume that a universal understanding of justice will not be present in any given society and thus a process that cannot incorporate multiple understandings of justice will meet with a variety of responses, including resistance. If we analyse these responses as other points of view, we can avoid the missed opportunity of merely dismissing them as actions of spoilers and those who have something to fear from justice.

With these assumptions as a starting point, the chapter now goes on to examine what it means to resist transitional justice. Here we look at the literature, which has referred to resistance and transitional justice and the ways in which it is limited by a concern with spoilers and acts of self-preservation. The chapter argues that we need to build on this but also move beyond it with our analysis. Drawing on work on resistance from geography and anthropology, the author argues that it is more analytically illuminating to understand resistance in subjective terms rather than as an objective act, which can be identified and described as an empirical fact. With this as an analytical foundation the chapter then moves to the case study of Côte d'Ivoire. Following a brief background section the chapter focuses on actors who self-identify as 'resisters' in terms of how they understand their acts, how they are understood by other actors, and what this means for the subjectivity of resistance to transitional justice in this context. The concluding discussion returns to the more general theoretical question of the value of bringing together resistance and transitional justice and the contributions this can make to the study of a 'just justice'.

Understanding resistance to transitional justice

It is important to understand transitional justice processes in the broader context of post-Cold War peace-building. Sriram (2009) has argued that if we accept that transitional justice is part of a broader liberal peace-building context then it too can be subject to similar critiques. These critiques include accusations that liberal peace-building may be prescriptive, instrumentalist, externally imposed, technical and underpinned by an agenda to transform attitudes, beliefs and domestic forms of governance (Duffield 2001; Goetschel and Hagmann 2009; Newman, Paris and Richmond 2009; Paris 2002). As Shinko highlights, there is a tension inherent in liberal internationalism which is that of the 'liberal proclivity to only grant respect to those in whom it recognises the self-same moral attributes and liberal

6 A working definition of resistance will be provided in the following section of the chapter.

commitments', coupled with a 'penchant for violence as a means to secure peace as a disciplinary order' (2008: 482).

If we accept this broader context of the nature of liberal internationalism and peace-building then we might expect that for a given peace-building intervention the responses of those implicated will be neither homogenous nor necessarily accepting. Peace-building as a normative endeavour – in seeking the prevention or reduction of different forms of violence (Goetschel and Pfluger 2014) – makes claims for others, which they may find neither palatable nor legitimate. Continuing this line of critique with reference to transitional justice, Leebaw (2008) has described the irreconcilable goals of transitional justice that aim at concurrently maintaining order, legitimising compromise, seeking consensus, exposing political violence and transforming the terms of debate over past human rights abuses.

Taking this as a starting point, one might wonder why 'resistance' as a concept has received relatively limited attention in peace-building literature[7] in general and transitional justice literature in particular. Leebaw addresses this gap in transitional justice scholarship by suggesting that: '[r]esistance is identified with an oppositional stance, rather than a constructive one, and generally construed as hostile to the prevailing order ... [which] sits uneasily alongside the goal of legitimating a new order' (2013: 244). As such, transitional justice has not dealt well with moral claims and agency outside of its own normative and policy frameworks (ibid). This means that, where resistance does appear, transitional justice scholars grapple with a dilemma that they rarely make explicit: whether resistance is *necessarily* an act of the disempowered against an oppressor. Studies of resistance have commonly associated acts of resistance with organised or everyday forms of resistance of the subordinate against the powerful, implying that the motivation is always empowering social, political and economic transformations (Fletcher 2001).

In transitional justice literature this distinction and discussion is relevant for Subotić's (2009) work on the subversive choices of the states of the former Yugoslavia vis-à-vis the International Criminal Tribunal for the Former Yugoslavia, in Thomson's (2011) work on the everyday resistance of Rwandans to the Gacaca courts, Jacob's (1997) work on the resistance of non-Aboriginal Australians to the state-led reconciliation process and Sriram's (2012) work on resistance against international actors in transitional justice contexts. But all too often the discussions centre in fact on whether those who resist are spoilers or 'bad guys' who have something to fear from a truth-telling process or prosecutions.

7 In peace-building literature a concern with resistance has been part of recent discussions on hybrid peace where it is of concern as one element in the local-international interactions and frictions which lead to forms of peacebuilding which fully reflect neither the international intervention nor the manifestation of local will, ie hybrid. The author has written more extensively on this subject matter elsewhere; see Jones, B. (2016) 'Hybrid Peace, Transitional Justice and Resistance'. *Conflict and Society* 2: 74–86.

However, recent work by geographers on resistance has highlighted the importance of standpoint and subjectivity in defining those acts that constitute resistance or not (see eg Keith 1997; Pile 1997). We can see such nuance in work that questions the easy moral assumption that those who resist the calls of justice and reconciliation are necessarily the 'bad guys'. Brudholm's work on South Africa and Germany leads him to assert that the refusal to forgive and reconcile 'can be the reflex expression of a moral protest and ambition that might be as permissible and admirable as the posture of forgiveness' (2008: 4). Also, seeking to complicate a resister/subordinate/good versus resisted/powerful/bad dichotomy, Palmer (2014) analyses the life history of one Rwandan and argues that a series of important yet neglected factors are relevant, such as power differentials within the 'subordinate' group, perspectives the individual may have regarding his or her own position of power and the values he or she draws on to inform an action of resistance or not.

Grappling with the moral posturing of an act of resistance seems vital for understanding resistance to transitional justice. Moving between the majority position in resistance studies of resistance as an act of the subordinate group, and in transitional justice literature of resistance coming from those who have something to lose from the process, we miss opportunities to illuminate the struggles over meaning and legitimacy in seeking justice in the aftermath of massive human rights violations. This has been illustrated in some of the work cited here. Connecting this with the starting point that transitional justice will prompt a series of varied and differentiated responses we are asked to look more closely and conceptually at resistance as one component of a broader analysis of what constitutes a just justice.

We can therefore pose a series of questions which inform the analysis presented here of the case of Côte d'Ivoire: where might contestations with the potential for resistance be located? Which actors understand themselves as resisting transitional justice? How do these actors understand their position of power? How might these subjective positions change over time and in context? As is implied by these questions, the approach taken in this chapter is not one of labelling an act or acts as 'resistance', nor of seeking to identify where resistance as an objective quantity can be found in current day Côte d'Ivoire. Rather, the purpose is to understand how 'resistance' to transitional justice is understood by different actors and what this means for their subsequent understanding of a just justice.

Resistance and transitional justice in Côte d'Ivoire

The context of Côte d'Ivoire

The fieldwork in/on Côte d'Ivoire was conducted over a one-year period from January 2014 and was qualitative in nature. The data was generated through semi-structured interviews, observations and focus groups, both in Côte d'Ivoire and with diaspora in the United States of America and the United Kingdom. The majority of the fieldwork was conducted by Adou Djané Dit Fatogoma (see

Chapter 2 in this volume), based at the Centre Suisse de Recherches Scientifiques in Abidjan, and in consultation with the author who joined him for two field visits and also conducted interviews with and on the Ivorian diaspora.[8]

Côte d'Ivoire was chosen as a case study for looking at resistance to transitional justice owing to some key characteristics. Following independence from France in 1960, Côte d'Ivoire was led by Houphouët-Boigny and his *Parti Démocratique de Côte d'Ivoire*,[9] which remained the only political party until 1990. This was seen by many commentators as a time of stability, management of ethnic tensions, and economic prosperity (Diallo 2005). Following the introduction of multiparty politics and Houphouët-Boigny's death in 1993, there were a series of political crises connected to ethnic divisions, regional splits and claims to autochthony (Bah 2010). A civil war in 2002 was followed by the creation of a unity government in 2003, a buffer zone between the north and south of the country, further violence and then, finally, the signing of the Ouagadougou Agreement in 2007.

The 2010 presidential elections (postponed from 2005) were intended to solidify unity within the country and to act as a formal end to the peace process. However, contested results in the second round of the presidential run-off led to both the incumbent Laurent Gbagbo and his opponent Alassane Ouattara declaring victory. The African Union (AU), the Economic Community of West African States (ECOWAS) and United Nations (UN) supported the election of Alassane Ouattara amidst high levels of post-election violence from 2010–2011. The crisis finally 'ended' on 11 April 2011 after the capture and house arrest of Laurent Gbagbo. The subsequent transitional justice process has consisted of ICC indictments for crimes against humanity regarding Laurent Gbagbo, his wife Simone Gbagbo (who has been convicted in Ivorian national courts and is serving a 20-year jail term[10]) and Charles Blé Goudé, a state-sponsored truth-seeking mechanism of the CDVR, a national commission of enquiry, and national prosecutions.

This brief summary can be given more depth by highlighting some aspects that are particularly significant for this chapter. First, Laurent Gbagbo had been declared the winner of the presidential election by the Ivorian Constitutional Council. Leaving aside debates over the extent of vote rigging and bias towards Gbagbo within the Constitutional Council itself, the decision of the UN Security Council to announce the election result in favour of Alassane Ouattara 'dismissed the validity of the Ivorian Constitutional Council's decision – a significant step for those

8 Interviews were conducted both in French and English and where necessary translated by Jacqueline Graves, a professional translator. All quotes from the data are presented in English for the purposes of this chapter.

9 Democratic Party of Côte d'Ivoire.

10 Simone Gbagbo was sentenced on 10 March 2015 for the crime of undermining state security during the period of violence which followed the 2010 presidential elections. The 20-year jail term has been perceived by her supporters as overly harsh, given that the prosecution had only requested a 10-year jail term for the crime of disturbing public order. For English language news coverage see www.bbc.com/news/world-africa-31809073 (last accessed 30 March 2017).

Council members formally committed to working on the basis of host state consent' (Bellamy and Williams 2011: 832). Secondly, the significant role of the former colonial power of France and her troops in using force to protect civilians and also in the arrest of Gbagbo 'blurred the lines between human protection and regime change…and [raised questions] about the place of neutrality and impartiality in UN peacekeeping' (ibid: 835). Thirdly, the controversies surrounding the election itself and subsequent intervention by French troops and UN peace-keeping forces have been followed by concerns coming from different actors that the transitional justice process as it is unfolding in Côte d'Ivoire represents a 'victor's justice'.

Amongst other international actors, the independent commission established by the Human Rights Council of the UN has expressed concern that investigations by the national military and public prosecutors have been limited to former officials and allies of Gbagbo (Baldo 2011; ICG 2011). McGovern, in his detailed anthropological work on the period preceding the post-election crisis, 'insists on a multicausal explanation of the Ivorian conflict' (2011: 25). In doing so he refuses to accept the tendency of both Ivorian and non-Ivorian analyses to seek 'neat' (ibid: 7) categories of ethnic, religious and political affiliation, which can explain a 'victor' and a 'loser'. However, the dominant discussion amongst actors both inside and outside of the country is the nature of the transitional justice process as biased in favour of Ouattara and his supporters.

Understanding resistance in Côte d'Ivoire

These aspects all tell us that, unsurprisingly, the Ivorian context is one in which the state-sanctioned transitional justice process is expected to meet with contestation and resistance. As such, we might see the transitional justice process as a focal point for continued discussions over the complex history of socio-political crises related to citizenship, autochthony and economic collapse (Akindès 2004), as well as the meaning of justice in Côte d'Ivoire today. Introducing resistance to this analysis offers an opportunity to say something concrete about the form that some contestation might take and the meaning given to the concept by the actors themselves. This chapter differentiates between resistance and other concepts such as contestation through an understanding of resistance as a purposeful act intended by the actor to work against, prevent or disrupt 'X', in this case the intended or implemented transitional justice process (Jones, Bernath and Rubli 2013). In this sense it is distinct from contestation, which is understood here to refer to divergences of perspectives, opinions and goals that are expressed in opposition to each other but which are not necessarily purposeful or designed to work against each other.

However, the content of the term 'resistance' should not be predetermined. What might be considered by one actor to be an act of resistance may not be so considered by another actor. In his work on political concepts, Heywood suggests that 'political argument often boils down to a struggle over the legitimate meaning of terms' (2000: 3). It is more fruitful in such complex and contested contexts as that of Côte d'Ivoire in transition to focus on the meaning given to the term by actors themselves, rather than to aim to pin down the exact meaning of resistance. In doing so we focus here on actors who self-identify as 'resisters' and what meaning they give to their acts through discursive strategies.

The analysis on this basis is informed by two main ideas. The first draws heavily on work by geographers such as Keith (1997) and Pile (1997) and holds that an understanding of what counts as resistance is subjective, meaning that actors will attribute a definition of 'resistance' to different acts depending on context, positionality and subjectivity. The second key idea has been mentioned in the introduction and is inspired by Jansen's work on resistance in another transition context of Serbia. Jansen looks at discursive strategies of resistance, 'which may strike us at first sight as emancipatory, progressive or liberating [but] may then be appropriated to serve oppressive purposes. This may be the result of conscious planning, but it can also form part of largely unintended everyday life coping strategies' (2000: 394). This allows for an understanding of resistance to be deployed by different actors in different contexts serving different agendas (ibid: 394).

Also connecting discourse and resistance, Lilja has explored discursive practices of Cambodian women vis-à-vis the Extraordinary Chambers in the Courts of Cambodia. Lilja observes that: '[r]esistance is, therefore, made possible by the ability of the subject to reflect upon prevailing discourses and to create new logics in the nexus of various contradictory discourses and subject positions' (2013: 2). Like Jansen, Lilja does not read discursive strategies as necessarily coherent and linear but understands them as bodies of representations which create meaning as they attach to matching objects, practices or bodies (ibid: 15 and 109).

Following Jansen and Lilja, the analysis presented here starts with an understanding of the actors as agents who are engaged in giving meaning to 'resistance' from their subjective positions. This meaning-making can be accessed in many different ways, and the entry point chosen here is that of the discursive strategies of resistance deployed by the actors. The subjective nature of the concept of resistance does not exclude a role for the researcher who, as will be shown in this chapter, can listen to and seek to understand the discursive strategies as an expression of meaning attributed to the concept of resistance by the actors themselves.

Such approaches to the study of resistance are particularly helpful in the context of resistance to transitional justice as they allow us to think beyond victor/loser and powerful/powerless dichotomies in societies that are changing rapidly perhaps as a response to experiences of massive human rights violations. This will help us to avoid two connected pitfalls of either championing all resistance as necessarily the act of an underdog, or of assuming that those who resist transitional justice are necessarily the 'bad guys' with something to lose. It is through such a frame that we can enter into a discussion of just justice and the discursive practices used to resist an 'unjust justice'.

Seeking a 'just justice' in Côte d'Ivoire

Interviews were conducted, among others, with actors who self-identified as resisters, and who use what Jansen (2000) has described as discursive strategies of resistance. This includes members of the diaspora group Committee of Actions for Côte d'Ivoire – USA (CACI–USA), the Abidjan-based *Congrès National pour La Résistance et la Démocratie* (CNRD)[11] and the political party of former President Laurent Gbagbo the *Front Populaire Ivoirien* (FPI).[12] This chapter focuses particularly on these actors and the perspectives of those who work with them, observe them, or seek to understand them. In doing so it is possible to bring to the front and centre the perspectives of those who 'resist' and how they make sense of this in a contested transitional justice context. In particular, this part of the chapter analyses ideas of the 'unjust oppressor' and the 'just cause', which together dominate the discursive practices of resistance explained by these actors in the interviews.

The unjust oppressor was an important figure in descriptions and explanations of resistance. This oppressor appeared not only as the target of the resistance, but the perceived unjust character of the oppressor was cited as a justification for the actions of those who resist. In this sense the 'unjust oppressor' and the 'just cause' are symbiotically connected in the actors' accounts of resistance. Such an understanding of the dynamics of resistance had two main elements: first, that President Ouattara and his supporters were not legitimate political actors; and, secondly, that the involvement of the UN and the French forces was motivated by illegitimate neo-colonial interference and a desire for regime change at the cost of Ivorian democracy.

When interviewing the Secretary General of CACI–USA it was possible to note his careful use of language. Referring to the current Ivorian president as 'Mr. Ouattara' and the ousted former president as 'President Gbagbo', the interview was framed from the very beginning in terms of a non-acceptance and, indeed, implied illegitimacy of the political status quo.[13] The Secretary General of the political party the FPI also used similar terminology, referring to the Ouattara government as 'a regime, which has been forced upon [us]',[14] rather than a government. The position of Ouattara as president after the contested elections, and the subsequent intervention of the UN and French troops, appeared to render illegitimate for these actors the transitional justice process as a whole.

The very understanding of transitional justice as a combination of both a transition towards democracy alongside addressing human rights violations of the past (see eg Arthur 2009; Bell 2009) was called into question by some of the actors interviewed. For them, the transition towards democracy in Côte d'Ivoire is a false one and it cannot therefore serve as a foundation for a reckoning with the past.

11 National Congress for Resistance and Democracy.

12 Ivorian Popular Front.

13 Interview conducted in English by phone on 29 May 2014.

14 Interview conducted in French in person on 26 March 2014, Abidjan.

Interviewees referred to Ouattara and his supporters not as president, politicians or officials but as 'rebels', as this quote from a member of the FPI illustrates: 'To my knowledge the FPI, in good faith, committed two errors. The first was to have accepted to enter into elections alongside armed rebels…The second, still in good faith, is to have accepted an electoral commission with all the rebels, who in reality are all RDR[15] supporters'.[16] If the president of the state is nothing more than a 'rebel leader', then what does this say about the legitimacy of his mandate to pursue transitional justice?

The strongly expressed feeling that Ouattara and his supporters were rebels who should have been suppressed and excluded from political office is sharpened by a perception that, in the words of one interviewee, 'Alassane Dramane Ouattara was forced on Côte d'Ivoire by the French army'.[17] A spokesperson for the CNRD claims that Ouattara was 'put there by a French coup d'état' as part of a 'menace of re-occupation'.[18] This interviewee explains the act of resistance in this context, arguing that: 'we had reason to call [our organisation] resistance for democracy because we are an occupied territory'.[19] In a press release by the *Comité de Pilotage des Actions de la Diaspora* (CPAD)[20] they state that 'all those in love with justice and democracy must resist' (Zokou 2012).

McGovern has written of the important role that the French rhetoric of revolution has played in the language of French-educated Ivorian intellectuals such as Laurent Gbagbo who utilise this 'rhetoric of root-and-branch cataclysmic change' (2011: 128). What is interesting is that this rhetoric of revolution and resistance has retained its importance through the struggle for independence from France, during the struggle for multiparty democracy, and now by supporters of Gbagbo who see themselves as resisting the illegitimate regime of Ouattara, a French supported 'rebel'. Some of the interviewees connected resistance against the Ouattara government and its form of transitional justice with an identity of being 'Ivorian patriots … who want democracy'.[21] In this way, calls for the release of Gbagbo from the ICC prison in The Hague are based not only on belief of his innocence but also that of a principle of democracy: 'the combat for the liberation of Laurent Gbagbo is a combat for the return of democracy'.[22]

Casting Ouattara as an enemy of democracy is achieved by connecting his status as an illegitimate rebel leader with his contested Ivorian identity, evidenced in the necessity for 'outsiders' such as the UN and France to put him in power.

15 Le Rassemblement des Républicains – Rally of the Republicans, which is the party of President Ouattara.
16 Interview conducted in French in person on 24 March 2014.
17 Interview conducted in French in person on 26 March 2014.
18 Interview conducted in French by phone on 13 October 2014. Author's own translation.
19 Ibid.
20 Diaspora Organising Committee.
21 Interview conducted in French by phone on 13 October 2014. Author's own translation.
22 Interview conducted in French by phone on 13th October 2014. Author's own translation.

Whilst some interviewees avoided the difficult subject of *ivoirité* ('the FPI does not identify with the concept of *ivoirité*. The RDR must ask the question of its ally the PDCI, which invented this concept. To come back to the subject …'),[23] others either alluded to its relevance in suggesting that Ouattara does not work in the interests of Ivorians and indeed attacks the fabric of Ivorian society (of which he is by implication not truly a part)[24] or suggest that he is indeed not eligible to stand for election in 2015 based on the constitution,[25] which since 1995 has required presidential candidates to have been born in Côte d'Ivoire. The support of Ouattara's claim to the presidency by actors such as the UN and France only serves to reinforce an understanding of resistance to Ouattara and his policies as in fact a support of democracy and the sovereignty of Côte d'Ivoire. Despite support for Ouattara also coming from the AU and ECOWAS the interviewees only mentioned the activities of the UN, France and their neo-colonial interference. This omission is interesting as it lends weight to the neo-colonial influence argument and in turn does not acknowledge the greater complexity that is introduced when we understand that Ouattara's claim to the presidency received support from some other African leaders.

The Secretary General of CACI–USA was explicit in describing their resistance as a common rather than a partisan cause: 'the question of the sovereignty, the authority and the capacity of the Ivorian people regardless of their political affiliation, to decide who should be the leader of their country'.[26] He goes on to say that: 'there will be no reconciliation with a regime that is illegitimate, that is in violation of the constitution, and that is what we are denouncing, this is our baseline of approach'.[27] Unsurprisingly CACI–USA as well as the Abidjan-based CNRD have refused to participate in the activities of the CDVR, be it the diaspora platform or gathering of testimonies in Côte d'Ivoire itself, because 'any organisation that was set up by the illegitimate president of the Ivory Coast, Mr. Alassane Ouattara, we have stayed away [from] because we don't trust the way it was put together, one, and we don't trust the mission'.[28]

Often, such declarations of resistance were accompanied by accusations of 'victor's justice'. One particularly vivid description of this comes from the Secretary General of the FPI when he says in response to the situation for Gbagbo supporters that: 'These are the unfortunate consequences of the governance inspired by disregard for one's adversaries. This is the pitiable result of political choices based on the art of conquering, not convincing. We can see that, under those people,

23 Le Parti Démocratique de Côte d'Ivoire (Democratic Party of Côte d'Ivoire). Interview conducted in French in person on 24 March 2014.
24 Interview conducted in French in person on 26 March 2014.
25 Interview conducted in French in person on 24 March 2014.
26 Interview conducted in English by phone on 29 May 2014.
27 Interview conducted in English by phone on 29 May 2014.
28 Interview conducted in English by phone on 29 May 2014.

Côte d'Ivoire has become a mother who buries her children'.[29] He goes on to say that: 'The victor's camp is made up of all those who are in the good graces of the government in all fields. On the other side are the vanquished'.[30]

Making sense of resistance to transitional justice in Côte d'Ivoire

Writing about resistance soon leads to a discussion of right and wrong, of powerful and powerless. This is the legacy of a rich and important field of study on resistance, and these are discussions that could valuably be brought into transitional justice literature, which is concerned with important debates over standpoint, marginalised voice and knowledge imperialism. Because of the normative project of transitional justice itself and its inherently political and thus contested nature, it makes sense that not everyone implicated in the process will agree with the motivations, management and goals that underpin it. However, to 'resist' transitional justice seems on the surface to be necessarily a position of the immoral, the unjust and the warmongering. The purpose of this chapter is not to become an apologist for all resisters of transitional justice, nor to dismiss and ridicule their claims. Instead, it has made an initial attempt to explore what we can learn if we seek to understand the discursive strategies of resistance that are employed, and how resistance is given meaning by those actors who may be otherwise identified as, to simplify, a problematic sticking point in the otherwise triumphant march of justice.

With these analytical goals in mind it makes sense to focus on those actors who identify as 'resisters', and this chapter has drawn on interviews with members of the diaspora organisation CACI–USA, and the Abidjan-based CNRD and FPI. The first observation we can make is that resistance to transitional justice, through eg refusal to respond to invitations to take part in CVDR consultations, is made sense of through a nuanced interconnection of a series of grievances which the actors are seeking to express and redress. It is somewhat obvious, and not at all new, to point out that transitional justice processes do not take place in an historical or contextual vacuum. However, to read commentary on Côte d'Ivoire from actors such as the UN one could be mistaken for thinking that the resistance of pro-Gbagbo supporters to the current situation was only to be understood as a refusal to accept defeat and their culpability for crimes against humanity committed as part of the post-election violence in 2010/11. If we solicit and listen to their stories of resistance, other factors come into play.

One interviewee representing the Civil Society Convention of Côte d'Ivoire made an interesting distinction between 'resistance' and 'opposition', saying that: 'Today the Civil Society is involved in the citizens' resistance, which should not be

29 Interview conducted in French in person on 26 March 2014.

30 Interview conducted in French in person on 26 March 2014.

confused with citizens' opposition. Citizens' opposition targets power, while the citizens' resistance means citizens' independence, making proposals on national issues'.[31] Indeed, within the interviews the different actors usually identified alternative courses of action to that which they are resisting. For example, the FPI has called for Estates General to be established, which would address violence of the past among other issues, and which its supporters believe would pave the way for 'reconciliation through sincere and inclusive political dialogue, and the estates-general of the Republic'.[32] This touches on a key grievance of those who identify as resisting: that of a closed public space for debating the terms of justice and peace. CACI–USA described a process of exclusion which they experienced based on the position of President Obama towards the election of President Ouattara. Their Secretary General explained that:

> [d]uring the time of the elections I was invited by Voice of America to give a position, and to speak on behalf of what we call quote unquote the pro-Gbagbos. And many times I had an opportunity to do that and I was interviewed also in a contradictors debate with other people. But right after April the eleventh all, those, doors, were, shut ... so there was a tacit boycott of anything that would be representing the views or dissenting views to the position taken by the US administration.[33]

The content of what the members of this organisation were saying had not in itself changed radically over the time period described, but the context had changed both in terms of national politics and geopolitics. It was this change of context which led to a change in perception of some US press actors, who no longer considered their activities to be legitimate or their views to be palatable.

The resisters cited here identify aspects of the transitional justice process that are also highlighted by more 'moderate' voices, such as the lack of transparency in the work of the CDVR,[34] the bias in national and international prosecutions towards supporters of Gbagbo, and a lack of communication and openness on the part of the UN in explaining its decision to declare Ouattara the winner of the presidential election. Concerns over these problematic aspects of the current transitional justice process led one interviewee to express concern that views of the political opposition and the experiences of their supporters were being eradicated from the broader public memory.[35] Tensions over the recent 2015 presidential elections demonstrate that contestations over position and control in the public political space have not been addressed by the transitional justice process, in part

31 Interview conducted in French in person on 12 May 2014.
32 Interview conducted in French in person on 26 March 2014.
33 Interview conducted in English by phone on 29 May 2014.
34 Representatives of both the United Nations and a UK NGO working with Ivorian diaspora groups as well as liaising with the CDVR expressed the same concerns to the author.
35 Interview conducted in French in person on 26 March 2014.

because it has failed to connect with the issues at stake for those who resist it. Sensitisation work for a violence free election as well as numerous candidates dropping out in protest over the process led to a peaceful and substantial win for the incumbent, Ouattara. Given this it is wise to consider what seeds of frustration might be being sown, even amongst sectors of the population and political elite considered to be the 'bad guys'.

However, this initial work raises a series of questions over how far we should take a concern with 'just justice'. Can we take at face value the motivations and intentions as expressed by those who resist? How can we take on board their perspectives, while maintaining a moral and juridical position on past violence? Can the language of resistance be used as a discursive strategy by those who wish to lend themselves a moral credence of the 'oppressed'? The answers to these questions are certainly not clear based on the analysis presented here, and more work needs to be done. However, it is the belief of the author that this subject warrants greater and more systematic attention by scholars of transitional justice as part of broader discussions of power and legitimacy, which dominate more critical searches for a 'just justice'. If we can start from a position of expecting forms of resistance to a necessarily contested process, then we should engage in detail with literatures on this subject. This chapter drew on work from geographies and anthropologies of resistance but these are surely not the only sources to which we can turn for our analysis.

Bibliography

Akindès, Francis. 2004. 'The Roots of the Military-Political Crises in Côte d'Ivoire'. Research Report No.128. Uppsala: Nordiska Afrikainstitutet.

Arthur, Paige. 2009. 'How "Transitions" Reshaped Human Rights: A Conceptual History of Transitional Justice'. *Human Rights Quarterly* 31: 321–67.

Bah, Abu Bakkar. 2010. 'Democracy and Civil War: Citizenship and Peacemaking in Côte d'Ivoire'. *African Affairs* 109/437: 597–615.

Baldo, Suliman. 2011. 'Ivory Coast must avoid Victor's Justice: Podcast with Suliman Baldo'. International Centre for Transitional Justice, In Focus, issue 3 http://ictj.org/content/ictj-focus-issue-3 (last accessed 30 March 2017).

Bell, Christine. 2009. 'Transitional Justice, Interdisciplinarity and the State of the "Field" or "Non-Field"'. *The International Journal of Transitional Justice* 3: 5–27.

Bellamy, Alex J and Williams, Paul D. 2011. 'The New Politics of Protection? Côte d'Ivoire, Libya and the Responsibility to Protect'. *International Affairs* 87(4): 825–50.

Bennett, Tom and others 2012. *African Perspectives on Tradition and Justice.* Cambridge, Antwerp and Portland: Intersentia.

Brudholm, Thomas. 2008. *Resentments' Virtue: Jean Améry and the Refusal to Forgive.* Philadelphia: Temple University Press.

Buckley-Zistel, Susanne and others. 2014. *Transitional Justice Theories.* Oxon and New York: Routledge.

Diallo, Youssouf. 2005. 'From Stability to Uncertainty: a Recent Political History of Côte d'Ivoire'. Working Paper No 74, Max Planck Institute for Social Anthropology Working Papers. Halle/Saale: Max Planck Institute.

Duffield, Mark. 2001. *Global Governance and the New Wars: The Merging of Development and Security*. London and New York: Zed Books.
Fletcher, Robert. 2001. 'What are we fighting for? Rethinking resistance in a Pewenche community in Chile'. *The Journal of Peasant Studies* 28(3): 37–66.
Goetschel, Laurent and Tobias Hagmann. 2009. 'Civilian Peacebuilding: Peace by Bureaucratic Means?' *Conflict, Security and Development* 9(1): 55–73.
Goetschel, Laurent and Sandra Pfluger. 2014. 'Assessing Quality in Peace Research'. In *Challenges of Peace Research*, edited by Goetschel, Laurent and Sandra Pfluger. swisspeace working paper 7/2014.
Heywood, Andrew. 2000. *Key Concepts in Politics*. London: Palgrave Macmillan.
Iliff, Andrew R. 2012. 'Root and Branch: Discourses of "Tradition" in Grassroots Transitional Justice'. *International Journal of Transitional Justice* 6: 253–73.
ICG (International Crisis Group) 2011. 'A Critical Period for Ensuring Stability in Côte d'Ivoire'. Africa Report No 176.
Jacobs, Jane M. 1997. 'Resisting Reconciliation: The Secret Geographies of (Post)Colonial Australia'. In *Geographies of Resistance*, edited by Pile, Steve, and Michael Keith, 67–89. London and New York: Routledge.
Jansen, Stef. 2000. 'Victims, Underdogs and Rebels: Discursive Practices of Resistance in Serbian Protest'. *Critique of Anthropology* 20(4): 393–419.
Jones, Briony, Bernath, Julie and Sandra Rubl. 2013. 'Reflections on a Research Agenda for Exploring Resistance to Transitional Justice'. swisspeace working paper 3/2013.
Kagoro, Brian. 2012. 'The Paradox of Alien Knowledge, Narrative and Praxis: Transitional Justice and The Politics of Agenda Setting in Africa'. In *Where Law Meets Reality: Forging African Transitional Justice*, edited by Okello, Moses Crispus and others, 4–52. Cape Town, Dakar, Nairobi and Oxford: Pambazuka Press.
Keith, Michael. 1997. 'Conclusion'. In *Geographies of Resistance*, edited by Pile, Steve, and Michael Keith, 277–86. London and New York: Routledge.
Leebaw, Bronwyn. 2013. 'Lost, Forgotten or Buried? Transitional Justice, Agency, and the memory of Resistance'. *Politica e Societa* 2: 237–64.
Leebaw, Bronwyn. 2008. 'The Irreconcilable Goals of Transitional Justice'. *Human Rights Quarterly* 30: 95–118.
Lilja, Mona. 2013. *Resisting Gendered Norms: Civil Society, the Juridical and Political Space in Cambodia*. Ashgate: Farnham and Burlington.
McEvoy, Kieran and Lorna McGregor. 2008. 'Transitional Justice from Below: An Agenda for Research, Policy and Praxis'. In *Transitional Justice from Below: Grassroots Activism and the Struggle for Change*, edited by McEvoy, Kieran and Lorna McGregor, 1–13. Oxford, Portland: Hart Publishing.
McGovern, Mike. 2011. *Making War in Côte d'Ivoire*. London: Hurst and Company.
Newman, Edward, Roland Paris, and Oliver P. Richmond. 2009. 'Introduction'. In *New Perspectives on Liberal Peacebuilding*, edited by Newman, Edward, Roland Paris, and Oliver P. Richmond, 3–25. Tokyo and New York: United Nations University Press.
Palmer, Nicola. 2014. 'Re-Examining Resistance in Post-Genocide Rwanda'. *Journal of East African Studies* 8(2): 231–45.
Paris, Roland. 2002. 'International Peacebuilding and the "Mission Civilisatrice"'. *Review of International Studies* 28: 637–56.
Pile, Steve. 1997. 'Introduction: Opposition, Political Identities and Spaces of Resistance'. In *Geographies of Resistance*, edited by Pile, Steve, and Michael Keith, 1–32. London, New York: Routledge.

Shaw, Rosalind, and Lars Waldorf, eds. 2010. *Localizing Transitional Justice: Interventions and Priorities after Mass Violence*. Stanford: Stanford University Press.
Shinko, Rosemary E. (2008). 'Agonistic Peace: A Postmodern Reading'. *Millennium: Journal of International Studies* 36(3): 473–91.
Sriram, Chandra L. 2012. 'Post-Conflict Justice and Hybridity in Peacebuilding: Resistance or Cooptation?' In *Hybrid Forms of Peace. From Everyday Agency to Postliberalism*, edited by Richmond, Oliver P., and Audra Mitchell, 58–72. Hampshire: Palgrave Macmillan.
Sriram, Chandra L. 2009. 'Transitional Justice and the Liberal Peace'. In *New Perspectives on Liberal Peacebuilding*, edited by Newman, Edward, Roland Paris, and Oliver P. Richmond, 112–30. Tokyo and New York: United Nations University Press.
Subotić, Jelena. 2009. 'The Paradox of International Justice Compliance'. *The International Journal of Transitional Justice* 3(3): 362–83.
Thomson, Susan. 2011. 'Whispering Truth to Power: The Everyday Resistance of Rwandan Peasants to Post-Genocide Reconciliation'. *African Affairs* 110(440): 439–56.
Zokou, Seri. 2012. 'Communiqué de Presse du Comité de Pilotage des Actions de la Diaspora (CPAD)'. (20 September 2012) www.civox.net/Communique-de-presse-du-Comite-de-Pilotage-des-Actions-de-la-Diaspora-CPAD_a1404.html (last accessed 30 March 2017).

Section introduction: Burundi

www.weltkarte.com/afrika/burundi/online-karte-burundi-politisch.htm (last accessed 30 March 2017).

13 October 1961: Assassination of Prince Louis Rwagasore.

1 July 1962: Independence.

1965: The failed Hutu gendarmerie *coup d'état* leads to retribution by the Tutsi dominated army against mainly Hutu civilians. A year later, Captain Michel Micombero takes over the government and declares the First Republic.

April–May 1972: As a response to a violent uprising by Hutu rebels, which target Tutsi, the army systematically kills or disappears around 80,000 educated Hutu.

November 1976: Colonel Jean-Baptiste Bagaza takes power in a bloodless *coup d'état.*

April 1980: Creation of the Palipehutu-FNL in Tanzanian Refugee Camps.

September 1987: Major Pierre Buyoya takes power in a bloodless *coup d'état.*

August 1988: FNL-Palipehutu kill Tutsi in the communes of Ntega and Marangara. This massacre is followed by violent retribution by the army.

November 1991: Palipehutu-FNL attacks the capital Bujumbura and the province of Cibitoke.

March 1992: Referendum for a new constitution that introduces the multiparty system.

July 1993: First democratic multiparty elections.

21 October 1993: Assassination of the first democratically elected Hutu President Melchior Ndadaye (FRODEBU) and of some of his followers. Massacre of Tutsi Students in Kibimba. Start of the civil war, which produces over 500,000 refugees and 800,000 internally displaced persons and in which 300,000 Burundians are killed.

July 1996: Major Pierre Buyoya successfully launches another *coup d'état.*

1998: The military wing splits from the political party CNDD and continues its armed fight as CNDD-FDD.

28 August 2000: Signing of the Arusha Peace and Reconciliation Agreement, which results from a two-year internationally mediated negotiation process. It is followed by a transitional period that lasts from 2001 until 2005, during which violence continues.

2003: Signing of a Global Ceasefire Agreement with the CNDD-FDD.

27 December 2004: Adoption of the law establishing the National Truth and Reconciliation Commission, which has never been implemented.

2005: The first post-conflict elections are largely won by the CNDD-FDD. Peter Nkurunziza is elected president.

2008: Following a previous ceasefire agreement (2006), the FNL-Palipehutu signs a peace agreement.

July–December 2009: National Consultation on Transitional Justice.

15 May 2014: Promulgation of the law establishing the Truth and Reconciliation Commission (TRC). Nomination of 11 commissioners and start of the four-year mandate of the TRC in December. Start of the TRC hearings in March 2016.

Chapter 4

Between resistance to and compliance with transitional justice: the case of political decision-makers in Burundi

Sandra Rubli

Introduction[1]

The formal transitional justice process in Burundi appears to have been blocked for a significant period of time. The mechanisms to deal with the legacies of the civil war and the different cycles of violence that Burundi has experienced following the country's independence in 1962 are a part of the Arusha Peace and Reconciliation Agreement, signed in 2000. This peace agreement was negotiated between different political parties and the Burundian government. While the agreement's provisions for transitional justice mechanisms were supposed to be implemented during the transitional period from 2001 until 2005, neither the Truth and Reconciliation Commission (TRC) nor the judicial mechanisms were set up within that time frame. It was only on 15 May 2014 – 14 years after the signing of the agreement – that the law on the creation, mandate, composition, organisation and functioning of the TRC was promulgated. However, there are currently no concrete efforts by the government or other political decision-makers to establish the Special Criminal Tribunal (SCT).

The fact that most of the provisions of the Arusha Agreement have been implemented, with the exception of those concerning transitional justice,[2] has led mainly civil society organisations and transitional justice advocates to conclude that the political will necessary for dealing with the legacy of the violent past in Burundi is missing. While the neglect of transitional justice can be the result of different priority setting in the reconstruction process, the Burundian government and political parties are said to have actively blocked, delayed and resisted transitional

1 This chapter has greatly benefited from the participants of the workshop held at swisspeace in March 2015. The author is grateful to them, in particular Briony Jones and Julie Bernath. The views expressed in this chapter are those of the author alone and do not represent positions of her associated institutions.

2 If one considers monuments also as a transitional justice mechanism, the national monument which was constructed in 2010 in Gitega constitutes a notable exception. However, owing to space limitations the erection of the monument is not analyzed here as a transitional justice moment despite the fact that it was contested by oppositional political parties. For an analysis see Rubli (2016).

justice.[3] Thus, at first sight, Burundi appears to be a typical case of the kind of resistance that is usually cited by transitional justice scholars: that of the powerful elite who resist formal dealing with the past mechanisms because of their fears over being held accountable for their role in past violence (e.g. Sriram 2012).

However, the accusations of elite resistance belie a more complicated story that deserves attention. While on the one hand the Burundian government seems to be reluctant to implement the formal transitional justice mechanisms included in the Arusha Agreement, the government and political parties have on the other hand shown some support for transitional justice on the rhetorical as well as on the material level. In December 2004, a law establishing the TRC was promulgated.[4] In June 2005, the Burundian government endorsed the Kalomoh Report, which resulted from a UN-led assessment mission and proposes an alteration of the transitional justice formula inscribed in the Arusha Agreement. Finally, in May 2014, the National Assembly passed a law on the establishment of the TRC, which is being gradually implemented, with the nomination of the commissioners in December 2014. In this regard, political decision-makers appear to be complying with the international norm on transitional justice.

This chapter speaks to the existing literature on transitional justice and resistance, which generally highlights that powerful actors oppose dealing with the past mechanisms. By focusing on these same political decision-makers, this chapter explores their actions, choices and potential motivations and seeks to understand the processes and contexts that inform their 'resistance' or 'compliance'. Thereby, this chapter does not seek to challenge this dominant narrative found in transitional justice literature, but rather seeks to add nuance and account for complexity. In doing so, the aim is to make more sense of the apparent contradiction of the Burundian case study in which we find political decision-makers resisting and at the same time implementing transitional justice institutions. Moreover, by looking at that which is being resisted, the chapter identifies aspects of transitional justice in Burundi for which there are political support, and those aspects that seemed to have met resistance. In doing so this chapter has relevance beyond the case study of Burundi by providing a more nuanced view on the resistance–compliance dynamic and taking into account the ways in which transitional justice is embedded in the broader political context of political party and governmental politics.

Following these introductory remarks, the chapter first outlines the conceptual background, including an overview of the relevant literature and some analytical and methodological reflections. The empirical analysis is divided into three parts, each focusing on a significant moment of Burundi's transitional justice process: first,

3 Interview by the author with civil society representative, Bujumbura 2009 (BUJ-I-b-1). See also UN representative, radio broadcast, La Benevolencija, 30 July 2010 (BUJ-II-x-6); Interview by the author with a representative of UPRONA (Union pour le progrès national), Bujumbura, by author, 2011 (BUJ-III-a-4); Human Rights Watch (2009).

4 Despite a call for candidates for the position of commissioners being released, the TRC has not been set up. The law of 2015 establishing the TRC consequently abrogates the 2004 law.

the negotiation of the transitional justice provisions during the Arusha talks and their implementation; secondly, the implementation of the Kalomoh Report's recommendations; and, thirdly, the setting up of the TRC. This structure is analytically helpful but is not intended to imply that these moments can be neatly separated, with each influencing the others as the discussion demonstrates. Each of these empirical sections first gives a description of the moment itself before turning to the exploration of the actions, choices and potential motivations of decision-makers and discussing them in terms of the resistance–compliance dichotomy. In the concluding remarks, the chapter points to the different insights from these empirical sections, which help to nuance the current conceptualisation of the resistance–compliance dynamic in transitional justice scholarship and practice.

Resistance and compliance within transitional justice

The UN has defined transitional justice as 'the full range of processes and mechanisms associated with a society's attempts to come to terms with a legacy of large-scale past abuses' (UN Secretary General 2004: para 8). This represents an international model of transitional justice based on international criminal law, human rights law and humanitarian law, which has emerged in the last 30 years (Nagy 2008; Sikkink 2008; Bell 2009; Rubli 2016). Such is the strength of the transitional justice discourse at this level that, from a moral and normative perspective, states emerging from conflict seem to be faced not with a choice of whether to engage in a transitional justice process or not, but rather with the choice of 'how much accountability when' (Bell 2009: 120). Although the implementation of a transitional justice mechanism is not an international obligation, it can be said that states emerging from conflict are expected to comply with this normative consensus and to address their legacy of past human rights violations through formal mechanisms.

From this normative consensus on the international level a distinct set of measures seen as legitimate has crystallised, sometimes referred to as a 'tool kit' (Roht-Arriaza 2006; McEvoy 2007; Thoms and others 2008; Arthur 2009). This comprises prosecutions, truth-telling, reparations and institutional reforms, including vetting, which are emphasised as the instruments of transitional justice available to countries (Joinet 1997; Sisson 2010). Transitional justice advocates, who are often international or local civil society organisations, but also international organisations or bilateral donor countries, actively promote this international model and emphasise its technical and legal approach to dealing with past human rights violations.[5] Despite an acknowledgement by such actors that context-specific and locally owned solutions are desirable (e.g. UN Secretary General 2004) such local transitional justice mechanisms are mostly only considered if they resonate with international standards and resemble Western courts and customary laws (Baines 2010).

5 For a critical reflection on this model and its practical application see Rubli (2012).

Within the transitional justice literature, we observe a rather clear distinction between compliance with and resistance to this international model of transitional justice. One reason for resistance that is often cited by scholars is the potential misfit between international models and local realities. For example, proposed transitional justice mechanisms may meet resistance because they are considered to be culturally inappropriate or because they interfere with existing local processes (Sriram 2012). This is a marked difference from the position taken by advocates of the international model who underline the universality of international humanitarian law upon which transitional justice is based (Vinjamuri and Snyder 2004; Buckley-Zistel 2009).

Another reason for resistance concerns the imposition of the international model by external actors mainly through financial conditions for budget support. Sometimes presented as a form of neo-colonialism (McEvoy and McGregor 2008; Shaw and Waldorf 2010), countries emerging from conflict evoke state sovereignty in order to resist this international imposition of transitional justice mechanisms. In contrast, states that adopt transitional justice mechanisms and comply with the normative consensus to deal with the violent past become accepted as full members of a peaceful world order and receive in return international financial support or other rewards (Subotić 2009; Bonacker and others 2011).

A third reason, which is probably the most cited in relation to resistance to transitional justice, is the fact that actors who have been implicated in past violence have little incentive to implement or support transitional justice processes. As potential perpetrators, parties to the conflict are said to fear prosecution and punishment by courts or to be held politically accountable for past human rights violations (Sriram 2012).

In this regard, transitional justice literature and practice usually locate resistance to transitional justice with powerful actors.[6] This includes former political elites and perpetrators of violence who particularly try to avoid prosecution and thereby may enjoy the protection of states (Subotić 2009). Resistance is also associated with the social groups who benefited from a regime involved in serious human rights violations (Mamdani 1996) or usual providers of justice, including state actors, because they see transitional justice mechanisms as 'incursions upon their sources of legitimacy, income, and power' (Sriram 2012). Thus, transitional justice literature and advocates ascribe resistance to powerful actors whose motivating impulse is the fear or the perception of having something to lose in the transition. Based on rational choice theory, the political elite and other powerful actors are portrayed as acting first and foremost out of self-interest and for their own advancement (Vinjamuri and Snyder 2004). Their resistance is not seen as something 'truly local' or motivated 'by any desire to defend the rights and claims of the local population' (Sriram 2012). Rather, they are cast as 'spoilers' of the

6 Thomson (2011) and Brudholm (2008) constitute notable exceptions.

process (Jones and others 2013), who do not understand the need for a profound social transformation after periods of massive human rights violations.

Thus, within the transitional justice literature we find a distinction between advocates of the process and those who either do not understand or support it. This has the effect of rendering those who resist as non-legitimate actors and their resistance as something that is inevitably deviant and in need of being 'fixed' (Jones and others 2013). This dichotomy between supporters and resisters of transitional justice is also implied in scholarship on compliance to transitional justice. In this regard, compliance with the transitional justice norm not only requires the set-up of legitimate mechanisms and institutions, but also implies that political decision-makers adhere and eventually internalise the goals and values of transitional justice. For example, Subotić (2014) speaks of instrumentalists whose compliance with transitional justice is driven by external incentives or pressure instead of justice acceptance and internalisation. This work illustrates that states and political elites are expected not only to comply with the international model of transitional justice on the legal and institutional level by setting up formal mechanisms, but also to act according to the 'correct' motivations.[7] If mechanisms are used to pursue goals other than justice and reconciliation, then the process is considered by its advocates to have been instrumentalised, hijacked or simply to be paying lip service to the values promoted by the internationalised norm (Murphy 2002; Subotić 2009).

Reflections on the analytical approach and methodology

In the analysis of this chapter the exploration of actions, choices and potential motivations of political decision-makers focuses on three different 'moments of transitional justice' in Burundi's dealing with the past process. They include the negotiations over the transitional justice provisions in the Arusha Agreement and attempts to implement them, the endorsement of the Kalomoh Report, which recommends a new transitional justice formula and, finally, the establishment of the recent TRC. Importantly, these moments occurred against a background of discussions over the nature of the transitional justice process being blocked, but are themselves full of action, negotiation and decision-making. This is analytically illuminative because these moments of transitional justice do not presume resistance at first sight. Thus, the chapter is less interested in discovering typologies of resistance than analysing actions, reactions and justifications of choices of political decision-makers in the context of the adoption and later implementation of a given transitional justice mechanism. In this sense, it is not the chapter's aim to make a claim as to whether a particular action or choice of a Burundian political decision-maker constitutes an act of resistance or compliance, but rather to

7 Subotić (2014) rightly highlights that different strategies of compliance matter because they influence the outcomes of transitional justice interventions.

problematise the resistance–compliance dynamic beyond the current discussion in the literature.

Burundian political decision-makers do not self-identity as resisting transitional justice: they do not use the term of resistance or any synonyms such as 'blocking', 'circumventing' or 'working against' to describe or justify their actions and choices. Rather, resistance is ascribed and identified by observers on the basis of the effects of their actions and choices regarding the implementation of the international transitional justice model.[8] This may then raise a methodological challenge for identifying potential motivations and intentions of those who resist or comply with a particular process or model of transitional justice. Can an observer ever grasp the real motivations of other actors or legitimately deduct and ascribe intentions to actors on the basis of their actions?

As shown earlier, most of the writings that foreground this compliance–resistance dynamic ascribe a certain set of motivations to powerful elite actors who are perceived to be resisting the effective setting up of transitional justice mechanisms. This chapter, however, aims to go beyond such a simplistic approach. Following a constructivist and interpretivist approach (Blaikie 2000; Guba and Lincoln 2005; McCandless 2007), it seeks to observe, listen and understand the ways in which decisions, negotiations and choices are being made in these three moments of transitional justice.

This approach implies that the exploration of actions, choices and potential motivations to resist or comply with transitional justice also need to be seen in the historical context. Resistance in Burundi was foremost associated with armed groups who opposed the state army and government (e.g. CNDD 2010). While organised violence is a highly visible form of resistance, in the context of past human rights violations carried out by authoritarian regimes there are also more subtle forms of resistance. For example, in the context of the events in 1972, family members of victims shaved their heads to resist the interdiction of mourning of those the regime considered 'traitors' (Vanderlick and Batungwanayo 2012). Recently, in 2015, Burundi experienced another form of resistance when many inhabitants of Bujumbura protested against the current president's ambitions to run for a third mandate. Thus, resistance in the specific context of Burundi has historically been associated with subalterns violently resisting the exercise of power (Fletcher 2001; Knight 2012), rather than with political elites.

As a methodological entry point, the chapter considers what are referred to as the potential 'objects' or 'targets' of resistance (and compliance) (Hollander and Einwohner 2004). Such objects of resistance may be particular aspects of a transition or a transitional justice process, including a particular mechanism, its composition or mandate. Such an approach is methodologically helpful for contexts in which transitional justice is not rejected per se or where we observe

8 As Hollander and Einwohner (2004) identify in their review article on studies of resistance, observers of resistance constitute one of the different levels for the recognition of resistance.

compliance with and at the same time resistance to transitional justice by the same group of actors, such as in Burundi.[9] This allows us to go beyond a simple resistance–compliance dichotomy and explore the actions, choices and potential motivations of Burundian decision-makers and to give a thick description of the three transitional justice moments.

The following empirical sections are largely based on data that was collected during doctoral fieldwork between 2009 and 2011[10] (Rubli 2016). It was collected with the aim of analysing the contestations and negotiations around transitional justice in the context of Burundi's post-conflict state-formation process. In order to analyse how transitional justice is used as an instrument for political struggles, I conducted around 100 semi-structured interviews with politicians and other actors involved in the transitional justice process and analysed reports, press statements and other documents. For newer empirical developments after mid-2014, the chapter relies on publicly available data, such as press releases or media articles.[11] Moreover, this chapter draws from the University of Antwerp's online collection of original documents on Burundi's transitional justice process.[12]

The Arusha Agreement: introducing transitional justice, but resisting its implementation

The Arusha Agreement, which resulted from a two-year long negotiation process between 17 political parties, the Burundian government and the National Assembly, was signed on 28 August 2000. Regarding dealing with past crimes, it foresees a TRC (Article 8), an International Judicial Commission of Inquiry (IJCI), which should be followed by an international criminal tribunal for acts of genocide, crimes against humanity and war crimes (Article 6), a national day of remembrance and a national monument remembering the victims (Article 6).[13]

9 For a further discussion of this dynamic in the Burundian context see the chapter by Birantamije in this volume.

10 The thesis has been conducted within the ProDoc 'Global Change, Innovation and Sustainable Development' as part of the research module 'Making Peace, Constructing States: Peace Agreements and the Dynamics of Statehood in post-conflict Africa' funded by the Swiss National Science Foundation (SNSF). In addition, the author benefited from being an associated member of the Swiss National Centre of Competence in Research (NCCR) North–South: Research Partnerships for Mitigating Syndromes of Global Change, which was co-funded by the SNSF and the Swiss Agency for Development and Cooperation (SDC). The author is grateful for their support.

11 Owing to a professional assignment, the author was not able to conduct interviews or collect further data for the analysis.

12 www.uantwerpen.be/en/rg/iob/centre-great-lakes/dpp-burundi (last accessed 26th October 2016, but now taken down).

13 The agreement did not speak explicitly of reparations. However, the day of remembrance and the national monument can be considered as symbolic reparations. Moreover, the agreement called for a commission of the reintegration of displaced persons and refugees which was replaced in 2006 by the National Commission for Land and other Goods. The aspect of institutional reforms,

Both transitional justice mechanisms, the TRC and the ICJI, were supposed to be set up during the transitional period from 2001 to 2005, which followed the signing of the Arusha Agreement. Conforming to the agreement, a technical judicial commission elaborated a draft law for establishing the TRC in 2002. This draft law was discussed by the Council of Ministers and the transitional National Assembly in May 2004 and was finally promulgated on 27 December 2004. In early 2005, the government issued a call for applications for the position of the commissioners.

Concerning the judicial mechanisms, and conforming to the Arusha Agreement, President Pierre Buyoya handed in a request to the UN Security Council to set up the IJCI in July 2002. The IJCI was supposed to investigate and establish facts regarding acts of genocide, war crimes and other crimes against humanity, classify them and determine those responsible (Arusha Agreement 2000: Article 6). However, as a response the UN sent an international mission to assess the advisability and feasibility of the IJCI. The resulting report, the so-called Kalomoh Report, proposed an alteration of the Arusha transitional justice formula (see the following section), including the abandonment of the IJCI.

On the formal level, the dealing with the past provisions in the Arusha Agreement comply with international requirements for transitional justice and thus include mechanisms which enjoy international legitimacy. The proposed TRC law of 2004 supposedly promotes the right to know by establishing the truth on serious acts of violence, qualifying crimes[14] and identifying those who are responsible, as well as victims. Moreover, the TRC is supposed to propose competent measures, decide on restitution and reparations for victims and propose all kinds of political, social or other appropriate measures for reconciliation (République du Burundi 2004). As such, the TRC law fulfils an obligation of the Arusha Agreement, respects the timing set by the negotiating parties and seems to have followed procedural aspects in the law-making process. The request to establish the IJCI conforms to the Arusha Agreement and can thus also be seen as an act of compliance with the Arusha requirements regarding transitional justice. Despite these efforts of the Burundian government to establish transitional justice mechanisms, neither the TRC nor the judicial mechanisms have been implemented in the transitional period (2001–2005) following the signing of the Arusha Agreement.

From the beginning of the negotiations in Arusha there was already a perceived tension between the aims of justice and political priorities. Some of the Hutu dominated negotiating parties; in particular, FRODEBU (*Front pour la Démocratie au Burundi*) called for an international tribunal, to judge those responsible for the assassination of the first democratically elected president issued from the ranks of

including the security sector, was also part of the agreement, but the provisions do not foresee any formal vetting process.

14 However, acts of genocide, crimes against humanity and war crimes have been excluded from the TRC's power to qualify crimes (Article 2).

FRODEBU and some of his followers in 1993. Citing the lack of prosecutions and justice after the assassination (e.g. FRODEBU 1997) their wish seemed to have been well reflected in the Arusha Agreement by the proposed IJCI and the international tribunal. However, some of the smaller Tutsi-dominated parties, which considered FRODEBU responsible for the massacres following the *coup d'état* in 1993, also requested an international tribunal, which should be implemented before the first post-conflict elections (ICG 2000; Rutamucero 2006). One of the underlying reasons for their call was that the Tutsi-dominated parties believed, or hoped, that the international criminal tribunal would mainly prosecute their adversaries in the Hutu-dominated parties, thereby eliminating them as political competitors in the elections (Vandeginste 2010). It is such machinations as this that have led to the accusations cited above of the cooption of the transitional justice process for political reasons.

In addition to concerns over cooption, the broader political and security contexts in Burundi are often seen as explanatory factors in the lack of political will to implement those mechanisms agreed upon in 2000. General insecurity and violence[15] still prevailed after the signing of the agreement (e.g. Assemblée Nationale du Burundi 2014) and, according to a representative of the FRODEBU delegation to the negotiations,[16] the priority was definitively to end the war rather than to set up transitional justice mechanisms. This prioritisation became visible through the fact that the so-called Pretoria Protocol, which was signed between the transitional government and the CNDD-FDD (*Conseil national pour la défense de la démocratie–Front pour la défense de la démocratie*) provided temporary immunity to the combatants of the CNDD-FDD, as well as to the security forces of the Burundian government (Pretoria Protocol 2003).

This has been interpreted as a flagrant contradiction of the rhetoric of transitional justice. As Nindorera (2004: 3) states: 'one cannot want one thing and its contrary. One cannot punish odious crimes, and at the same time, preconise provisional immunity, amnesty or the liberation of political prisoners who committed flagrant infractions whose qualification as war crimes and crimes against humanity seems to be evident'. Continuing such apparent contradictions, the first draft of the TRC law in 2002 stated that: 'in the actual context, this [setting up of the TRC] is a particularly difficult and delicate task' (République du Burundi 2002). Moreover, it specified that commissioners could only be nominated after the effective implementation of cease fire agreements (ibid). However, this article was later removed and the law promulgated in 2004 does not in fact explicitly mention political insecurity, despite the fact that only the CNDD-FDD signed a ceasefire agreement in 2003, while the other main armed group Palipehutu-FNL (Palipehutu–*Front national de la libération*) was still at war.

15 Insecurity was also evoked by oppositional parties in the context of setting up the TRC in 2014.
16 Interview by the author with a representative of FRODEBU, Bujumbura 2009 (BUJ-II-a-3).

Another reason that is often cited in relation to the resistance to implement transitional justice mechanisms in Burundi is that these mechanisms are (perceived to be) imposed from the outside by the 'international community' (Taylor 2013). Indeed, bilateral donors and international organisations repeatedly call for accountability of human rights violations and remind the Burundian government of its obligations emanating from the Arusha Agreement, the ratification of the Rome Statute or its rhetorical commitment to establishing transitional justice mechanisms. Such a perception of an international imposition is most relevant for the Arusha Agreement, which was facilitated by an international mediation team and the Kalomoh Report.[17] However, the notion that the Burundian decision-makers resist the implementation of transitional justice because they perceive it to be an international imposition is mainly ascribed to observers rather than being cited by these decision-makers themselves. For example, the Minister of Justice stated during the endorsement of the Kalomoh Report (see below) that transitional justice mechanisms should not be seen as the result of international intervention, calling for Burundians to be included in the discussion (United Nations 2005).

On a rhetorical level it is important for politicians in Burundi to assert national ownership of the process, suggesting as others have done that the narrative of international imposition has come to constitute a myth in analyses of transitional justice in Burundi (Taylor 2013). It also suggests ways in which we can start to be wary of observers keen to ascribe resistance to powerful elites, even when their words and actions do not always confirm to such expectations.

While Burundian political decision-makers had indeed changed their stance, in particular after the first post-conflict elections in 2005, and began to speak of transitional justice as an international imposition, it was still these same decision-makers who firmly requested the inclusion of at least a provision for an international tribunal in the agreement. This is despite the fact that some of the negotiating parties might themselves become the target of such accountability mechanisms. Clearly, we need to look further than accounts of self-preservation to explain these resistance–compliance dynamics and towards political dynamics, as already explored by Subotić (2009) with regard to the Balkans, where she identified motivating factors such as domestic political actors using transitional justice mechanisms for gaining international legitimacy or for removing of political opponents. We can see such interplay between political context and moments of transitional justice continue as we move chronologically through the Burundian process.

Finally, the prevailing violence in the aftermath of the signing of the Arusha Agreement that was cited as a reason for not implementing the transitional justice mechanisms adds a nuance to the resistance–compliance dichotomy. This is not unique to Burundi, since insecurity and ongoing violence are often cited as reasons

17 In contrast to the Arusha negotiations, the elaboration of the new transitional justice formula did not include Burundian participation.

for not establishing transitional justice provisions or leaving them completely out of peace agreements (Sriram 2012). This has been reflected in the so-called 'peace versus justice' debate. There is indeed an existing discourse within the transitional justice field, which says that providing justice is only possible if there is peace and stability, and yet, justice itself can hinder the achievement of (at least 'negative') peace (e.g. Sriram and Pillay 2009).

In using the argument that prevailing violence prevents the implementation of transitional justice mechanisms, actors may thus resort to this existing discourse to justify their resistance to the implementation of transitional justice. Similarly, regarding resistance to international law, we learn from Rajagopal (2003) that: 'the main filter through which Third World resistance is admitted to be legitimate is the discourse of human rights'. This resort to existing discourses or 'dilemmas' thus point to what are considered to be 'legitimate' acts or motives of resistance in transitional justice or in other particular fields. This might even go as far as stating that those choices, actions or behaviours are not even recognised or considered to be resistance (by transitional justice advocates).

The Kalomoh Report: compliance with its recommendations and resistance to their implementation

As a response to the request by Pierre Buyoya to set up the IJCI, in 2004 the UN sent an assessment mission to evaluate the advisability and feasibility of this body (Vandeginste 2010). The so-called Kalomoh Report was published in March 2005 and represents an important moment of transitional justice in Burundi insofar as it called for a reconsideration of the Arusha transitional justice formula. Instead of a TRC, IJCI and international criminal tribunal, it proposed a twin mechanism, consisting of a TRC and a Special Chamber integrated into the Burundian court system, which was, however, later abandoned in favour of a SCT (Ndikumasabo and Vandeginste 2007). As one Burundian politician states: '[i]t is the Kalomoh Report which in fact has defined the prescriptions of a transitional justice' process.[18]

The Kalomoh Report was eventually endorsed by the UN Security Council in a session of June 2005. The Burundian government was represented by its Justice and Keeper of the Seals Minister, Didace Kiganahe, who approved the proposed idea of the TRC and the Special Chamber. He underlined the insufficiencies of the proposed mechanisms of the Arusha Agreement and agreed with the Kalomoh Report that having both commissions would risk overlap in terms of their material and temporal competences (United Nations 2005). However, this endorsement only came some months before the first post-conflict elections took place in 2005. In the meantime, the former armed group CNDD-FDD had transformed into a political party and some months later won the parliamentary

18 Inverview by the author with a representative of UPRONA, Bujumbura 2009 (BUJ-II-a-7).

and communal elections, which gave it a mandate to put forward a presidential candidate from the party ranks.[19]

Thus, the TRC law of 2004 was promulgated 'at the end of the mandate of the transitional regime, but the latter has yielded its place to the new institutions without undertaking something to implement the said law' (Assemblée Nationale du Burundi 2014), according to the minister for National Solidarity, Human Rights and Gender from the party CNDD-FDD.[20] The newly elected government, which was dominated by the CNDD-FDD who did not sign the Arusha Agreement, did not undertake any immediate efforts to implement the Kalomoh Report's recommendations. Instead, the Burundian government and the UN conducted negotiations over the implementation of the Kalomoh Report's recommendations in March 2006 and 2007.

While the endorsement of the Kalomoh Report by the outgoing Burundian government appears to constitute compliance with the international model of transitional justice, several objects of resistance became immediately visible in the endorsement session of the Security Council in June 2005 and later in the context of the negotiations between the Burundian government and the UN.

A first object constitutes the relationship between the TRC and the judicial mechanisms, thus the special chamber or the SCT. This includes important questions such as the qualification of events as particular crimes, whether one of the bodies will be bound by the conclusions of the other or whether they are independent from each other, and whether information that was gathered by one institution can be used as probative value by the other. During the endorsement session, the Justice and Keeper of the Seals Minister, who represented the government, asked for a clarification of the relationship between the TRC and the special chamber (United Nations 2005). The relationship and the independence of the tribunal's prosecutor was thus also an issue during the negotiations between the Burundian government and the UN in order to implement the Kalomoh Report's recommendations (Vandeginste 2010), but no agreement could be reached. Even in the context of the set-up of the TRC, the missing reference to the special criminal tribunal in the TRC law generated much criticism, mainly from opposition parties and civil society organisations and has been seen as an attempt by the government to circumvent this judicial mechanism (e.g. Iwacu 2012; Ndabashinze 2014).

A second object of resistance emerged around the means to achieve reconciliation and forgiveness. For example, the Burundian Minister of Justice and Keeper of the Seals stated that the proposed TRC does not sufficiently take into account the aspect of reconciliation and called for a structure that would be in charge of

19 In 2005 the president was elected by indirect suffrage, while in 2010 he was directly reelected by the population.

20 This was during the explanations of the law to establish a TRC in the parliamentary session in 2014.

national reconciliation (United Nations 2005). In a memorandum issued in May 2007, the CNDD-FDD stated that:

> There is a choice to be made between the way of national reconciliation through the Truth and Reconciliation Commission or the way of repression through a Special Criminal Tribunal. Another way to explore consists of privileging the way of reconciliation and to submit those litigations which could not be solved by the way of reconciliation to the tribunal.
>
> (CNDD-FDD 2007)

Instead of prosecuting and punishing those responsible for serious crimes, the CNDD-FDD favours the South African model in which those who confess their crimes in front of the TRC would benefit from an amnesty (ibid). Based on this memorandum, opposition parties and civil society organisations considered the CNDD-FDD to be resisting one substantial component of the planned transitional justice mechanisms – the SCT – and to be trying to circumvent justice by prioritising forgiveness (e.g. Ndagijimana 2007).

A third issue that appeared in the context of the endorsement of the Kalomoh Report (cf. United Nations 2005) and the negotiations between the Burundian government and the UN were the national consultations. The Burundian government and the UN agreed, in May 2007, to hold national consultations on the modalities of establishing transitional justice mechanisms.[21] They eventually took place between July and December 2009, as well as in March 2010 for the Burundian diaspora. Some opposition parties as well as civil society organisations, however, criticised the consultations for either being a farce[22] or a means to further delay the implementation of the TRC and the SCT.[23]

Indeed, the consultations did not have any tangible influence on the design of the future TRC, not least because their recommendations were not compulsory. However, during the initiation phase, the Burundian government intended for the national consultations to determine the objective of the transitional justice process, its mechanisms and their mandate (Vandeginste 2010; Batumubwira 2006).[24] This led opposition politicians and civil society representatives to suspect that the CNDD-FDD-dominated government attempted 'to find an opportunity to eliminate certain mechanisms that they do not want such as the special tribunal'.[25]

21 Interview by the author with Member of CPT (*Comité de Pilotage Tripartite*), Bujumbura 2009 (BUJ-I-b-3).

22 Interviews by the author with a representative of UPRONA, Bujumbura 2009 (BUJ-II-a-7); and a representative of FRODEBU, Bujumbura 2011 (BUJ-III-a-1).

23 Interviews by the author with a representative of UPRONA, Bujumbura 2009 (BUJ-II-a-7); civil society representative, Bujumbura 2009 (BUJ-I-b-1); civil society representative, Bujumbura, 2010 (BUJ-II-b-1).

24 Member of CPT, radio broadcast, La Benevolencija, 30 July 2010 (BUJ-II-x-7).

25 Interviews by the author with civil society representative, Bujumbura 2009 (BUJ-I-b-1). See also interviews by the author with a representative of UPRONA, Bujumbura, 2009 (BUJ-II-a-7); a

However, the consultations eventually excluded a question over whether to have a TRC and/or a SCT and the TRC was eventually set up in 2014 (see below).

The national consultations can be seen as a transitional justice practice, which is part of the international model of transitional justice and draws from international human rights law (Rubli 2016). Consultations and meaningful participation in decisions that affect one's life are a means to fulfil the right of every citizen to take part in the conduct of public affairs, an element of human dignity and key to empowerment (International Covenant on Civil and Political Rights 1966; Kenny 2000). Thus, by organising national consultations, the Burundian government seems to comply with this requirement. However, if we consider the opposition parties' perception of the national consultations as a delaying tactic or an attempt to prevent or circumvent mechanisms by the government, then the national consultations appear to them as an act of resistance. Thus, the government appeared rather as 'instrumentalists', in Subotić's (2014) words: whilst mechanically complying with a transitional justice practice, the actual transformation that would be required if these consultations were taken seriously is not embraced. This example highlights well the importance of considering the cited or underlying reasons for decisions taken by political elites in order to understand apparently contradictory observations about compliance and resistance.

Furthermore, both aspects, the sequencing of the TRC and the STC, inluding their relationship, and the question of how to achieve reconciliation, are considered by opposition parties as resistance by the government or the ruling CNDD-FDD party to the judicial element of transitional justice. Considering the fact that the CNDD-FDD, as a former rebel group, is supposedly responsible for past violent events, this seems to resonate well with the dominant narrative within transitional justice literature that powerful elites resist transitional justice because they fear prosecutions. However, different meanings and comprehensions of reconciliation, justice and forgiveness might underlie these debates over the suitability, for achieving reconciliation, of a certain body or a sequencing of different mechanisms. For instance, the CNDD-FDD considers reconciliation as a form of continiuing *rapprochement* between Hutu and Tutsi, which would be prevented by a STC since it would (again) oppose perpetrators and victims, or Hutu and Tutsi.[26] Thus, the tribunal, by delivering somewhat punitive justice, is not considered to be an appropriate instrument for the CNDD-FDD's conception of restorative or reconciliatory justice.[27] The reasons to resist particular transitional justice mechanisms might not necessarily be motivated by diverging appreciations of the most appropriate ways to achieve justice and reconciliation, but by diverging understandings of these goals themselves.

Burundian expert, Bujumbura 2009 (BUJ-I-d-1); a member of CPT, Bujumbura 2009 (BUJ-I-b-3); and a civil society representative, Bujumbura 2010 (BUJ-II-b-2).

26 Interview by the author with a representative of CNDD-FDD, Bujumbura 2009 (BUJ-II-a-6).

27 Representative of CNDD-FDD, radio broadcast, La Benevolencija, 22 January 2011 (BUJ-III-x-1). See also Rubli (2011).

Since (objects of) resistance might point to divergent or alternative understandings of reconciliation, peace and justice, we can learn from taking into account those who resist in the analysis that 'the local context' is not homogenous and that opinions, visions and meanings of reconciliation, peace and justice diverge among various local actors. This certainly also applies to the so-called powerful elite; even if different groups were responsible for human rights violations, they might have different perceptions of reconciliation, justice and peace and of the most appropriate means to achieve these aims.

Resistance in the context of setting up a Truth and Reconciliation Commission

A third relevant moment of transitional justice in Burundi is the recent establishment of the TRC. This moment includes the elaboration of the organic law that was prepared by a technical committee in 2011 and which was eventually adopted in 2014, followed by the nomination of commissioners.[28] About six months after the publication of the final report of the national consultations, President Nkurunziza nominated by decree a technical committee that was supposed to propose methodological directions for the TRC and adapt the legal and regulatory texts of the conclusions of the national consultations and the TRC law of 2004 (République du Burundi 2011). In October 2011, at the end of its mandate, the technical committee proposed a draft law on the creation, mandate, composition, organisation and functioning of the TRC (Comité technique 2011). During the formal legislation process in the Council of Ministers, the National Assembly and the Senate, this draft law was amended several times until the Parliament adopted it on 17 April 2014 and the president eventually promulgated it on 15 May 2014. Around two months later, the call for commissioners was publicly launched and finally, on 3 December 2014, 11 commissioners were nominated.

By setting up the TRC, the Burundian government complies with one of the requirements of the Arusha Agreement and the Burundian president fulfilled a political promise that he frequently repeated (e.g. Ikoraneza 2011). This seems surprising since the ruling CNDD-FDD party has not signed it and does not appear to stick much to the content of the agreement (*The Economist* 2011). However, we can only speculate about the reasons and it is important that they be seen in the wider political context. The law was promulgated in only a year, and the commissioners were nominated in only six months, before the elections in 2015 for which President Nkurunziza could not run again, according to a certain

28 There might be further resistance to be observed when the TRC will start its actual work of choosing complaints and hearings of victims, witnesses and alleged authors of crimes. However, at the time of writing (December 2015) the TRC was only conducting preparatory activities such as elaborating the internal organisation, searching funds and organizing awareness campaigns.

interpretation of the constitution.[29] It is important to remember that since the elections in 2010, the CNDD-FDD holds a majority in the Parliament and therefore controls much of the legislative process, including the elaboration of the TRC law. The extra-parliamentary coalition of opposition parties, ADC-Ikibiri (*Alliances des démocrates pour le changement Ikibiri*), suspected that: 'the setup of the TRC would follow the ideals of some members of UPRONA (*Union pour le progrès national*) and CNDD-FDD who would not wish for the real truth to be revealed one day' (*ARIB News* 2012a).

While most of the political parties, the government as well as civil society in general seem to agree with the international normative expectation to deal with the past through a formal body such as a TRC, the process met some resistance. Some of the objects of resistance, including the relationship between the TRC and the SCT or the political context already surfaced in the context of the implementation of the Arusha Agreement or the Kalomoh Report's recommendations. Therefore, this section does not further elaborate on them, but focuses on two other objects of resistance.

A first object of resistance, which is specific to this transitional justice moment, can be located in the way the TRC has been set up. The technical committee, which prepared a draft of the law, was composed of representatives of political parties, including CNDD-FDD, UPRONA and FRODEBU and one history professor, who withdrew citing too much work.[30] The composition of the committee was heavily criticised by representatives of civil society organisations as well as opposition political parties complaining that they were excluded in the elaboration of the TRC law (e.g. FIDH 2011; *ARIB News* 2012c). For example, the vice president of FRODEBU, which is part of the extra-parliamentary coalition ADC-Ikibiri, speculated that the government wanted to prepare the law alone, without consulting the UN or the population (*ARIB News* 2012b).[31]

In addition, the way in which future commissioners should be chosen was criticised on the grounds that it would exclude certain actors. While the initial draft law (Comité technique 2011: Article 15) foresaw that the commissioners should be selected after a large consultation with the government, political parties, parliamentary and extra-parliamentary opposition, religious communities and civil society organisations, the ad hoc commission, which preselected 33 candidates out of the around 700 applications, was only composed of parliamentarians and senators (Commission ad hoc 2014). Thus, during the voting session of the law on 17 April 2015, some deputies of UPRONA and FRODEBU-Nyakuri protested with their

29 Nkurunziza was reelected as president in July 2015, which plunged Burundi into a major political and violent crisis.

30 Interview by the author with a Burundian historian, Bujumbura, 2011 (BUJ-III-d-1).

31 However, the technical committee eventually consulted the group of civil society organisations GRJT and international experts (Ntazina and Gahungu 2011).

absence[32] against the lack of a consensus following what they considered as the interruption of the inter-parliamentary dialogue by the ruling party (Xinhua 2014) and the ruling party's wish unilaterally to designate the commissioners (IRIN 2014).

A second object of resistance was then also the composition of the TRC; this concerns both the actual commissioners who were finally chosen as well as the sole Burundian composition of the TRC. By referring to the results of the national consultations, representatives of opposition parties as well as of civil society organisations complained that the TRC would not be a mixed commission composed of Burundian and international commissioners (Ntazina and Gahungu 2011). Regarding the composition, some voices suspected that the 'right' persons (or those who enjoy the confidence of the government and the ruling party) had not yet applied for the position of the commissioners as the initial deadline for the call for applications as commissioners was extended for another two weeks. The final selection of the commissioners also created an outcry; in particular, civil society organisations were concerned that the commission was composed of 'politicians and religious actors' (Ngendakumana 2014). Indeed, out of 11 commissioners, four have a political background and six commissioners are representatives of religious communities.

When the selection of commissioners was announced, media and statements by different actors almost exclusively mentioned the political or religious background as well as respect for ethnic and gender criteria[33] of the selected commissioners. The main focus was on their political and religious background, since both politics and religion have been cited as having played a significant role in the past violence. For example, the fact that the commission's president, Jean-Louis Nahimana, is a so-called victim of 1972, or that during the mandate of the then justice minister, Clotilde Niragira (secretary general of the TRC), a massacre was committed, has led some to ask whether they would not take a biased stance towards the different cycles of violence or even try to hide or distort evidence (Impunity Watch 2014). Other qualifications, such as their experience in dealing with the past processes or their motivations have rarely been discussed.

Both objects of resistance underlie a crucial element in particular of truth commissions and transitional justice mechanisms. Transitional justice does not only address the past, but also constitutes the future, and thus its mechanisms therefore respond to today's perceived needs for the future (Leebaw 2008). The design and the composition of a TRC largely influence the truth that will be 'found' and officially acknowledged. They thus might be a powerful instrument of

32 The National Assembly adopted the law on the creation of the TRC with 81 votes in favour and one vote against on 17 April 2015 (Assemblée Nationale du Burundi 2014). However, 21 parliamentarians of the oppositional parties UPRONA and FRODEBU-Nyakuri refrained from voting and the single vote against the adoption of the law was from a member of UPRONA (Xinhua 2014).

33 The law of the TRC specified that its composition needs to respect the constitutional equilibrium and must contain at least four women and one member of the Batwa community (Articles 10 and 11). The commission is composed of six Hutu and four Tutsi, which corresponds to the ethnic quota of 60 per cent Hutu and 40 per cent Tutsi for state institutions such as the National Assembly.

those who dominate the legislative process (Rubli 2016) and might be coopted for political reasons. It seems only rational that the CNDD-FDD-dominated government nominated those members of the technical committee and the ad hoc selection commission who enjoyed its confidence in order to control the process that will acknowledge a certain truth. The resistance from opposition parties against both committees might thus rather come from the fact that they could not participate in the elaboration of the draft law of the TRC and the selection of the commissioners owing to the exclusion in the technical committee and the ad hoc committee rather than against the committee's members.

However, their members might also have been the target of resistance, which is even more the case for the selected TRC commissioners (see the second object of resistance above). The commissioners' anticipated and perceived lack of 'impartiality', a criterion that is highlighted by almost every writing on 'good' transitional justice practice, has been used to question the legitimacy of certain personalities to serve as commissioners. However, would it be possible ever to find completely 'impartial' or 'neutral' personalities in contexts such as Burundi where almost everybody has been affected by the past violence, either as a victim, a perpetrator or as a bystander? How would such past experiences influence the work of a commissioner? Moreover, the composition of the Burundian TRC has been criticised for its dominance of religious actors who are perceived to promote forgiveness. In contrast, the South African TRC, to which Burundian actors often make reference, has relied heavily on religious actors. This points to the importance of credibility and legitimacy in transitional justice, which includes questions such as who has the right to decide about those processes or who has legitimacy to say something about the past (Bernath and Rubli 2016). This certainly needs to be seen also in the specific context in which a TRC is operating.

Concluding reflections

By giving a thick description of three decisive moments of Burundi's transitional justice process, this chapter has explored actions, choices and potential motivations of political decision-makers with regard to resistance to and compliance with transitional justice as an international norm. Thereby this chapter adds nuance and complexity to the compliance versus resistance dichotomy that we find in transitional justice literature, and which often posits that it is the powerful elite who resist transitional justice out of fear of prosecution. Instead of ascribing simplistic motivations, we need to take a closer look at the actions and choices that political decision-makers have to make with regard to various aspects of a transitional justice process in order to understand the complexity of the resistance–compliance dynamic regarding the international model of transitional justice.

First, some of the choices that need to be made seem to be rather technical, such as the sequencing of different transitional justice institutions. However, the resistance they met in Burundi points to the fact that those decisions may greatly influence the outcome of the transitional justice process. Thus, transitional justice is not simply a technical process of holding accountable those who committed crimes; instead, it is a political process and a social engineering project (Nagy 2008; Rubli 2012).

Secondly, examining the choices and the underlying potential motivations of political decision-makers also tells us something about the conceptualisation of key concepts of transitional justice, such as justice, reconciliation and peace. For example, the fact that some of the Burundian decision-makers argued that the planned transitional justice mechanisms did not sufficiently consider the aspect of reconciliation might highlight the existence of different understandings of what reconciliation means and how it can be achieved. Or, the perception of an international imposition of transitional justice can point to a misfit between local realties, values and beliefs. However, we also need to remind ourselves that 'the local context' is not homogenous and even the so-called 'powerful elite' is not a unified group with the same interests, but instead the local context, including transitional justice policies, is the product of negotiations.

Thirdly, some of the resistance to transitional justice we can observe in Burundi might arise from the fact that some political actors were excluded from the decision-making process, such as the setting up of the TRC or the selection of its commissioners. Thus, resistance might not be so much about transitional justice itself, the TRC or the legitimacy of the commissioners, but rather about how political decisions are generally taken and how policies are implemented. Finally, we need to remind ourselves that a transitional justice process does not take place in a vacuum, but instead is embedded in a particular political context and transition. This is exemplified by the reasons of resistance that have been put forward with regard to the timing of the transitional justice mechanisms, which were supposed to be set up during the transitional period after the signing of the Arusha Agreement. By referring to the 'peace versus justice' discourse, Burundian political actors evoked the volatile situation and the ongoing violence to motivate the postponing of the transitional justice provision of the Arusha Agreement. Any analysis of actions, choices and potential motivations of political decision-makers must be seen in the broader political post-conflict context in which actors negotiate, compromise and struggle for power, status and legitimacy.

Thus, a particular transitional justice process should rather be seen as a product of different actions, choices and motivations than in terms of simple compliance with or resistance to the international model. This is certainly valid for political decision-makers or any other actors working for or against the implementation of transitional justice mechanisms. Instead, factors such as the political background, the nature of decision-making processes and the domestic struggles, compromises and negotiations for power, legitimacy, the definition of values and the understandings of justice, peace and reconciliation nuance and provide additional explanatory value to the simplistic resistance–compliance dichotomy that we find within the transitional justice literature.

By taking into account those actions, choices and potential motivations, this chapter draws attention to the fact that in Burundi, transitional justice per se does not seem to be resisted, but instead different aspects of the whole process might become the object or the target of resistance. Transitional justice might not be pursued by some actors for the sake of justice, but rather for other reasons and thus become coopted. However, underlying this is the assumption that transitional justice needs to be pursued with the 'correct' motivations to make a social transformation effective and thus be more than a 'mechanistic compliance' on the formal level with setting up transitional justice institutions. This also points to the questions, which certainly deserve future research, of what counts as resistance in a particular field, such as transitional justice, and who defines what legitimate and illegitimate resistance is.

Bibliography

ARIB News. 2012a. 'Nouvelles locales du jeudi 27 décembre 2012'. *ARIB News*, 27 December 2012. www.arib.info/index.php?option=com_content&task=view&id=6424&Itemid=1 (last accessed 30 March 2017).

ARIB News. 2012b. 'Nouvelles locales du lundi 24 décembre 2012'. *ARIB News*, 24 December 2012. www.arib.info/index.php?option=com_content&task=view&id=6408&Itemid=1 (last accessed 30 March 2017).

ARIB News. 2012c. 'Nouvelles locales du vendredi 28 décembre 2012'. *ARIB News*, 28 December 2012. www.arib.info/index.php?option=com_content&task=view&id=6433&Itemid=1 (last accessed 30 March 2017).

Arthur, Paige. 2009. 'How "Transitions" Reshaped Human Rights: A Conceptual History of Transitional Justice'. *Human Rights Quarterly* 31: 321–67.

Arusha Agreement. 2000. *Arusha Peace and Reconciliation Agreement for Burundi*, signed on 28 August 2000 in Arusha.

Assemblée Nationale du Burundi. 2014. *Analyse et adoption du projet de loi portant Création, Mandat, Composition, Organisation et Fonctionnement de la Commission Vérité et Réconciliation.* Bujumbura.

Baines, Erin. 2010. 'Spirits and Social Reconstruction After Mass Violence: Rethinking Transitional Justice'. *African Affairs* 109(436): 409–30.

Batumubwira, Antoinette. 2006. *Lettre au Secrétaire Général Adjoint aux Affaires Juridiques Nicolas Michel, Conseiller Juridique des Nations Unies.* Lettre No 204.01/374/RE/2006, Bujumbura.

Bell, Christine. 2009. 'The "New Law" of Transitional Justice'. In *Building a Future on Peace and Justice: Studies on Transitional Justice, Conflict Resolution and Development: the Nuremberg Declaration on Peace and Justice*, edited by Kai Ambos, Judith Large and Marieke Wierda, 105–27. Berlin, Heidelberg: Springer Verlag.

Bernath, Julie, and Sandra Rubli. 2016. 'Adopting a Resistance Lens: An Exploration of Power and Legitimacy in Transitional Justice'. *Conflict and Society: Advances in Research* 2: 87–104.

Blaikie, Norman. 2000. *Designing Social Research.* Cambridge: Polity Press.

Bonacker, Thorsten, Wolfgang Form, and Dominik Pfeiffer. 2011. 'Transitional Justice and Victim Participation in Cambodia: A World Polity Perspective'. *Global Society* 25(1): 113–34.

Brudholm, Thomas. 2008. *Resentment's Virtue: Jean Améry and the Refusal to Forgive.* Philadelphia: Temple University Press.

Buckley-Zistel, Susanne. 2009. 'Transitional Justice in Divided Societies: Potentials and Limits'. Paper presented at the 5th European Consortium for Political Research General Conference, 10–12 September 2009, Potsdam.

CNDD-FDD. 2007. *Mémorandum du parti CNDD-FDD sur la commission vérité et réconciliation et le tribunal spécial pour le Burundi*. Bujumbura.

CNDD. 2010. *Demain, le Burundi: Les chantiers de demain: 111 engagements fondamentaux du parti CNDD et de son président Léonard Nyangoma pour la paix, et le développement du Burundi*. Bujumbura.

Comité technique. 2011. *Rapport du comité technique chargé de la préparation de la mise en place des mécanismes de justice transitionnelle*. Bujumbura.

Commission ad hoc. 2014. *Rapport de la Commission ad hoc chargée de la préselection des candidats commissaires de la Commission Vérité et Réconciliation*. Bujumbura, File with author.

FIDH (Fédération Internationale des Ligues des Droits de l'Homme). 2011. 'Burundi: le processus de mise en place des mécanismes de justice transitionnelle mal embarqué'. *ARIBNews*, 8 July 2011. www.arib.info/index.php?option=com_content&task=view&id=3687 (last accessed 30 March 2017).

Fletcher, Robert. 2001. 'What are We Fighting For? Rethinking Resistance in a Pewenche Community in Chile'. *The Journal of Peasant Studies* 28(3): 37–66.

FRODEBU, Bureau du Secrétaire Général. 1997. *Memorandum: Du débat national: Les points de vue du Parti Sahwanya-FRODEBU*. Bujumbura.

Guba, Egon G. and Yvonna S. Lincoln. 2005. 'Paradigmatic Controversies, Contradictions, and Emerging Confluences'. In *The Sage Handbook of Qualitative Research*, edited by Norman K. Denzin, and Yvonna S. Lincoln, 191–215. Thousand Oaks, London, New Delhi: Sage Publications.

Hollander, Jocelyn A., and Rachel L. Einwohner. 2004. 'Conceptualizing Resistance'. *Sociological Forum* 19(4): 533–54.

Human Rights Watch. 2009. *Burundi: Seek Justice for War Crimes Victims*. www.hrw.org/news/2009/08/13/burundi-seek-justice-war-crimes-victims (last accessed 30 March 2017).

ICG. 2000. *The Mandela Effect: Prospects for Peace in Burundi*. Nairobi: International Crisis Group.

Ikoraneza, Jean. 2011. 'Discours à la Nation de SE Pierre Nkurunziza à l'occasion de la célébration du premier anniversaire de son investitutre à la tête du Burundi pour un second mandat'. *Burundi Info*, 29 August 2011.

Impunity Watch. 2014. *Policy Brief: Sincerity of Burundi's Commitment to TJ under Scrutiny as TRC Commissioners Sworn In: Four-Year TRC Mandate Officially Begins*. Bujumbura.

International Covenant on Civil and Political Rights. 1966.

IRIN (Integrated Regional Information Networks). 2014. 'Paix et processus de réconciliation en péril au Burundi'. *IRIN*, 17 July 2014. www.irinnews.org/fr/report/100384/paix-et-processus-de-r%C3%A9conciliation-en-p%C3%A9ril-au-burundi (last accessed 30 March 2017).

IWACU. 2012. 'Vers une CVR, mécanisme de Justice de Transition, sans justice ...'. *IWACU*, 4 December 2012. www.iwacu-burundi.org/vers-une-cvr-mcanisme-de-justice-de-transition-sans-justice/ (last accessed 30 March 2017).

Joinet, Louis. 1997. *Revised Final Report. Question of Impunity of Perpetrators of Human Rights Violations (Civil and Political)*. E/CN.4/Sub.2/1997.20. New York: United Nations.

Jones, Briony, Julie Bernath and Sandra Rubli. 2013. 'Reflections on a Research Agenda for Exploring Resistance to Transitional Justice'. swisspeace working paper 3/2013. www.swisspeace.ch/fileadmin/user_upload/Media/Publications/WP_3_2013.pdf (last accessed 30 March 2017).

Kenny, Karen. 2000. 'The Right to Participate in International Human Rights Fieldwork'. *International Human Rights Network* 18.

Knight, Alan. 2012. 'Rethinking Histories of Resistance in Brazil and Mexico'. In *New Approaches to Resistance in Brazil and Mexico*, edited by John Gledhill and Patience A. Schell, 325–53. Durham, London: Duke University Press.

Leebaw, Bronwyn Anne. 2008. 'The Irreconcilable Goals of Transitional Justice'. *Human Rights Quarterly* 30(1): 95–118.

Mamdani, Mahmood. 1996. 'Reconciliation without Justice'. *South African Review of Books* 46 (November–December): 3–5.

McCandless, Erin. 2007. 'Selected Research Perspectives and Paradigms'. In *Peace Research for Africa: Critical Essays on Methodology*, edited by Mary E. King and Ebrima Sall, 111–24. Addis Ababa: Africa Programme, University for Peace.

McEvoy, Kieran. 2007. 'Beyond Legalism: Towards a Thicker Understanding of Transitional Justice'. *Journal of Law and Society* 34(4): 411–40.

McEvoy, Kieran, and Lorna McGregor, eds. 2008. *Transitional Justice from Below: Grassroots Activisim and the Struggle for Change.* Oxford, Portland: Hart Publishing.

Murphy, Matt. 2002. 'Political Justice and Regime Change: A Case for Transitional Justice as a Foundational Rather Than Transitional Act'. Paper presented at the Annual Meeting of the American Political Science Association Boston, August 2002.

Nagy, Rosemary. 2008. 'Transitional Justice as Global Project: Critical Reflections'. *Third World Quarterly* 29(2): 275–89.

Ndabashinze, Rénovat. 2014. 'Vers une CVR amputée d'un aspect judiciaire? Un recul, selon la société civile'. *IWACU*, 3 January 2014.

Ndagijimana, Philippe. 2007. *Déclaration no 0001.* Bruxelles: SurviT-Banguka, Association internationale pour la sécurité et la solidarité de la communauté Tutsi du Burundi.

Ndikumasabo, Méthode and Stef Vandeginste. 2007. 'Mécanismes de justice et de réconciliation en perspective au Burundi'. In *L'Afrique des Grands Lacs: Annuaire 2006–2007*, edited by Stefaan Marysse, Filip Reyntjens and Stef Vandeginste, 109–33. Paris: L'Harmattan.

Ngendakumana, Philippe, 2014. 'Une CVR faite de politiques et de religieux'. *IWACU*, 9 December 2014.

Nindorera, Eugène. 2004. *La réconciliation au Burundi est-elle en marche?* Bujumbura. On file with author.

Ntazina, Barnabé, and Barthélemy Gahungu. 2011. *Rapport des travaux de la journée d'information sur le rapport du comité technique chargé de la préparation de la mise en place des mécanismes de justice transitionnelle au Burundi*, Bujumbura.

Pretoria Protocol. 2003. *The Pretoria Protocol on political, defence and security power sharing in Burundi.* Signed on 8 October 2003 in Pretoria.

Rajagopal, Balakrishnan. 2003. *International Law from Below: Development, Social Movements and Third World Resistance.* Cambridge: Cambridge University Press.

Republique du Burundi, Cabinet du Président. 2002. *Projet de loi portant missions, compositions, organisation et fonctionnement de la Commission Nationale pour la Vérité et la Réconciliation.* Bujumbura. On file with author.

République du Burundi, Cabinet du Président. 2004. *Loi no 1/018 du 27 Décembre 2004 portant missions, composition, organisation et fonctionnement de la commission nationale pour la vérité et la réconciliation.* Bujumbura.

Republique du Burundi, Cabinet du Président. 2011. *Décret no 100/152 du 13 juin 2011 portant création et nomination des membres du comité technique chargé de la préparation de la mise en place des mécanismes de justice transitionnelle.* Bujumbura.

Roht-Arriaza, Naomi. 2006. 'The New Landscape of Transitional Justice'. In *Transitional Justice in the Twenty-First Century: Beyond Turth versus Justice*, edited by Naomi Roht-Arriaza and Javier Mariezcurrena, 1–16. Cambridge: Cambride University Press.
Rubli, Sandra. 2011. 'Knowing the Truth: What For? The Contested Politics of Transitional Justice in Burundi'. *Journal für Entwicklungspolitik* 27(3): 21–42.
Rubli, Sandra. 2012. 'Transitional Justice: Justice by Bureaucratic Means?' swisspeace working paper 4/2012.
Rubli, Sandra. 2016. 'Transitional Justice as an Instrument for Political Struggles: Dealing with the Past and State-Formation in Burundi'. PhD diss., University of Basel.
Rutamucero, Diomède. 2006. *Pour une paix durable et une véritable reconciliation au Burundi*. Bujumbura: Puissance d'autodefense Amasekanya.
Shaw, Rosalind, and Lars Waldorf. 2010. 'Introduction: Localizing Transitional Justice'. In *Localizing Transitional Justice: Interventions and Priorities after Mass Violence*, edited by Rosalind Shaw, Lars Waldorf with Pierre Hazan, pp 326. Stanford: Stanford University Press.
Sikkink, Kathryn. 2008. 'From Pariah State to Global Protagonist: Argentina and the Struggle for International Human Rights'. *Latin American Politics and Society* 50(1): 1–29.
Sisson, Jonathan. 2010. 'A Conceptual Framework for Dealing with the Past'. *Politorbis* 50: 11–15.
Sriram, Chandra Lekha, and Suren Pillay. eds. 2009. *Peace Versus Justice? The Dilemma of Transitional Justice in Africa. Scottsville, South Africa*: University of KwaZulu Natal Press.
Sriram, Chandra. 2012. 'Post-Conflict Justice and Hybridity in Peacebuilding: Resistance or Cooptation?' In *Hybrid Forms of Peace: From Everyday Agency to Post-Liberalism*, edited by Oliver Richmond, and Audra Mitchell, 58–72. Hampshire: Palgrave Macmillan.
Subotić, Jelena. 2009. *Hijacked Justice: Dealing with the Past in the Balkans*. Ithaca, London: Cornell University Press.
Subotić, Jelena. 2014. 'Bargaining Justice: A Theory of Transitional Justice Compliance'. In *Transitional Justice Theories*, edited by Susanne Buckley-Zistel and others. Oxon, New York: Routledge.
Taylor, David. 2013. '"We Have No Influence": International Discourse and the Instrumentalisaton of Transitional Justice in Burundi'. *Stability: International Journal of Security & Development* 2(3): 1–10.
The Economist. 2011. 'Burundi politics: Ruling party rules'. *The Economist*, http://viewswire.eiu.com/index.asp?layout=VWcountryVW3&country_id=110000011 (last accessed 30 March 2017).
Thoms, Oskar N.T., James Ron and Roland Paris. 2008. *The Effects of Transitional Justice Mechanisms: A Summary of Empirical Research Findings and Implications for Analysts and Practitioners*. Ottawa: Centre for International Policy Studies, University of Ottawa.
Thomson, Susan M. 2011. 'Whispering Truth to Power: The Everyday Resistance of Rwandan Peasants to Post-Genocide Reconciliation'. *African Affairs* 110(440): 429–56.
United Nations. 2005. *Le Conseil commente avec le Ministre Burundais de la Justice la proposition de créer au Burundi une Commission de la Vérité et une Chambre Spéciale chargée des crimes graves: Communiqués de presse*. CS/8413, Bujumbura.
UN Secretary General. 2004. *The rule of law and transitional justice in conflict and post-conflict societies*. S/2004/616, New York: United Nations.
Vandeginste, Stef. 2010. *Stones Left Unturned: Law and Transitional Justice in Burundi*. Antwerp, Oxford, Portland: Intersentia.

Vanderlick, Benjamin, and Aloys Batungwanayo. 2012. *Lieux de mémoire, Commemorative Initatives and Memorials to Burundi's Conflicts: Invisible and Permanent Memories*. Utrecht: Impunity Watch.

Vinjamuri, Leslie, and Jack Snyder. 2004. 'Advocacy and Scholarship in the Study of International War Crime Tribunals and Transitional Justice'. *Annual Review of Political Science* 7: 345–62.

Xinhua. 2014. 'Burundi: l'Assemblée nationale adopte le projet de loi portant création de la CVR'. *Xinhua*, 18 April 2014, http://fr.africatime.com/burundi/articles/burundi-lassemblee-nationale-adopte-le-projet-de-loi-portant-creation-de-la-cvr (last accessed 30 March 2017).

Chapter 5

Civil society organisations and transitional justice in Burundi: when making is resisting

Gérard Birantamije

Introduction

> [T]here are organisations that are claiming that if there is no tribunal, then no more TRC. The report of the TRC could be used against alleged perpetrators. We say, let's move. At least there are victims who could succeed.[1]

> When you consider the law, forgiveness is almost imposed; victims are almost obliged to grant forgiveness. Our organisation insists that the person who committed the crime apologise and it is up to the victim to pardon.[2]

Since the signing of the Arusha Peace and Reconciliation Agreement in Burundi in 2000, the country has been committed to implementing transitional justice mechanisms, based both on the evolution of the local political situation and on international standards. Within this process many actors, including civil society organisations, are involved in the construction of a Burundian transitional justice model, an idea over which there is in fact limited consensus as the quotes cited above illustrate.

This chapter explores and highlights how civil society organisations are resisting the idea and attempted practice of a Burundian transitional justice model in their role as in fact 'makers' of this very same model. In doing so there are two main parts to the chapter. The first provides an historical background to the transitional justice process in Burundi with regard to the global transitional justice paradigm. The second analyses Burundian civil society organisations as actors of transitional justice, with a particular focus on their resistance through 'making'. The analysis highlights how the method of implementation favoured by the Burundian government and the international community motivates and shapes this form of resistance. Methodologically, the analysis is based on grey literature, critical literature

1 Interview conducted in person in French with J N, Civil society organisation, Bujumbura, 8 January 2015 (Author's translation).

2 Interview conducted in person in French with C G, Civil society organisation Forum, Bujumbura, 14 January 2015 (Author's translation).

on transitional justice and 13 semi-structured interviews conducted with key civil society organisations in Burundi.

Transitional justice as public policy in Burundi

In Burundi, the Arusha Agreement provides the foundation for transitional justice as public policy. There are three important arguments for thinking about transitional justice in Burundi as a public policy. The first one is that ethnic and political problems have been identified by Burundian politicians as the main causes of different crises that Burundi has been facing for the last 40 years. The second argument is that different decision-makers had proposed transitional justice as one of the main solutions to the Burundian crises. The third one is that there is an attempt to deal with many problems that have arisen from these crises by implementing the transitional justice mechanisms, and in particular by looking at whether there could be a Burundian model of transitional justice (Pohu and Klimis 2013). So far, different actors and organisations have been focusing their debate on both the implementation of these mechanisms and on the development of operational approaches that could fit the national context as well as respond to international standards of transitional justice. In this context, transitional justice is to be seen as a hybrid public policy.

The transitional justice process and mechanisms of Burundi, according to the Arusha Agreement, will deal with human rights violations committed during an unusually long period from independence on 1 July 1962 to 4 December 2009, the date of the end of belligerence between the Government of Burundi and the last rebel group: FNL Palipehutu (Global Rights 2014). In its recommendations, the four pillars of transitional justice that are dominant in international models (truth, justice, reparation and guarantees of non-recurrence) (Joinet 1997) are emphasised by and indeed structure the policy-making around transitional justice that is recommended in the agreement. The agreement further states that the negotiating parties recognise that: 'genocide acts, war crimes and other crimes against humanity have been committed in Burundi against Hutu and Tutsi ethnic communities since Burundi achieved independence' (Arusha Agreement: 16). With regard to such serious aspects, this agreement advocated three mechanisms that would constitute the backbone of transitional justice in Burundi in order to establish truth about the various crises, identify the different responsibilities and persecute where relevant and promote reconciliation.

They were mechanisms such as (i) an International Judicial Commission of Inquiry on genocide, war crimes and other crimes against humanity; (ii) an International Criminal Tribunal to try and convict the guilty once the report of the Commission had established the existence of acts of genocide, war crimes and other crimes against humanity; and (iii) the National Commission for Truth and Reconciliation.

Since the inclusion of this transitional justice policy plan in the Arusha Agreement, there has been mixed progress towards implementation, with some aspects advancing and others appearing to be blocked (see Rubli's chapter in this volume). The implementation of this policy began on 24 July 2002, when the Burundian government requested that the UN establish an International Judicial Commission of Inquiry to investigate the events that had plagued Burundi since its independence (United Nations 2005, Report S/2005/158 § 1; Global Rights 2014: 1). Then, its mandate covers the main events of 1965, when many Hutu politicians and military were killed in the wake of a *coup* attempt against King Mwambutsa; 1972, when a rebel attack in Rumonge, a province in the south of Burundi, was followed by massacres of Hutu intelligentsia (Ngayimpenda 2005; Lemarchand 2004); 1988, with the main FNL Palipehutu attack against Tutsi families, followed by the government army's repressions in the Northern provinces (Chrétien, Guichaoua and Le Jeune 1989); and 1993 to 2009, when it was observed that massacres had taken place against both Hutu and Tutsi by fellow civilians, army personnel and different rebel groups. This request was made in the context of the implementation of the Arusha Agreement and the role that the UN played as one of the guarantors of the agreement (Arusha Agreement 2000: 3).

However, the way in which the UN established the basis of this commission and the resulting conclusions in its report were contradictory to the government request. In fact, the UN did not opt to establish the International Judicial Commission of Inquiry but requested that the Secretary General send a 'Secretariat assessment mission' to Burundi to examine the desirability and feasibility of the establishment of such a commission. This mission, led by Tuliameni Kalomoh, recommended a two-phase approach: the establishment of a non-judicial accountability mechanism in the form of a truth commission, and the establishment of a judicial accountability mechanism in the form of a special chamber within the court system of Burundi (United Nations 2005, Report S/2005/158: 18).

Despite this potential setback to the government's intended policy on transitional justice, a series of laws were passed in relation to the establishment of various transitional justice mechanisms. In particular, on 8 May 2003, it enacted a law to suppress acts of genocide, crimes against humanity, and war crimes, emphasising limitations in testifying against such crimes. Further, the government passed three additional related laws: the Law on the Ratification of the Rome Statute of 30 August 2003 that created the International Criminal Court; the 22 September 2003 enactment that created the Observatory for genocide prevention and eradication, war crimes, crimes against humanity and exclusion; and the 27 December 2004 law that established the National Truth and Reconciliation Commission (NTRC) (Global Rights 2014).

These government initiatives with regard to implementing transitional justice policy as agreed at Arusha take place within a context of negotiation between the government and the UN, and by extension between nationally led approaches and internationally led approaches. Such points of tension have led to different forms of opposition. In particular, the two mechanisms recommended by the Kalomoh Report have for a long time only existed in debate between the Burundian government and the UN. The Burundian government has held the position that there is a choice between either *justice* or *reconciliation*, as this statement made by President Pierre Nkurunziza illustrates: 'After the statement of facts by the CVR[3] (Truth and Reconciliation Commission), we will know the following steps: either reconciliation or justice'. This places reconciliation and justice in direct opposition to each other, in stark contrast to the holistic approach pursued by the UN and based on the four pillars of justice, namely truth, justice, reparation and guarantees of non-recurrence (Lambourne 2014: 41–60).

Such a position was also defended by the ruling CNDD-FDD party,[4] which has, since 2007, focused mostly on 'forgiveness and reconciliation' as it appeared in its 2007 memorandum:

> '[t]he National Truth and Reconciliation Commission [*the name given to the Commission in the Arusha Agreement*] will provide opportunities for reintegration to authors who have confessed their crimes while keeping in perspective the criminal sanctions against those who committed crimes and refuse to cooperate or recognise their crimes' and that 'only the NTRC should then have the quality to cease the special court and determine the crimes to submit to its jurisdiction'.

This position of the ruling party was akin to the one defended by the government in all international arenas, although according to the power-sharing mechanism institutionalised by the Arusha Agreement, the government is a coalition of those political parties which received at least five per cent of the votes in the legislative election. This suggests that the government position on the main public policies such as transitional justice must be one of consensus between the government's members and their political parties. The CNDD-FDD party's position has thus ultimately strengthened the government's position in its pursuit of the implementation of transitional justice mechanisms, politically supporting forgiveness and reconciliation over justice and truth. But this position has proven difficult to implement owing to differing positions of other political parties, and the system of power-sharing based on political and ethnic quotas has led to stalemate and blockage.

In this context, some aspects of transitional justice have been implemented but their meaning and impact are much debated. For example, memorialisation initiatives and reparations programs for victims exist, but many consider them to be unable to achieve transitional justice goals owing to lack of consensus: a national memorial was constructed in Gitega in central province but is still closed; and the resolutions of a national commission on land and other goods are being contested. Furthermore, other political parties also have their own positions on transitional

3 Commission de Vérité et Réconciliation.

4 Conseil National pour la Défense de la Démocratie-Forces de Défense de la Démocratie (CNDD-FDD).

justice and some of them, including UPRONA,[5] support judicial mechanisms in addition to a truth commission. According to UPRONA's stated political position, the process of transitional justice in Burundi must look to the future as the result of a working justice vis-à-vis the perpetrators/victims, address all forms of violations and promote measures of memory, reconciliation and acts of reparation (UPRONA 2013).

This means that hybrid approaches that result from the Kalomoh Report have generated de facto competing rationalities (Matignon 2014: 55–80) based on the different objectives of actors and organisations. Thus, as a public policy, transitional justice is stuck between a rock and hard place. In fact, it has to appear to be in conformity with the national needs of truth, justice and reconciliation as expressed in the Arusha Agreement, with the international standards on transitional justice which form an international public policy being implemented in Burundi, and negotiate between the differing and contested positions of Burundian political actors.

Burundi's transitional justice model and the global paradigm

Transitional justice with its four pillars has emerged as a new paradigm from its exceptionalist origins to become something that is normal, institutionalised and mainstreamed (McEvoy 2007: 412). Its aims are now in this sense rather broad and it can be evoked in response to different kinds of transitions from war, mass atrocities or the crimes of past regimes. The paradigm emphasises that no post-conflict country can achieve sustainable peace and democratic transition if questions of truth, justice and reconciliation for past crimes are not taken seriously (McEvoy 2007; Fletcher, Weinstein and Rowen 2009: 163–220; Baines 2010: 409–30).

Despite this internationalisation of the transitional justice paradigm, scholars have shown that many questions remain, especially when assessing implementation in a variety of cases. Some scholars have asked for whom and for what transitional justice is implemented, and have highlighted how transitional justice has been used by political regimes in transition actually to promote amnesia and retain some level of authoritarian control (Lefranc 2002: 239). Others have emphasised the legalism of transitional justice mechanisms, which belies the political parameters that actually fundamentally determine these processes (Osiel 1999, quoted in McEvoy 2007; see also Cohen 2002). Most critically, transitional justice standards are considered to be a kind of 'westoxification' with 'the west' imposing standards of rights and justice on 'the rest' (Baxi 2012), despite limited empirical evidence that transitional justice mechanisms either positively or negatively improve lives, foster social reconstruction or promote peace (Thomas, Ron and Paris 2008: 31) or indeed

5 There are two mains political parties that were representing Hutu and Tutsi communities in the Arusha negotiations: Union pour le Progrès National (UPRONA) and Front pour la Démocratie au Burundi (FRODEBU).

that they are able to promote accountabilty for crimes (Sriram 2012: 61). It has been noted that in many cases of transitional justice the views of affected people are not taken into account, arguing that global efforts are too foreign and dislocated from the realities of the everyday survivor (Baines 2010; Shaw and Waldorf 2010: 6).

The Burundian transitional justice process, which is in line with the international paradigm, has been facing the same criticisms and limits. Indeed, the Government of Burundi has demonstrated a reluctance to implement the model of transitional justice that is being promoted by international actors, most notably the UN. In fact, after the UN Kalomoh Report the government organised national consultations, which had the aim of, among other things, involving the population in the reconciliation process and creating an environment conducive for national ownership of the transitional justice mechanisms (Republic of Burundi and United Nations 2010). These consultations directly raised the issue of whether transitional justice policy in Burundi was to be determined globally (within international standards), nationally (government approaches according to the political transition) or locally (populations, ie both victims and perpetrators) (Betts 2005: 745–52).

What is interesting to note for the purposes of this chapter is the disjuncture between the views expressed during these consultations and the decisions taken by the government with regard to specific transitional justice policies. For example, the national consultations returned a preference for a TRC with a mixed national and international composition but the government opted to create an entirely Burundian commission. In addition, while more than half of those consulted did not agree with the involvement of political parties in the selection committee for the TRC, the law establishing the TRC provides all rights to parliamentary and extra parliamentary parties to choose the members. Finally, the national consultations showed that about 93 per cent of respondents believed in the value of participation of civil society organisations in the composition of the TRC[6] and about 85 per cent preferred a civil society representative to be given the role of TRC President. In contrast, the government did not provide for any formal inclusion of civil society organisations in this way.

By disregarding the national consultation results, the Burundian government revealed its transitional justice agenda. One interpretation could be that the government acted in the way which could be expected of an actor involved in the crimes considered under the remit of the TRC or tribunal. As noted by Lambourne (2014: 49), 'this development was disturbing but not surprising given that the government comprises a number of former rebel leaders who could be accused of genocide, war crimes and crimes against humanity through the CVR …'.

Whether or not this is a direct causal factor in the government's policy-making, it is possible to say that the law establishing the TRC was shaped by the political demands of the ruling party and a balancing act between the demands of the

6 The draft law proposed by the Technical Committee in its Report intended that the selection procedure must involve only the parliamentary and extra-parliamentary political parties.

international community, the views of the local population and the implications of certain mandates for the mechanisms. The response of the government in disregarding the national consultations and UN reports in its decision-making may be disturbing as Lambourne (2014) suggests, but it is certainly not without its challengers. As with other forms of domination we can read in the Burundian process forms of resistance to the government. In particular, resistance which is articulated in the very process of making and implementing the transitional justice process dominated by the government.

Transitional justice and resistance

The previous two sections have illustrated that transitional justice like other public policies remains exposed to resistance as many actors with different interests and agendas are involved. It is necessarily contested as it involves negotiation and compromises over legal, political and even moral aspects. Moreover, transitional justice as a form of justice faces realpolitik (Lefranc 2002: 75) as different parties attempt to consolidate their power in the face of a political transition and a shifting political landscape. Thus, the new attempts to achieve a balance of power create in themselves dominators and resistors; as Michel Foucault pointed out: '[w]here there is power, there is resistance' (Foucault, as quoted by Hollander and Einwohner, 2004: 548).

The resistance that is analysed in this chapter is understood not in terms of violent protest against the way the Burundian government is conducting the transitional justice process but rather in terms of soft mechanisms, likely to influence the government's position in moving towards international standards considered to be more or less legitimate. This approach is influenced by the work of scholars such as James Scott, who writes of 'infrapolitical dominated groups' who develop secret forms of everyday resistance (Scott 2008: 33). In the Burundian context it is civil society groups who most closely match this actor description and who leverage their position as 'makers' of transitional justice to be 'resistors' of the transitional justice that is being offered to them. Their acts of resistance take place within discourse and by taking part in the implementation of transitional justice mechanisms, opportunities which are used to deconstruct social myths of ethnicity, to shape the process to move it away from government aims and to challenge the procedures taking place. Before analysing this in more detail we first need to understand the nature of civil society in Burundi and how civil society organisations operate as transitional justice actors.

Civil society organisations in Burundi as transitional justice actors

Civil society organisations are almost a new phenomenon in Burundi. They date back to the 1990s with the wave of democratisation in many African countries (Gillet 1997: 65). In fact, there are five mains groups with different implications at different levels: community-based organisations and associations; political or social organisations mainly located in urban areas, specifically in the capital Bujumbura; trade unions; religious organisations; and media[7]. Whilst of course many differences exist between these organisations (legal status, paid staff, missions and geographical locations), the main difference is their political participation or their intervention in political issues such as transitional justice. Community-based organisations are located mainly in rural areas with their influence on transitional justice limited and mainly pursued through relationships with international organisations.

The UN transitional justice unit located in BNUB[8] created the FONAREC/TJ[9] in order to involve community-based organisations as community facilitators in the transitional justice process.[10] They contribute to capacity building in transitional justice, especially in the area of memorialisation. Members of FONAREC and people in rural areas participate in identifying mass graves in different localities of the country.[11] Other organisations located in urban areas are mostly engaged in advocacy and play a significant role in the transitional justice process, as we will see in the analysis that follows. Religious organisations also play a significant role in the community-based reconciliation process by organising meetings and fora on issues related to transitional justice, such as the *Commission Episcopale Justice et Paix* of the Catholic church of Burundi.[12] The media is also part of the transitional justice process as different outlets organise debates on transitional justice and related issues.

Civil society organisations in Burundi as a whole are playing a significant role in the development of the political landscape and peace-building policies in Burundi. Overall, they have been contributing to the formation of public opinion and popular involvement in political issues, especially those close to the transitional justice process. In particular, civil society organisations have been performing three main functions most relevant to the discussion here. Firstly, civil society in Burundi has been consistently considered to be a public space for the denunciation of government abuses and thus, as a space for advocating for change. Secondly, they have been playing a role as observers and controllers of government and population behaviors that do not comply with Burundian and international norms and legislation by organising workshop training, norm dissemination, monitoring of implementation processes, surveys and above all publishing reports on related issues. And thirdly, they have played a role in the socialisation of the population towards political participation (PRIME ACBF 2011).

7 The media is sometimes considered to stand outside of civil society but in the Burundian context it makes sense to include it as a civil society actor.

8 Bureau des Nations Unies au Burundi (United Nations Office in Burundi).

9 Forum National des Relais communautaires pour la Justice de Transition (FONAREC/JT).

10 Interview conducted in French with T K, Tutsi, member of a civil society organisation, Bujumbura, 14 January 2015. See also Lambourne 2014, 50–51.

11 T K, Interview, Bujumbura, 14 January 2015.

12 For more information, see the commission's website www.paxchristi.net/member-organizations/burundi/126 (last accessed 30 March 2017).

The relationship between civil society organisations and successive Burundian governments since the Arusha Agreement has been strained. This has required civil society organisations to adopt strategies to organise themselves in coalitions based on specific peacebuilding issues. Among others there is the *Forum pour le Renforcement de la société civile* (FORSC),[13] created in 2002, the ambition of which is to strengthen the organisations of civil society in Burundi, the *Coalition des organisations de la Societé civile pour le Monitoring des Elections* (COSOME),[14] created in 2005, which handles election monitoring, the *Observatoire de l'Action Gouvernementale* (OAG)[15] for the observation of government actions and, recently, the *Groupe de Réflexion sur la Justice Transitionnelle* (GRJT).[16] This strategy has also been reinforced by the media, which has always organised itself in synergy with civil society coalitions on sensitive issues such as elections, corruption and transitional justice. Indeed, civil society organisations in Burundi are considered to be the main actors who interplay with government policies.

Generally speaking, the principal activities of these organisations are training and advocacy. With regard to training, workshops are organised with a focused expertise on topics related to national issues. In addition, these organisations produce annual reports, organise media debates, press releases and often send advocacy memoranda to the government and the international community. All these activities mean that civil society organisations are key actors of transitional justice, even though their legitimacy is challenged by the government position on these transitional justice issues. The important role that civil society organisations play is evidenced in the fact that much of what the population knows about transitional justice in Burundi is from civil society activities rather than from government. Indeed, when the government was organising national consultations before implementing transitional justice mechanisms, people did not hesitate to ask that the process be led by civil society and churches (Republic of Burundi and United Nations 2010).

This role for civil society is at odds with a national government that wants to organise and control the debate on sensitive issues such as the establishment of transitional justice. Despite including civil society organisations in the transitional justice process the government has at the same time passed new laws on associations and the press in order to restrict the scope of their activities. In addition, new organisations allied with the government have been set up to help to sabotage other civil society organisations' actions.[17] The absence of a civil society representative in the TRC, and the distance which the government has put between itself and the national consultations' report which was in favour of a strong role

13 Forum for the Reinforcement of the Civil Society (FORSC).

14 Coalition of Civil society organisations for Elections Monitoring (COSOME).

15 Observatory of Government action (OAG).

16 Reflexion Group on Transitional Justice (GRJT).

17 Interview with V.N., Tutsi, Male, member of a civil society organisation's Forum; Bujumbura, 10 January 2015.

for civil society organisations, has been transformative in galvanising the forms of resistance which are the focus of this chapter.

Civil society organisations' resistance: making as resisting

In this chapter I focus on the 'resisting by making' of civil society organisations active in transitional justice in Burundi. The 'Making as Resisting' as an approach to Burundian transitional justice process has similarities to the everyday resistance of James Scott. While Scott analyses 'resistance' in the context of complete domination such as slavery, I analyse civil society organisations' resistance in line with political participation rules in democratic society. In a context such as Burundi, where the government is powerful enough to ignore the views of civil society organisations, then these same organisations, which are recognised as actors in processes of democratic participation, can be analysed as dominated actors.

Three main similarities can be outlined between this 'making as resisting' approach that I am developing here and Scott's analysis of everyday resistance. First, Burundian civil society organisations as a dominated group in the transitional justice implementation process produce a text which remains hidden from the eyes of the dominant and which constitutes a critique of power as it is the result of power relations (Scott 2008: 12). Second, civil society organisations resist by avoiding open confrontations with authority structures to which they have opposing views (ibid 101). The making as resisting which we analyse in this part of the chapter consists of managing ironic messages on the established order (the transitional justice process in this context). Third, the practices initiated by civil society actors express the refusal to reproduce hegemonic appearances, as they gradually create social spaces for a culture of dissent (ibid 123). This has led to the exploration of new avenues to deal with the dominant government's approach. As we can see, civil society organisations write press releases, hold memoranda, conduct surveys, organise workshops and send suggestions to the government. The main purpose of such activities is to encourage the government to consider alternatives to its approach to transitional justice and to alter policy course accordingly.

The only important difference between Scott's model of resistance and 'making as resisting' which I also want to emphasise is linked to the existence of a public space of contestation owing to the fact that democratic participation permits open contestation within organised movements such as civil society organisations. This space is exploited by civil society in order to influence the transitional justice debate that is dominated by the government. The signing of the Arusha Agreement did not close political debate on transitional justice. The ruling parties faced debate and opposition from other parties, with diverse perspectives on how Burundi should deal with its past.

For the main political parties representing the two ethnic groups (Hutu and Tutsi), the positions are entrenched. For the CNDD-FDD, which has been the dominant party since the 2005 election and may be said to represent 'Hutu interests' and a

'Hutu vision' of transitional justice, all mechanisms should lead to reconciliation, an end goal that can be achieved even without justice (CNDD-FDD 2007). But for the UPRONA party that represents the Tutsi minority, there can be no reconciliation without judicial forms of justice for the victims identified in the 1995 international inquiry report, ie the Tutsi (United Nations 1996). For UPRONA the truth as such is already known, and any policy that pursues only reconciliation is considered to be legitimising impunity and negating the rights of victims (UPRONA 2013).

This kind of debate is in contradiction with the international standards as outlined above. As Pablo de Greiff[18] has stated, truth, justice, compensation and guarantees of non-recurrence should be thought of as components of an overall policy, not as a menu from which national governments can select one preferred element (UN Special Rapporteur 2014: 1). As mentioned above, the activities of civil society actors vis-à-vis the transitional justice process in Burundi have been aimed at moving the government's policies towards a standardised international position, not by standing outside of the process but by engaging in ways which can subtly alter the course of the process. This resistance has operated with a series of key aims, which are analysed in the rest of this chapter.

'Depoliticisation' of the transitional justice debate

By understanding 'depoliticisation' of the debate on transitional justice as an act of resistance we want to stress what many interviewees have shown: the way civil society organisations have tried to reconnect grassroots communities to transitional justice and to move the transitional justice debate away from political parties and their interests. This depoliticisation can be seen in exploring the media debate on transitional justice and interventions of civil society organisations in these debates; and the sensitisation of the population to transitional justice via plays.

Apart from the somewhat patchy consultations with the population, civil society raised the population's awareness both of the evolution of transitional justice mechanisms and, above all, what could be expected from the government with regard to these mechanisms. Through these public yet subtle actions, the influence of political actors over the process has gradually weakened as people have had access to more information about their transitional justice needs, and specifically those needs as advocated for by civil society organisations. According to one interviewee:

> No one was able to say what transitional justice is before the media had organised debates. Even politicians were not informed about what these mechanisms would provide for the population. Some were saying, people need justice, truth and reconciliation, but it was as though people are equal to politicians. Do you think CNDD-FDD [*party*] opinions are for all Burundians?

18 The UN Special rapporteur on the promotion of truth, justice, reparation and guarantee of non-recurrence since 2012.

> If UPRONA or FRODEBU say no transitional justice, do you really think people don't need it anymore? Politicians have their own agenda, mostly different from the need of populations.[19]

As other interviewees added, the media diffused in the population at large information about the transitional justice mechanisms and the debate between politicians, which was of distinct value because 'people really understand the different positions of representatives of political parties and compare these with expert views on the same problems'.[20] The idea behind these debates which were mainly organised in coordination with media, is that transitional justice has been for a long time a preoccupation for 'politicians who are seeking legitimacy and votes',[21] but 'not to elucidate the events that Burundi has experienced and that people have had to suffer'.[22] Specific debates have been organised such as '*Akahise kadasorongoye*' (the unsolved past)' and '*si ma mémoire est bonne*' (if my memory is good) in order to explicitly depoliticise the debate on Burundian contemporary history (La Benevolencija 2015). In line with Scott's work, this constitutes a refusal to reproduce hegemonic appearances built by government actors in this transitional justice process.

The second aspect that highlights resistance by moving the debate away from the control of the political parties is the use of socio-cultural mechanisms such as 'catharsis' plays (Matignon 2014: 82, 131; Rosoux 2007: 101–10), mostly followed by community discussion groups which address the content of the plays and the possibility of different outcomes and actions. Civil society organisations such as AMEPCI,[23] *Réseau des Citoyens Network* (RCN *Justice et Démocratie*) or Trauma Healing and Reconciliation Services (THARS) are mostly known to have developed this strategy. This generated a common understanding of the pillars of transitional justice and especially that none of them can be neglected in favour of the others. The main output was that at the time of national consultations, people expressed their wishes and expectations on the subject of each pillar and on the transitional justice mechanisms as whole as previously outlined.

Struggling for the non-instrumentalisation of the transitional justice mechanisms

Even though civil society has not been able to control the political agenda of transitional justice (Vandeginste 2009) its resistance to the political instrumentalisation

19 Interview conducted in French with J-N B, Tutsi, Male, member of a Victim's Association, Bujumbura, 15 December 2014.

20 Interview conducted in French with A B, Hutu, Male, member of a Victim's Association, Bujumbura, 29 December 2014.

21 C G, Interview, Bujumbura, 14 January 2015.

22 Interview conducted in French with T M, Tutsi, Male, Victim's Association, Bujumbura, 31 December 2014.

23 AMEPCI means *Association pour la Mémoire et protection de l'humanité contre les crimes internationaux*. It is a Burundian civil society organisation involved in memory and memorialisation issues.

of transitional justice arose at the beginning of the Arusha Agreement. Two attitudes illustrate this.

First, civil society has engaged in an intense resistance against policies granting political immunity and provisional immunity to government-defined 'political' prisoners. It was said that 'immunity is the breeding ground of impunity and the dependence of justice on politics'[24] and, as one leader of a civil society organisation has noted:

> Justice acts as a deterrent, if people began to kill, what would prevent the same crimes being repeated. Justice is one of the guarantees of non-recurrence; it would also be an opportunity to give a new beginning, that is to say, another basis for the functioning of justice.[25]

Secondly, many civil society organisations believe that if there is no independent justice, transitional justice will fail. This can be seen in the denouncement of judicial decision-making, as three particular cases illustrate well. Faced with two instances of prisoner release (first 673, then 780 prisoners) decided by the government in 2006 (Republic of Burundi, Decree no 100/2 of 2 January 2006), AC Genocide Cirimoso, the association against genocide, protested against the release of criminals who had been convicted in Burundian courts. The group perceived this action to be an infringement of the principle of the separation of powers, a final blessing for the crime of genocide, and an affront to the lives of survivors who had testified against such criminals (AC-Genocide 2006: 1).

In the same vein, the *Association des Chrétiens pour l'Abolition de la Torture* (ACAT-Burundi)[26] did not mince its words: 'The Ministerial Order No. 550/18 of 9/1/2006 on provisional political prisoners' release from the jails of the Republic of Burundi is a consecration of impunity, a blatant breach of laws and constitutional principles as well as a denigration of victims' (ACAT-Burundi 2006: 1). This resistance against a political measure considered by the political class as a prelude to reconciliation culminated with a condemnation of the prisoner release orders as unconstitutional by the *Forum pour le Renforcement de la Société Civile*, the Burundian Human Rights League Iteka, and the Observatory of Government Action (OAG), three other civil society organisations significantly involved in transitional justice.

What is important in this kind of resistance is that these different civil society organisations do not have enough power to contest or even to make the government change the decision taken, but they act as actors invested with the legitimacy to contest government decisions. In their different press releases or memoranda, it was clear that civil society organisations expressed the need for a holistic approach to transitional justice whereas the government was focusing on a 'piecemeal'

24 T K, Interview, Bujumbura, 14 January 2015.
25 T M, Interview, Bujumbura, 31 December 2014.
26 Christians' Association for the Abolition of Torture (ACAT-Burundi).

approach that helped them to justify the primacy of reconciliation over justice in negotiations with the UN on transitional justice mechanisms (Ligue Iteka 2014). It is as though the transitional justice mechanisms as they are standardised gave an opportunity to the government to implement pillars that would serve its own interests, especially those permitting government actors to escape from prosecution (Ndabashinze 2014).

Collaboration between 'intimate enemies'

In a country torn apart by ethnic conflict, civil society is not immune to or detached from ideologies mobilised according to ethnic group identity. Expectations of unanimity amongst Hutu and Tutsi mean that while civil society organisations are not structured as either defending a Hutu or Tutsi cause, they are still labelled as such by each other. This situation is a challenging one in which to work as one civil society actor observed:

> Burundian civil society organisations reflect the experiences of Burundian society as a whole. They are implemented by Hutu and Tutsi who were struck by the different tragedies and are still suffering from the effects of this painful past. Some associations were created to defend a particular group of survivors and to seek justice for them, and thus use the label of a Hutu or Tutsi cause. Do you see for example that AMEPCI is speaking up for 1972 victims more and globally for Hutu victims, whereas AC Genocide-Cirimoso is focusing more on the 1993 Tutsi massacres? This means that they are not seen favorably by this or that group.[27]

For many interviewees, this labelling impacts on processes of reflecting on, and memorialising, the past. When on 21 October each year, AC Genocide-Cirimoso commemorates the 1993 Tutsi genocide, only Tutsi go to the memorial at Kwibubu. In the same vein, when Hutu associations commemorate 1972 victims, Tutsis do not attend.[28] This situation has been greatly exploited by politicians. It was common to see Tutsi political parties participate in 21 October 1993 commemorations and Hutu political parties saying they would not commemorate that day. The government has erected a monument at Kwibubu and has also participated in these commemorations but, since 2005, the government has refused to send a representative to the memorial. This has been interpreted by Tutsi as a sign of 'denial' of the Tutsi genocide that was recognised by the UN in 1996 (United Nations, Report S/1996/682; Decaux 1997: 33).

27 T M, Interview, Bujumbura, 31 December 2014.
28 A B, Interview, Bujumbura, 29 December 2014.

However, one interviewee said that collaborative engagement between victims' associations invited them to synergise their efforts and transcend personal and group pains and interests because no ethnic group or political party can claim to have the monopoly on suffering.[29] In order to resist such processes of labelling which occur in the realms of civil society and political parties, the solution has also been sought in working with civil society and two institutions have been established with this aim in mind: the GRJT and the Collective Victims' Associations (CARAVI).

Comprising representatives from the executive body (Ministry of Human Rights, Ministry of Justice), legislative (the National Assembly and the Senate) and independent special committees (Independent National Commission for Human Rights), civil society,[30] international non-governmental organisations[31] and the UN (BNUB Transitional Justice Unit), the GRJT, which was created in 2006, is a think tank which draws its legitimacy from gathering different actors with diverse perspectives on transitional justice. The confidence in this group can be measured in terms of the place held during the consultations organised by the Technical Committee in charge of the establishment of transitional justice mechanisms (République du Burundi 2011: 122–25). Its reputation also rests with its recommendations to that committee (GRJT 2011) as well as the memoranda it sent to the parliament and the government before the appointment of the commission members (GRJT 2014). In this Memorandum, the GRJT explains the need to communicate the list of 33 commissioners from which the Parliament ad hoc group would choose the 11 commissioners to be appointed to the TRC.

According to the GRJT, this would offer to the population an opportunity to appeal against the risk of election of members who do not fulfill the conditions required by Article 13 of the Act creating the TRC. Furthermore, this civil society organisation called all parliament groups to participate in the ad hoc commission so that there can be a debate during the selection process of the commissioners, giving more credibility to the future TRC (ibid 2–3). The government did not accept the suggestion, and for now the selection of the commissioners has raised concerns.[32]

Even if most of its expertise was rejected by the government,[33] the GRJT remains the most listened to group. It is considered to be impartial and representative of all the opinions of Hutu and Tutsi communities with regard to transitional justice. Notably before its creation, the party in power, the CNDD-FDD, and the government created their own organisations in order to challenge civil society organisations engaged in transitional justice. These organisations called 'Government-organised Non-governmental Organisations' or GONGOs (Steinberg 2001), are associations

29 J-N B, Interview, Bujumbura, 15 December 2014.

30 That is FORSC, AMEPCI-Girubuntu, THARS, FONAREC-JT, MIPAREC, FOCODE, conseil national des Bashingantahe, Commission Episcopale pour la Paix, PISC-Burundi, etc.

31 It is the case of Impunity Watch, Global Rights, RCN justice et Démocratie and La Benevolencija.

32 C G, Interview, Bujumbura, 14 January 2015.

33 Interview conducted in person in French with J N, Civil society organisation, Bujumbura, 8 December 2014 (Author's translation).

or organisations created by a political or ethnic group with the sole purpose of combating actions advanced by civil society on a given political issue.

At this level, this group has allowed civil society to resist internal dissent related to ethnicity as each of them are somewhat affected by one of the Burundi's main crises as a Hutu or a Tutsi. For example, the CNDD-FDD party and its satellite organisations constituted by former Hutu political actors and combatants have been arguing that the TRC would be a political organ constituted only by former belligerents, a kind of return to the conflict between Hutu and Tutsi. This would create dissent in the GRJT as different members of GRJT are Hutu or Tutsi and are somewhat affected by that opposition as members of an ethnic community. But intervening in media, members of GRJT have shown the danger of this approach in the search for truth. According to them, everyone would blast the investigation of crimes committed in his own camp (Mbazumutima 2013a). Unanimously, they showed that it would endanger the entire process of finding the truth, which must be not that of Hutu or Tutsi, as one interviewee noticed:

> In the GRJT, we are Hutu and Tutsi. And when a member is speaking, he is maybe a Hutu or a Tutsi but he is not for the payroll of Hutu or Tutsi. That is the force of this group. We all work for a real transitional justice process. For Hutu or for Tutsi, truth is truth. …[34]

The second civil society group that resists communitarianism are the victims' associations. Currently eight associations have emerged to fight for victims' rights within a Support and Thinking Centre for Victims' Associations (CARAVI). Like GRJT, CARAVI is not legally recognised.[35] This support centre gathered all the victims' associations and brought together the choices made with respect to the four transitional justice pillars.

The interviews made it clear that the victims' associations share an understanding that the four pillars are complementary. On this topic, one interviewee questioned:

> What is truth without justice? And without vetting institutions? What is reparation without justice as we noticed with monuments? I think we need a clear policy that internalises international standards, which puts them into practice and shows how international standards are rigorous towards transitional justice. These four mechanisms are like the wheels of a car.[36]

Another interviewee added:

> Our organisation has protested against forced forgiveness, and seeks to encourage not only the knowledge of the truth but also justice for the victims.

34 A B, Interview, Bujumbura, 29 December 2014.
35 ibid.
36 ibid.

> When you look at the law, forgiveness is almost imposed, victims are almost obliged to give forgiveness. We insist that the person who committed the crime and asks for forgiveness, it is up to the victim to forgive. Victims are both Hutu and Tutsi, we need a common process.[37]

From the first steps of the implementation of the Arusha Agreement's transitional justice policy, there has been a lack of a shared vision of the transitional justice pillars. Before the creation of CARAVI, communitarianism was at its height. Some organisations advocated for the search for truth, others for compensation, still others for justice. These diverse understandings resulted in the victims' commemorations being held separately early on in the transitional process, because some organisations think the truth is known, whereas others express the need to know exactly what happened. For example, the AC-Génocide consider the debate of Tutsi in 1993 closed as the UN resolution recognised it in 1996. So what they seek is justice. However, there are organisations such as the Association of 1972 Victims (Kazirukanyo 2015) or the Association of Victims of Ntega-Marangara (Ngabire 2013) that understand their work as seeking the truth.

These organisations have long been commemorating separately as if the Hutu victims' suffering was not the same as the Tutsi's. Sometimes such activities are brought back to moments of denial, believing each group has a monopoly on suffering. In order to resist this, CARAVI has organised since 15 December 2013 joint commemorations at which testimonies are delivered by both Hutu and Tutsi victims (CARAVI 2014). These joint commemorations are also an occasion to celebrate the 'unsung heroes', ie those Hutu or Tutsi who saved people from their opposite community from massacres.[38]

This kind of celebration driven more recently by civil society organisations, apart from resisting communitarianism as they permit the transcendence of differences as victims' organisations, also permits working together for the interest of all victims, such as in the process of identifying mass graves.[39] This can also be interpreted as resistance to the government's option of not participating in or organising commemorations. Indeed, it appears that the government dominated by Tutsi did not permit any act of memorialisation of Hutu community but accepted and organised commemoration for Tutsi community since 1994. From 2005, when the government came into the hands of the former Hutu armed opposition movement CNDD-FDD, the government had neither participated in nor organised any commemoration of victims.

37 C G, Interview, Bujumbura, 14 January 2015.
38 J.-N B, Interview, Bujumbura, 15 December 2014. See also Ngabire 2014a.
39 T K, Interview, Bujumbura, 14 January 2015. See also Mbazumutima 2013b.

Exploring new avenues while dealing with the government approach to transitional justice

Following the discussion of how civil society is 'making by resisting' through its participation in and attempts to reshape the transitional justice process this chapter now turns to the important role that civil society organisations are playing following the government's creation of the TRC. The 2014 establishment of the TRC by the Government of Burundi resulted from the challenges of civil society as one of the main actors invested in transitional justice, and their scathing criticism of the government. Specifically, the criticisms focused on the composition of the TRC and the option of forgiveness privileged by the law. Indeed, in a press release, the Forum for Civil Society Reinforcement attacked one of the commissioners, Mrs Clotilde Niragira, accusing her of lack of competency, honesty and integrity. For evidence, FORSC recited a series of her failures, including support for impunity in crimes against human rights, arbitrary imprisonment, and her appointment of inexperienced judges to high judicial responsibilities when she was Minister of Justice (FORSC 2014a). Different civil society actors who were interviewed stressed that the composition of the TRC indeed raises many concerns. For example:

> The knowledge of the truth which will be endorsed by the government remains fragmented. The TRC will initiate further guidance. The Commissioners do not inspire any confidence. This is the case of Clotilde [Niragira, TRC Secretary] or someone who worked at the President Bagaza cabinet, these are people who are involved in many cases of the Burundi crisis. Does their past not hinder research?[40]

Another civil society activist added:

> We're not totally satisfied with the way things are conducted. The establishment of the TRC was made in violation of the popular consultations. Art 10 of the memorandum between the United Nations and Burundi was not respected. For example, any member of the SC is not a member of the TRC ... With respect to the composition, it should be first civil society, religious commissioners. But beyond some members are not credible .... The commission taken globally is somewhat not satisfactory. In fact, even if members have been approved, the media had already reported the names. So it seems that the appointment was made elsewhere ...The commission is composed mainly of the victims of 1972, the procedure is almost biased.[41]

Claims that each commissioner has been implicated in past violations (Ngendakumana and Bigirimana 2014) led some to conclude that these commissioners should in fact be among those being heard by the commission rather than

40 J N, Interview, Bujumbura, 8 January 2015.
41 J-N B, Interview, Bujumbura, 15 December 2014.

among those conducting the hearings.[42] The second criticism regarding the composition concerns the commissioners' ideological affiliation. Made up of 50 per cent religious representatives and 50 per cent politicians, the TRC was intended to be a deal between the two groups. However, in many ways the approaches advocated by both religious leaders and political parties are similar and suggest a coincidence of perspectives which lends further support to the government's attempts to control the process. For example, forgiveness has a central role for both the religious representatives and those politicians close to the CNDD-FDD. According to the government, forgiveness is necessary in order to avoid destabilising the country.

The ruling party CNDD-FDD in its statement of 2007 noted that: 'Instead of favoring the path of repression by the simple legal procedure, the CNDD-FDD party believes that mutual forgiveness is the most appropriate way to ensure reconciliation and lasting peace in Burundi (CNDD-FDD 2007: 5–6). Such a sentiment has been repeated by key religious groups in Burundi (Conférence des Evêques catholiques du Burundi 2014: 5). This coincidence of positions taken by religious leaders and politicians – to forgive and to liberate rather than administer punitive justice – has forced civil society to work with members of the TRC as a form of resistance.

In order to collaborate more directly with the TRC civil society organisations have undertaken a series of activities such as the elaboration and publication of a citizens' guide on the TRC (FORSC and Nindorera 2015). This guide is a tool for use by each citizen as a victim, witness or alleged offender to know his/her rights as provided for in the TRC Law. Even though not each civil society organisation has faith in the TRC commissioners, they still advocate for ensuring that the process be as effective as possible in contributing to justice in Burundi, and in so doing to be moved further away from the control of the government. As one interviewee said:

> [T]here are organisations that are claiming that if there is no tribunal, then no more TRC. The report of the TRC could be used against alleged perpetrators. We say, let's move. At least there are victims who could succeed.[43]

Concluding remarks

In his book, Scott (2008: 220) notes that it is one thing not to greet a superior using the appropriate formula, and it is another to deliberately refuse to greet him. This passage reflects the kind of resistance initiated by Burundian civil society to the state sanctioned transitional justice process. Civil society does not deliberately refuse the approaches initiated by the government from the signature of the

42 T M, Interview, Bujumbura, 31 December 2014; J.N., Interview, Bujumbura, 8 January 2015.
43 J N, Interview, Bujumbura, 8 January 2015.

Arusha Agreement in 2000 but resists them by highlighting and advocating for alternatives both within and outside of the process.

Various positions taken have drawn Burundian civil society organisations close to the positions taken by the UN and international standards without firmly making open opposition to the government. In a situation where there are no checks and balances on government power, this form of resistance is not insubordination, but accommodation to the status of secondary actor to play its full role of rectifying state wrongs. If the results of this resistance are scarce in relation to the recent establishment of the TRC, what is important is that the new TRC and the future other mechanisms are subject to citizen oversight as people, politicians and the whole society are constantly informed and asked to contribute through civil society activities and initiatives. One could ask if this indeed does constitute resistance, as the government continues to dominate and ensure that its own approach to transitional justice is reflected in policy-making.

At the same time, some people now realise that the debate on transitional justice has been relocated (Impunity Watch and APRODH 2010); local communities are now the most concerned (Beoloquy 2013). If all the activities that are to be organised by the TRC are to be oriented to people as victims, witnesses or perpetrators, the 'resisting by making' approach of civil society organisations would create new spaces of negotiation between the population and the TRC. That is what Jean-Louis Nahimana, president of the new TRC, seemed to say when he claimed that success is linked to the way in which they will win the confidence of all those who still doubt (Ngabire 2014b). Civil society organisations are among those who doubt and who are the most resistant (Ngendakumana and Bigirimana 2014), especially by showing what needs to be done to dispel these doubts (FORSC 2014b). This case of civil society organisations could inspire other actors who invest in other public policies, such as governance, the fight against corruption and the responsibility to protect.

Bibliography

AC Génocide-section Jeunesse Universitaire. 2006. Déclaration, Bujumbura, 20 February 2006.

ACAT-Burundi. 2006. Position Statement on the Ministerial Order No. 550/18 of 9 January 2006 on provisional release of political prisoners, Bujumbura, 13 January 2006.

Arusha Agreement in Burundi, Protocol I, article 3, point 3, p.16.

Baines, Erin. 2010. 'Spirits and Social Reconstruction after Mass Violence: Rethinking Transitional Justice', *African Affairs* 109(436): 409–30.

Baxi, Upendra. 2012. *The Future of Human Rights*, 3rd edition, Oxford: Oxford University Press.

Betts, Alexander. 2005. 'Should Approaches to Post-conflict Justice and Reconciliation be determined Globally, Nationally or Locally?', *European Journal of Development Research* 17 (4): 745–52.

Boloquy, Mathieu. 2013. 'Les victimes à la Une: Perceptions des victimes burundaises vis-à-vis des mécanismes de justice transitionnelle', Rapport, Impunity Watch, Bujumbura.

CARAVI. 2014. 'Ensemble pour les droits des victimes (Together for the victims' rights)', Common Commemoration of victims of the different crises that bereaved Burundi, organised by CARAVI from 15 to 16 December 2014.

Chrétien, Jean-Pierre, Guichaoua, André, and Le Jeune, Gabriel. 1989. *La crise d'Août 1988 au Burundi*, Paris, Ed. Afera, Karthala, Cahiers du CRA, n°6.

CNDD-FDD. 2007. *Mémorandum du Parti CNDD FDD sur la Commission vérité et Réconciliation et le Tribunal spécial pour le Burundi*, Bujumbura, 5 May 2007.

Cohen, Stanley. 2002. *States of denial: knowing about atrocities and suffering*, Cambridge, Polity Press.

Conférence des Evêques catholiques du Burundi. 2014. 'Message des Evêques Catholiques du Burundi concernant la Commission Vérité et Réconciliation, Ngozi, le 4 septembre 2014'. (Original message in Kirundi).

Decaux, Emmanuel. 1997. 'Les Nations unies dans la Région des Grands Lacs', *Politique africaine, 'Politiques internationales dans la région des grands Lacs'* 68: 32–39.

Fletcher, Laurel E, Weinstein, Harvey and Rowen, Jamie. 2009. 'Context, Timing, and the Dynamics of Transitional Justice: a Historical Perspective', *Human Rights Quarterly* 31: 163–220.

FORSC 2014a. Press Release about the Elections of the TRC Members, Bujumbura, 12 October 2014.

FORSC. 2014b. 'The Role of the Civil Society in Supporting the Process of Truth Search by the Truth and Reconciliation Commission in Burundi', Bujumbura.

FORSC and Nindorera, Louis Marie. 2015. 'Moi et la Commission Vérité et Réconciliation du Burundi. Guide du citoyen', Bujumbura.

Gillet, Eric. 1997. 'Les droits de l'homme et la justice pour fonder l'avenir', *Politique africaine, 'Politiques internationales dans la région des Grands Lacs'* 68: 61–68.

Global Rights. 2014. *Transitional Justice in Burundi. Chronology of Facts and Events in Relation with the Transitional Justice in Burundi*, Bujumbura.

GRJT. 2011. 'Observations sur le Rapport du Comité technique chargé de la préparation de la mise en place des mécanismes de justice transitionnelle, Bujumbura' (Observations on the Report of the Technical Committee for the Preparation of the Establishment of Transitional Justice Mechanisms), 7 December 2011, Bujumbura.

GRJT. 2014. 'Le Parlement et le Gouvernement à la croisée des chemins' (Parliament and the Government at the Crossroads), Memorandum published with the approach of the election of the Truth and Reconciliation Commission members, Bujumbura.

Hakizimana, Dieudonné. 2015. 'Le processus de la mise en place de la CVR biaisé', *Journal Iwacu*, 9 December 2014.

Hollander, Joselyn A. and Einwohner, Rachel L. 2004. 'Conceptualizing Resistance', *Sociological Forum* 19(14): 533–54.

Impunity Watch-APRODH. 2010. La justice de transition dans une perspective communautaire, unpublished study on file with author.

Joinet, Louis. 1997. *Question de l'impunité des auteurs des violations des droits de l'homme, civils et politiques, Rapport final en application de la décision 1996/119 de la Sous-commission*, United Nations, E/CN.4/Sub.2/1997/20 et E/CN.4/Sub.2/1997/20/Rev.1.

Kazirukanyo, Martin 2015. 'Pour le Génocide de 1972, il faut crever l'abcès. 42 ans déjà! Rappel des faits'. https://clubbujumburanews.wordpress.com/2014/04/18/pour-le-genocide-de-1972-il-faut-crever-labces-42-ans-deja-rappel-des-faits/ (last accessed 30 March 2017).

La Benevolencija 2015. *'Ninaba nibuka-Si ma mémoire est bonne', Compilation de 24 articles sur l'histoire récente du Burundi*, Bujumbura, Editions Iwacu.

Lambourne, Wendy. 2014. 'What are the Pillars of Transitional Justice? The United Nations, Civil Society and the Justice Cascade in Burundi', *Macquarie Journal of Law* 13: 41–60.

Lefranc, Sandrine. 2002. *Les politiques du Pardon*, Paris: Presses Universitaires de France.

Lemarchand, René. 2004. *Burundi, Ethnic Conflict and Genocide*, Woodrow Wilson Center Press and Cambridge University Press.

Ligue Burundaise des Droits de l'Homme Iteka. 2014. 'La CVR va-t-elle réellement réconcilier les Burundais ?', Press release, 4 December 2014.

Matignon, Emilie. 2012. *La justice en transition. Le cas du Burundi*, Thèse de doctorat en droit privé et sciences criminelles, inédit, 2012.

Matignon, Emilie. 2014. 'La justice en mutation au Burundi : les défis du pluralisme juridique', *Afrique contemporaine* 250: 55–80.

Mbazumutima, Abbas. 2013a. 'Amener les Burundais à commémorer ensemble les victimes des différentes tragedies', *Journal Iwacu.* www.iwacu-burundi.org/amepci-gira-ubuntu-amener-les-burundais-a-commemorer-ensemble-les-victimes-des-differentes-tragedies/ (last accessed 30 March 2017).

Mbazumutima, Abbas. 2013b. 'Vers une CVR "Nyakuri"', *Journal Iwacu.* www.iwacu-burundi.org/vers-une-cvr-nyakuri/ (last accessed on 30 March 2017).

McEvoy, Kieran. 2007. 'Beyond Legalism: Towards a Thicker Understanding of Transitional Justice', *Journal of Law and Society* 34(4): 411–40.

Ndabashinze, Rénovat. 2014. 'Vers une CVR amputée de l'aspect judiciaire ? Un recul selon la Société civile », *Journal Iwacu*, 4 January 2014. www.iwacu-burundi.org/cvr-sans-aspect-judiciaire-recul-societe-civile/ (last accessed 30 March 2017).

Ngabire, Elyse. 2013. '25 ans après les massacres de Ntega-Marangara, les victimes réclament la mise sur pied de la CVR', *Journal Iwacu*, 19 August 2013.

Ngabire, Elyse. 2014a. 'Massacres de 1972. "Honorer des Héros non chantés"', *Journal Iwacu*, 5 May 2014. www.iwacu-burundi.org/?s=H%C3%A9ros+non+chant%C3%A9s (last accessed 30 March 2017).

Ngabire, Elyse. 2014b. 'Notre pari, c'est de gagner la confiance de tous ceux qui doutent encore', *Journal Iwacu.* www.iwacu-burundi.org/notre-pari-cest-de-gagner-la-confiance-de-tous-ceux-qui-doutent-encore/ (ast accessed 30 March 2017).

Ngendakumana, Philippe and Bigirimana, Christian. 2014. ' Une CVR qui ne rassure pas', *Journal Iwacu.* www.iwacu-burundi.org/une-cvr-qui-ne-rassure-pas/ (last accessed 30 March 2017).

Ngayimpenda, Evariste 2005. *Histoire du conflit politico-ethnique burundais. Les premières marches du calvaire (1960–1973)*, Bujumbura: Editions de la renaissance.

Pohu, Anne-Aël and Klimis Emmanuel (eds), 2013. *Justice Transitionnelle. Oser un modèle burundais. Comment vivre ensemble après un conflit violent?*, Bruxelles: Facultés Universitaires Saint-Louis.

Présidence de la République 2002, *Lettre du Président de la République du Burundi du 24 juillet 2002*, S/2005/158.

PRIME ACBF. 2011. *Etude sur la société civile*, Rapport 2011.

République du Burundi. 2006. *Décret n°100/2 du 03 janvier 2006 portant immunité provisoire des prisonniers politiques détenus dans les maisons de détention de la République du Burundi.*

République du Burundi. 2011. *Rapport du comité technique chargé de la mise en place des mécanismes de justice transitionnelle*, Bujumbura.

Republic of Burundi and United Nations. 2010. *Rapport sur les consultations nationales sur la mise en place des mécanismes de Justice de transition au Burundi*, Bujumbura.

Rosoux, Valérie. 2007. 'Art et résolution des conflits', in Françoise Massart-Piérard (ed.), *Culture et relations internationales. Liber amicorum Jean Barréa*, Louvain: Presses de l'UCL, 101–10. www.academia.edu/5398616/Lart_et_r%C3%A9solution_des_conflits (last accessed 30 March 2017).

Scott, James C. 2008. *La domination et les arts de la résistance. Fragments d'un discours subalterne*, Paris: Ed. Amsterdam.

Shaw, Rosalind and Waldorf, Lars. 2010. 'Introduction. Localizing Transitional Justice', in Rosalind Shaw, Lars Waldorf with Pierre Hazan (ed.), *Localizing Transitional Justice. Interventions and Priorities after Mass Violence*, Stanford: Stanford University Press, 3–26.

Sriram, Chandra. 2012. 'Post-conflict justice and hybridity in Peacebuilding: Resistance or Cooptation', in Olivier P. Richmond and Audra Mitchell (eds), *Hybrid Forms of Peace. From Everyday Agency to Post-Liberalism*, London: Palgrave.

Steinberg, Nathalie. 2001. 'Background paper on GONGOs and QUANGOs and Wild NGOs', World federalist movement institute of global policy. www.globalpolicy.org/component/content/article/177-un/31600-background-paper-on-%5Ccongos-and-quangos-and-wild-ngos.html (last accessed 30 March 2017).

Thomas, Oskar N T, Ron, James and Paris, Roland. 2008. 'The Effects of Transitional Justice Mechanisms', *CIPS working paper* www.cips-cepi.ca/publications/the-effects-of-transitional-justice-mechanisms/ (last accessed 30 March 2017).

UN Special Rapporteur on the Promotion of Truth, Justice, Reparation and Guarantees of Non-Recurrence. 2014. Preliminary Conclusions and Observations of Burundi Visit report, 8–16 December 2014, Bujumbura.

United Nations. 2005. Report on the Assessment Mission on the Establishment of an International Judicial Commission of Inquiry for Burundi, Report S/2005/158, 11 March 2005.

United Nations. 1996. Report S/1996/682, 23 July 1996.

UPRONA. 2013. 'La position sur la justice transitionnelle', Bujumbura, 8 October 2013.

Vandeginste, Stef. 2009. 'Le processus de justice transitionnelle au Burundi. L'épreuve de son contexte politique.' *Droit et Société* 3(73): 591–611.

Section introduction: Cambodia

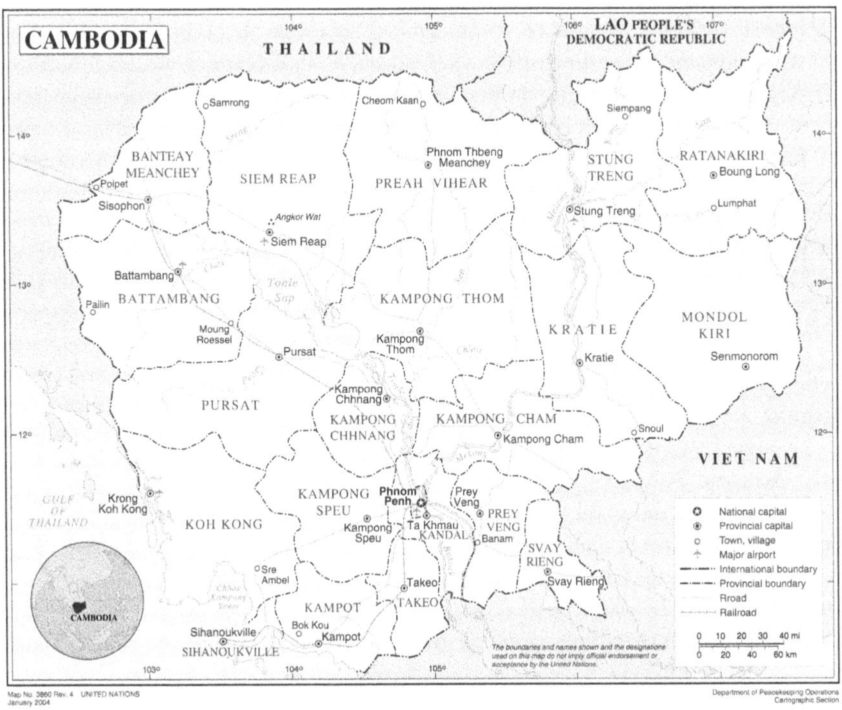

Map of the UN Geospatial Information Section, 2004 www.un.org/Depts/Cartographic/map/profile/cambodia.pdf (last accessed 30 March 2017). This map does not include the new province of Tboung Khmum that was established by royal decree in December 2013.

1953: Independence.

1969–1973: US bombing of Cambodia in the context of the US–Vietnam war.

1970: *Coup* by Marshal Lon Nol against head of state Sihanouk and proclamation of the Khmer Republic.

17 April 1975–January 1979: Khmer Rouge (KR) regime.

1979–1990: The army of the Socialist Republic of Vietnam puts an end to the Khmer Rouge regime, with the support of the United Front for the National Salvation of Kampuchea. Proclamation of the People's Republic of Kampuchea, which will last until 1989.

23 October 1991: Adoption of the Comprehensive Cambodian Peace Agreement and establishment of the UN Transitional Authority of Cambodia (UNTAC).

May 1993: First democratic elections overseen by UNTAC.

11 April 1997: Adoption of resolution 1997/49 by the UN Human Rights Commission, requesting that the Secretary General examine any request from Cambodia for assistance in creating an accountability mechanism for past serious violations of Cambodian and international law.

21 June 1997: Request to the UN by the two Cambodian co-Prime Ministers, Norodom Ranarridh and Hun Sen, for assistance to bring to justice those responsible for crimes under the KR regime.

13 July 1998: Appointment of a Group of Experts for Cambodia by the UN Secretary-General.

February 1999: Incorporation of the last KR remnants into the Royal Cambodian Armed Forces.

February 1999: Publication of the report of the Group of Experts.

August 1999: Creation of the Royal Government Task Force for the Khmer Rouge Trials to draft a law on the establishment of Khmer Rouge Trials.

July–August 2001: Approval of the draft law by the Cambodian National Assembly, Senate and Constitutional Court.

February 2002: The UN mission, led by UN Legal Counsel Hans Corell, ends the negotiations with the Cambodian Government.

December 2002: Adoption of resolution 57/228 sponsored by Japan and France to resume negotiations between the UN Secretariat and the Cambodian Government.

June 2003: Final agreement between the UN and the Royal Government of Cambodia.

October 2004: Promulgation of the amended Law on the Extraordinary Chambers in the Courts of Cambodia (ECCC).

2006: The ECCC becomes operational.

Chapter 6

Civil party participation and resistance at the Khmer Rouge tribunal

Julie Bernath

Introduction[1]

Despite an increased focus on victims in transitional justice scholarship and practice (Bonacker 2013), scholars and practitioners do not necessarily conceive of victims as having legitimate reasons to resist transitional justice. As key beneficiaries of transitional justice processes that are necessarily 'doing good', what reasons could they have to oppose and resist these processes? As a result, transitional justice institutions repeatedly list the multiple benefits which transitional justice supposedly entails for victims (see e.g. Brounéus 2007; Mendeloff 2004). Those victims who do oppose transitional justice processes or do not comply with expectations of what a victim should be in the aftermath of massive human rights violations may then become cast as 'recalcitrant' or 'bad' victims (Madlingozi 2007; Hamber and Wilson 2002; Meister 2002).

This chapter proposes to explore and thicken these perceptions of resistance with regards to victims in transitional justice, focusing on victims as agents of both participation and resistance. It develops a case study of civil party participation at the Extraordinary Chambers in the Courts of Cambodia (ECCC). Civil party participation constitutes the most visible form of participation for victims at this hybrid court and initially also provided the 'most progressive mode of victim participation' in internationalised criminal tribunals (Thomas and Chy 2009: 231). As civil parties, victims of the Khmer Rouge (KR) regime are allowed to participate in court proceedings in order to support the prosecution and to seek collective and moral reparations.[2] Initially, civil parties were granted participation rights as equal party to the proceedings, however the scope of civil party representation was progressively, yet significantly, reduced (Ciorciari and Heindel 2014: 216–25).

1 The author thanks Dr Briony Jones and Dr Chris Tenove for valuable comments on earlier drafts of this chapter. The fieldwork which this chapter draws from is part of the author's PhD research conducted in the framework of the research project 'Resistance to Transitional Justice? Alternative Understandings of Peace and Justice' funded by the Swiss National Science Foundation, and completed with funding from the University of Basel Research Fund for Early Career Researchers.

2 Rule 23, ECCC Internal Rules, Rev. 8.

In Case 001, 90 civil parties participated in the trial proceedings, out of which 76 were admitted by the Supreme Court Chamber Judgment, whilst 3,866 civil parties were admitted to participate in Case 002.

This chapter analyses civil party participation at the ECCC as a space for resistance and negotiation of victim subject positions. Caution is needed when equating acts with either compliance or resistance, as this may be reductive of the significant nuances of human activity which exist in between this oppositional binary (MacGinty 2012: 168). Resistance is therefore not defined as one extreme in a continuum between compliance or participation *vs* resistance, but rather as a subtle form of engaging with transitional justice processes. Since civil parties always navigate within discourses of what is expected of victims in transitional justice processes, as well as discourses on justice and the past produced through transitional justice or dominant in the national context, this chapter pays particular attention to discursive strategies of resistance.[3]

This approach is based on the idea that victims are central objects of transitional justice discourses (see e.g. Bonacker 2013; McEvoy and McConnachie 2013: 490) and that these discourses produce victim subject positions, i.e. the idea(l)s of what a victim should be (see e.g. Kesselring 2015). Discursive resistance then becomes a way of rejecting the expectations victims are facing when participating in transitional justice processes, or the delimited role they are given therein. This relates to what some scholars in resistance studies (Hollander and Einwohner 2004: 537) refer to as 'identity-based resistance', i.e. resistance against the 'resister's expected or attributed identity'. However, discursive resistance may also more broadly constitute a way of speaking back to the analytical categories which govern the discourses and practices of transitional justice (Moon 2012). This chapter argues that the analysis of such forms of resistance, which exceed the limits set by transitional justice processes, enables a decentring of the study of transitional justice, as well as the identification of the victim subject positions produced in these contexts and their articulation in relation to discourses on justice and the past.

This chapter draws from qualitative fieldwork conducted in Cambodia between 2013–2016, both in the capital Phnom Penh and in rural communities across eight provinces. It is mainly based upon in-depth, semi-structured interviews conducted with diverse actors engaged in the state-sanctioned transitional justice process in Cambodia, including ECCC staff members, civil parties and civil society actors. Research interviews are themselves considered spaces of resistance, since each interview 'reflects, reproduces and produces and/or challenges the discourses of the society' and is 'informed by, as well as forming social practices and "truths"' (Lilja 2013: 9).

3 See also chapter three by Jones in this volume.

This chapter further draws from non-participant observation of two regional civil party forums[4] and the analysis of transcripts of public hearings at the ECCC. It focuses on two main themes of civil party resistance at the ECCC: resistance for individual, financial reparations and resistance against the ECCC's limited temporal jurisdiction. Navigating between the visibility and invisibility of resisting acts, claims of civil parties and their meaning in transitional justice processes, it concludes that resistance in civil party participation enables the creation of spaces for discussion and dissent and, as such, a higher degree of participation.

Claims for individual and financial reparations: resisting from within

From individual contestations to collective demonstrations

The ECCC constitutes one of the few internationalised tribunals to hold a specific reparations mandate. Reparations have however been a contested issue since the start of the ECCC proceedings and a regular topic of discussion amongst civil party lawyers and advocates of victim participation inside and outside of the ECCC. The ECCC's rules of procedure indeed only envisage 'collective and moral' reparations.[5] The category of 'moral' reparations, unprecedented in international or domestic legal frameworks, has been clarified by the Supreme Court Chamber as referring to 'the aim of repairing moral damages rather than material ones' (ECCC [SCC] 3 February 2012: §§ 658–59).[6] As for the category of 'collective reparations', it is used so as to affirm 'the unavailability of individual financial awards' (ibid).[7] With this exclusion of individual, monetary reparations, the ECCC deviates from civil claims under domestic law in Cambodia.[8] The Trial Chamber judges explained this as follows:

> Such departures from national law were considered necessary in view of the large number of Civil Parties expected before the ECCC and the inevitable difficulties of quantifying the full extent of the losses suffered by an indeterminate class of victims. Reparations before the ECCC were therefore intended

4 These civil party forums were organised by the Victims Support Section of the ECCC in Phnom Penh on 23 December 2013 and in Kampot on 29 November 2013.

5 Rule 23 *quinquies* (1), ECCC Internal Rules, Rev. 8.

6 See also Appeal against Judgment on Reparations, Co-Lawyers for Civil Parties Group 2, 2 November 2010, F13, §94–110. An international judge at the ECCC noted that many civil parties spoke of the loss of assets during the Khmer Rouge regime: 'We constantly hear "and I lost all my land and I lost my cattle and I lost my home" and so on. We can't deal with that, because we have no money to compensate'. Personal interview, 29 January 2014, Phnom Penh, Cambodia.

7 *Case of Kaing Guek Eav alias Duch*, 001/18-07-2007/ECCC/SC, Appeal Judgment, 3 February 2012, F28, §§ 658–59.

8 This exclusion was explicitly formulated in the 6th revision of the Internal Rules, with Rule 23 *quinquies* (1) stating: 'these benefits shall not take the form of monetary payments to civil parties'.

> to be essentially symbolic (aimed at conferring official recognition upon victims, and assisting to restore dignity and preserve the collective memory) rather than compensatory.
>
> (ECCC [TC] 26.07.2010: §661 n 1144)

Nonetheless, the exclusion of individual, financial reparations for civil parties remains one aspect of the transitional justice process that has been repeatedly contested by civil parties. The few quantitative surveys on civil party participation at the ECCC have also consistently shown a desire for individual, monetary compensation amongst civil party applicants and Cambodian citizens more generally. In a 2010 study, for instance, more than one-third of the respondents amongst civil party applicants (38.9%) preferred individual over collective reparations, while 30.3 per cent stated that they wanted individual monetary compensation (Stammel and others 2010: 35–36; see also Pham and others 2009: 43–44; Pham and others 2011: 35–37).

Several civil parties have on numerous occasions, including at civil parties' forums, thematic conferences, press conferences or meetings with their lawyers, continued to claim for individual, financial reparations, although it has been explicitly excluded from the realm of possibilities at the ECCC. This chapter analyses these instances as forms of discursive resistance through which civil parties resist from within, yet against the terms set for the state-sanctioned transitional justice process. The following quotes from civil parties at conferences and civil parties' forums between 2008 and 2013 illustrate such a discursive resistance:

> Even though I survived, I am dead … I lost my husband at S-21. I want reparations for all victims, especially widows like me who have suffered the most … because we had to combine so many roles in our life after the Khmer Rouge.[9]

> There is no financial or individual reparation to improve the living standards of the civil parties … I am an orphan; I lost my family, my house … My wife also is an orphan. I agree that we want stupas [*Buddhist shrines*] for the young generation to see, but we also need reparations to improve our living standards … Millions have been spent already and it takes so long.[10]

9 Conference on 'Reparations for Victims of the Khmer Rouge Regime' organised jointly by the ECCC Victims Unit and the Cambodian Human Rights Action Committee on 26 November 2008 in Phnom Penh, Cambodia. Notes on file with author. See also conference quotes in Mohan (2009: 760, 764) or the Conference Report by CHRAC/ECCC Victims Unit (edited by Christoph Sperfeldt and Vinesh Winodan), Phnom Penh, May 2009, pp 10–11.

10 Regional civil party forum, Phnom Penh, 23 December 2013, notes on file with author. Traditionally, Cambodians use *stupas*, i.e. Buddhist shrines, in order to contain the cremated remains of their family members.

These discursive forms of resistance then took a collective, visible turn when 150 to 200 civil parties staged a demonstration at the gates of the ECCC during the opening of the evidentiary hearings in Case 002/02 on 18 October 2014, holding signs in Khmer and English reading: 'We are the civil parties. We need individual reparations'.[11] Threatening to retrieve their civil party application if their claims were not heard, the civil parties tried to enter the ECCC compound in order to submit their petition but were prevented from doing so by security officers. Their petition asks for US$13,500 for each member lost during the KR regime, an amount calculated on the basis of the compensations which were awarded to victims of the Koh Pich (Diamond Island) stampede during the Khmer Water Festival celebrations on 22 November 2010. With this petition, civil parties thus question the claim of the extraordinary nature of justice which transitional justice supposedly provides, since they explicitly refer to the domestic justice system that foresees individual, financial compensation. They thereby reject that victims be treated any differently than in other instances of victimisation in Cambodia.

A mere matter of communication and expectation management?

For practitioners working with civil parties in Cambodia, such claims for financial reparations, since they clearly expand the 'realm of the possible' at the ECCC, mainly constitute a matter to be addressed by adequate communication. Mohan (2009: 761), for instance, quotes a local civil society leader who argues that simply informing civil parties of the ECCC's limits with regard to reparations is not enough:

> With victims, their emotions overwhelm them and even if you tell them once that there will be no money, because they want it, their mind is set, they hear you but then it's lost … it needs to be repeated again and again. The lawyers think 'Oh I said it!' but that does not mean it was effectively communicated … You need to know whether it has been received at a level that sticks and can be accepted and internalised by the victims.

This challenge has been exacerbated by the fact that civil claims under domestic law in Cambodia provide this possibility, but also by the implication of some form of monetary payment in the Khmer term used to speak of reparations (*somnâng*, literally 'compensation').[12] However, to practitioners working with civil parties at the ECCC, it is also a matter of expectation management. Many practitioners

11 Journalists have given different accounts of the number of civil parties present during the protest. See White (18 October 2014) and Kuch (18 October 2014).

12 All transliterations are based on Franklin E. Huffman's Franco-Khmer transcription system, as reproduced in Heder and Ledgerwood (1996, xvii).

indeed understand that, in any given context, victims will generally have many expectations which cannot be fulfilled by the transitional justice mechanism:

> You always have to deal with the expectations of victims, which are always enormous and will go far beyond what will be possible … and so at some point in time you have to make them understand that we will enter into a [judicial] framework, and that this framework will forcibly limit their expectations … and cannot answer to everything … It's all the finesse of a civil party lawyer, from my point of view.[13]

It thus becomes the responsibility of those working with victims, including civil party lawyers, to carefully manage victims' expectations so as not to create frustration and disappointment. Initially, this was not adequately recognised at the ECCC, as one civil party lawyer regrets:

> I think the biggest problem was created in 2007 … when people in United Nations cars arrived in the villages and said that now there would be a tribunal … 'Civil parties, come, reparations!' They did not explain exactly what we would have. This has made our work much more difficult.[14]

Whilst financial and individual reparations remain excluded at the ECCC, advocates of victims' participation inside and outside the ECCC have successfully lobbied for the improvement of the ECCC's interpretation of the provision for 'collective and moral' reparations. Indeed, the Internal Rules initially only allowed for reparations 'awarded against, and … borne by convicted persons'.[15] In Case 001, the accused was found indigent and the Trial Chamber, later confirmed by the Supreme Court Chamber, only awarded two reparations measures to the civil parties: the compilation and publication of statements of apology made by the accused during the trial; and the inclusion of civil parties' names and those of the immediate victims in the judgment. This decision on reparations was widely criticised as 'really the most minimal, most conservative, and perhaps it's fair to say unimaginative that could have been ordered'.[16] In anticipation of the second trial, the judges subsequently extended the ECCC's provisions on reparations in two significant ways during the 7th and 8th plenary session.[17]

First, the Trial Chamber expanded the Victim Support Section's (VSS) mandate to develop and implement, together with governmental or non-governmental

13 Personal interview, international civil party lawyers, Phnom Penh, Cambodia, 20 November 2013.

14 ibid.

15 Rule 23 (11), ECCC Internal Rules, Original version.

16 Quote from Karim Kahn, International Civil Party Co-Lawyer in Civil Party Group 1, ECCC Press Conference, 26 July 2010. Notes on file with author. See also O'Toole (27 July 2010).

17 For more detail on the evolution of the procedural rules on reparations at the ECCC, see Sperfeldt (2012) or Ciorciari and Heindel (2014, 225–29).

partners external to the ECCC, 'non-judicial measures addressing the broader interests of victims'.[18] Secondly, the Trial Chamber was granted the authority to recognise reparation projects designed together with the VSS when external funding has been secured, thereby introducing a new avenue for financing reparations beyond the conviction-borne form of reparations.[19] In Case 002/01, the co-lead civil party lawyers, together with the civil party lawyers, VSS and local civil society organisations, developed their reparations requests following careful consultation with civil parties both in and outside Cambodia in order to render these meaningful.[20] The Trial Chamber judgment in Case 002/01 granted 11 out of the 13 reparation measures submitted by the co-lead civil party lawyers.

Significant efforts were thus carried out in order to introduce more meaningful and transformative reparation measures for civil parties within the limits set by the tribunal. Claims for individual, financial reparations are thus seen as clearly exceeding the limits of the ECCC and brought forward by those victims who 'always want more' and therefore are seen as 'not clearly understanding' the process.[21] Some even argue that the benefits provided to civil parties participating in the ECCC proceedings, such as daily allowances or visits to the country's capital where the ECCC is located, in fact constitute some form of individual and financial reparation, although not officially or explicitly named as such nor perceived by civil parties as such.[22] Nonetheless, this chapter argues that 'allowing victims to "speak back to" the analytical categories' that structure transitional justice discourse and practice (Moon 2012: 190–91) highlights how victims are negotiating and resisting the victim subject positions that are produced in these processes.

Negotiating and resisting victim subject positions

Civil parties participating in the ECCC proceedings have to conform to the expectations of what a 'good victim' should be in the transitional justice process in Cambodia; expectations which become visible in those moments where there is a 'discrepancy between those who conform and those who do not' (Moon 2006: 273–74).

Because transitional justice processes are often conceived of as being inherently positive and beneficial to victims (Rubli 2012: 10), they are expected to be thankful merely for the ECCC taking place. This is illustrated in following quote from an

18 Rule 12 bis (3), ECCC Internal Rules, Rev. 5.

19 Rule 23 *quinquies* (3.b), ECCC Internal Rules, Rev. 6.

20 See e.g. *Case of Nuon Chea et al*, 002/19-09-2007/ECCC/TC, Doc. E125/2, 'Initial Specification of the Substance of the Awards that the Civil Party Lead Co-Lawyers intend to seek – Hearing of 19 October 2011', 12 March 2012.

21 Informal discussion with a national judicial staff member of the ECCC Victims Support Section, November 2014, Phnom Penh, Cambodia.

22 Personal interviews, national civil party lawyer, 23 December 2013; and national VSS staff member, 3 February 2014, Phnom Penh, Cambodia.

ECCC investigator, who shares his surprise when he was first faced with the absence of gratitude from, and the emotional position taken by, victims:

> In my experience, a problem arises when you think that because you are trying to help and include them that they should line up and nod politely to you. Often they do not. They shout. They express their individualism. They have deep feelings that are beyond my comprehension.
>
> (as quoted in Mohan 2009: 767)

Victims are furthermore expected to be reasonable in their claims and in the use of their emotions (Lefranc, Mathieu, and Siméant 2008). Because some are, however, 'overwhelmed by emotions', as the civil society leader argues above, they not only require continued communications efforts from their lawyers but are sometimes not deemed to be in a position to make reasonable demands. This highlights the particular and difficult role which civil party lawyers, and others working with civil parties, have in terms of mediating and conveying the limits of the transitional justice process to the victims, as we have seen above. However, this role can also be practiced as a way of 'pacifying' or 'containing' the victims, i.e. of erasing any form of excessive reactions, claims or emotions of victims which are not accepted in the transitional justice process. One national civil party lawyer, for instance, told me that because she was very skilled in calming victims down, she was often called by ECCC administrators during the first trial, something she was proud of:

> Some civil parties, when they attend public hearings, they make very dreadful and very violent gestures. They are extremely angry towards the defence and do not understand the rights of the accused to be defended this way. They do not understand that the defence lawyers are just doing their jobs. They only remember from certain confrontations with the defence that the 'defence is rejecting them', and are very angry.[23]

This quote clearly shows how transitional justice processes involve a specific channelling of emotions, i.e. they exclude certain emotions, such as anger, for being negative and thus not acceptable (Brudholm 2008: 2). When claiming for individual, financial reparations, civil parties are moreover addressing not only a measure which has been explicitly excluded at the ECCC but are also making claims in terms perceived by many as being clearly unethical. Indeed, financial reparations, when asked in compensation for the loss of life rather than the loss of assets, 'performs a strange transubstantiation in which money granted in recompense for the dead makes their bodies exchangeable for, or "turns them into", other commodities such as food', as Moon (2012: 195) notes. During the November 2008 Conference on 'Reparations for the Victims of the Khmer Rouge Regime'

23 Personal interview, national civil party lawyer, 23 December 2013, Phnom Penh, Cambodia.

held in Phnom Penh, a Buddhist monk invited to give the 'Buddhist perspective on reparations', admonished the civil parties for claiming individual monetary reparations in similar terms: 'Does it match the loss of lives of the beloved ones? What has money to do with feelings of the heart?'[24]

This challenge posed in ethical terms to the claim of individual, financial reparations seems to be acknowledged by civil parties protesting for such monetary reparations. One of the civil parties, who took the floor at the 2008 Reparations Conference in Phnom Penh, for instance, implicitly acknowledged the impossibility of quantifying the loss of life – in this case, his wife's – and used this impossibility to argue that the amount he asked for was thus in fact very reasonable: 'I want a compensation of US$50,000 for my wife's death. [Duch] executed my wife. If it happened to the judges' wives, how would they feel? Would US$50,000 be enough?'[25]

Moreover, the civil parties whom I interviewed amongst the group who signed the petition for individual, financial reparations also seemed aware of this ethical challenge. They would indeed consistently avoid mentioning any specific amount during the discussions and interviews in relation to their claims for individual, financial reparations and rather underlined how they would use this money to pay respect to their loved ones through religious ceremonies and the building of *stupas*.[26]

The question of distributing financial reparations at the ECCC is thus perceived by practitioners as opening a 'Pandora's box' of uneasy questions, including that of quantification. One national staff in the VSS argued that it was thus better to focus on 'national reconciliation':

> We try to manage their expectations, that they are going to receive only collective and moral, rather than individual, reparations and this is leading to national reconciliation. It is difficult to determine any individual compensation! Because then people would say 'I'm handicapped, I have a problem with my leg, I want to get US$1,000'. The people who have problems with their ears would say 'Ok, I need US$1,000 too'. And then others would ask 'Why do those with problems with their ear get compensation, while I have problems with my eyes?' It's a mess, you know it's a mess. So the provisions for reparations in the ECCC system are collective, they focus on preserving the collective memory, improving the dignity, and they're good for younger generations as a whole too.[27]

The resistance of civil parties at the ECCC to forms of reparation which exclude the individual, financial thus contributes to locating the victim subject

24 'Reparations for Victims of the Khmer Rouge Regime' Conference (n 9).

25 ibid.

26 Personal individual and group interviews, Civil Parties, 28 and 29 November 2014, Siem Reap, Cambodia.

27 Personal interview, national VSS staff member, February 2014, Phnom Penh, Cambodia.

positions they have to conform to when participating in the state-sanctioned transitional justice process in Cambodia. In making claims for individual, financial reparations, civil parties are possibly seen as ungrateful, unreasonable or unethical. However, engaging with these forms of civil party resistance also enables us to challenge some core assumptions of the transitional justice field.

Resisting the compartmentalisation of transitional justice

These forms of resistance to transitional justice in Cambodia indeed raise questions of priorities in the design of transitional justice processes and of spending high amounts of money in contexts of high poverty. The following quote from a female civil party participating in the protest illustrates the disconnect between the realities of civil parties and the millions spent on the judicial process at the ECCC:

> They said that NGOs help. Help, help, help, but [we] don't see. [We] people know nothing. I heard that America helps. And others help, help, help, but we don't see any money. Help, but we do not get any of the money, so where does all the money go? Is that not for victims? Victims that lost husbands, children, relatives. All of us want that funding to release our minds, we don't want to be stressed. It's been already eight years that we've held on. Now they said it's finished [there's a] judgment. If they have finished, it means it's the end of the story, what else?[28]

Population-based, quantitative surveys in Cambodia have indeed shown that 'while respondents viewed accountability as important and frequently wanted to see former Khmer Rouge tried and punished for past crimes, justice was not a priority for most respondents' since it was superseded by priorities revolving around 'basic needs and livelihoods concerns' (Pham and others 2009: 34–35; Pham and others 2011: 19–20). These surveys for instance indicate that in 2008, 83 per cent of respondents mentioned 'economy, jobs and poverty' as a priority (a figure that increased to 98% in 2010), followed by services to meet basic needs such as health (20%) and food (17%). The number of respondents who would have preferred that the money spent on the ECCC was spent on 'something else' even increased from 52.6 per cent in 2008 to 63 per cent in 2010.

These findings thus question spending high amounts of money on judicial processes in contexts where poverty remains high. However, significantly, in framing issues of justice and development as 'either-or' survey questions, such studies seem to prevent multifaceted understandings of justice in developing countries (Mani 2008) and to reproduce the 'invisibility of economics' in transitional justice as a field of knowledge, practice and policy-making (Franzki and Olarte 2014; Miller

28 Translation from Khmer taken from the PP Post video report, see White (October 18, 2014).

2008). The transitional justice process in Cambodia thus reproduces the equation of justice as criminal accountability while some victims and survivors may rather frame their claims for justice in terms of livelihood needs, underlining the psychological and physical harm they suffered under the Khmer Rouge regime, but also the loss of livelihoods and opportunities. One civil party from Siem Reap province who signed the petition for individual, financial reparations but did not join the protest in the capital on 18 October 2014 for instance said to me:

> Since I was born, I have suffered … I am very tired with my life. As a child, I could not have a good education. I was at school only from 1969 to 1972 … so I only studied very briefly, for four years … And then there was war, for such a long time … Only in 1980, after getting married, did I come back from the refugee camp at the Thai border … So as a result, my life has not ever been good. I don't want to live any more lives after this one, as it is envisaged in Buddhism's belief in reincarnation; this one life is more than enough for me![29]

Robins (2012: 21) has similarly shown how indigenous victims of the Maoist insurgency in Nepal express their claims for justice in terms of addressing basic needs, in stark contrast to the legalistic agenda of human rights agencies and transitional justice practitioners which, he argues, 'continue to prevent the emergence of a practice that can deliver a broader justice after conflict that includes addressing the social injustices that led to conflict' in Nepal.

This compartmentalisation of transitional justice versus development is also visible in the debates on collective and moral reparations. Civil parties have indeed repeatedly requested the construction of new infrastructure – such as irrigation systems (Ly 2011: 8) – or educational and health institutions as forms of 'collective and moral reparations'. However, these requests are seen not only as exceeding the terms of the existing process, but as constituting an entirely separate form of 'needs' which is to be addressed by a different field of intervention, the development industry. This compartmentalisation can be illustrated with the following quote:

> Survivors commonly request schools, roads, hospitals, wells, bridges and housing. In light of the poverty plaguing most survivors, their focus on *developmental needs* is unsurprising. Many do, however, suggest *victim-centred forms* of reparations, including ceremony halls, memorials and statues, genocide education, mental health clinics and the construction of temples, pagodas and stupas.
>
> (Thomas and Chy 2009: 249)

29 Personal interview, Civil Party in Case 002 (male, age 57), 30 November 2014, Siem Reap, Cambodia.

Transitional justice processes of course cannot be expected to deliver an answer to all needs of victims in the aftermath of mass atrocity. However, engaging with civil party resistance for individual financial reparations raises the question of how transitional justice as an industry has come to prioritise certain measures and mechanisms over others, whilst the compartmentalisation of development versus accountability is not necessarily reflected in the needs and claims of those most affected by past human rights violations.

Engaging with civil parties' resistance thus allows us to decentre the study of transitional justice and become 'other-focused' rather than purely 'self-focused' (Lambourne 2012: 257). This chapter now moves to a second key theme of civil party resistance at the ECCC, that of the temporal jurisdiction.

Claims for more comprehensive discussions of past conflicts

Resisting the cutting into pieces of the 'crocodile' in the ECCC's temporal jurisdiction

The temporal jurisdiction of the ECCC is limited only to 17 April 1975 to 7 January 1979, i.e. the timeframe during which the Communist Party of Kampuchea (CPK), known as the Khmer Rouge, held power over the entire country.[30] Scholars have previously shown how the specific framing of the Cambodian conflict adopted at the ECCC, in that it focuses on particular actors whilst excluding others, constitutes a significant exercise of power (Hughes and Pupavac 2005: 875–76). During negotiations over the establishment of the ECCC, the temporal jurisdiction was from the outset limited to 1975–1979, as it was indeed very clear that 'to widen the scope would be a recipe for no result' (Hammarberg 2001: 6). Countries such as the US clearly wanted to avoid consideration of crimes before 1975, as this would include the abuses of the US-backed Lon Nol regime and the massive bombing of Cambodia from 1969 to 1973 by US B-52s (Ciorciari and Heindel 2009: 73; Jarvis and Fawthrop 2004: 5–6). The Cambodian government unsuccessfully proposed several times to widen the scope to include other crimes such as the US carpet bombing of Cambodia and the Chinese support for the Khmer Rouge into the 'package' (Hammarberg 2001). However, the issue of temporal jurisdiction would not become too controversial as the Cambodian government too was concerned with enlarging the scope as it could draw attention to the crimes committed during the Third Indochina War (Ciorciari and Heindel 2009: 73).

This temporal limitation has been criticised by many civil parties in diverse spaces such as civil parties' forums, thematic conferences, press conferences,

30 The Khmer Rouge forces controlled significant portions of Cambodia's territory prior to 1975 and after 1979. In 1993 for instance, when UNTAC pulled out, the Khmer Rouge forces still controlled one sixth of Cambodia's territory. See e.g. Richer (2009, 98).

meetings with their lawyers, and research interviews. One civil party for instance complained to me:

> The Court … only looks at 17 April 1975 to 7 January 1979, only this, it doesn't talk about before and after! But to have justice, we need to know [everything], from the beginning until the end! We cannot only look at the middle, at one part of it only. This is not justice![31]

With the main interest of many civil parties being to understand 'Why did Khmer kill Khmer?', which cannot be answered only when looking at the timeframe of 1975 to 1979, civil parties engage in discursive forms of resistance to repeatedly raise the broader implications of the Khmer Rouge regime. At a regional civil party forum in Kampot, for instance, one civil party specifically enquired about the United Nations' involvement in the conflict, confronting the international members of staff who were present with the following question: 'Was the United Nations created before Democratic Kampuchea? If yes, why did the United Nations do nothing? Why did they authorise the crimes committed under the Khmer Rouge?'[32] Civil party lawyers also face these questions, as one national civil party lawyer describes:

> [Civil parties] still want to add more [to the trial], the facts out of the scope of investigations or beyond the limitation of the period to the Khmer Rouge regime … They want to know more about the destruction and war crimes committed from 1970 until 1975 during the civil war between the Khmer Rouge and the Lon Nol regime … Because they all say that this is also the responsibility of the Khmer Rouge …! And some civil parties want to confront Vietnam, China, America … all of the countries related to supporting the Lon Nol regime and the Khmer Rouge regime and responsible for the war in Cambodia which destroyed the country. But I tell them that we cannot [do this] because this Court limits the temporal and personal scope of the trial …[33]

In these forms of discursive resistance, some civil parties adopt the narratives of the accused, in particular one of them, Nuon Chea, former Deputy Secretary of the CPK, who has a defence strategy designed precisely to break with the temporal limitations laid out at the ECCC. One of the metaphors used during his opening statements in Case 002/01 where he paternalistically addressed his 'beloved Cambodian people' and 'Khmer children' as a former senior political leader, was particularly repeated by civil parties:

> I, Nuon Chea, have been given an opportunity today which I have been waiting for so long. That is, to explain to my beloved Cambodian people and

31 Personal interview, civil party in Case 002 (male, age 57), 30 November 2014, Siem Reap, Cambodia.

32 Regional civil party forum, Phnom Penh, 29 November 2013, notes on file with author.

33 Personal interview, national civil party lawyer, 30 January 2014, Phnom Penh, Cambodia.

> the Khmer children the facts [which] occurred in Cambodian history. As I clarified, if my health is fine, I will try to explain and to provide resolutions to all the problems in order [to explain] our history, which is a proper history, [and] not for the purpose of serving any particular tendency. I am of the opinion that this Court has been unfair to me since the beginning because only certain facts are to be adjudicated by this Court. I must say *only the body of the crocodile is to be discussed [at this Court], not its head or the tail* … the root causes and its consequences are those that happened pre-1975 and post-1979 [but they] are ignored by this Court.[34]

This metaphor of the crocodile was repeatedly mobilised by civil parties during interviews, when they criticised the ECCC for not addressing the entire story of the conflict:

> This Court is only looking at one piece. As Nuon Chea mentioned, there are three pieces of a crocodile, but they only look at one piece only. It's injustice already. But I want to know about the Khmer Rouge, this is why I became a civil party. First, I want to know who created the Khmer Rouge? And then, from 1975 to 1979, why did they kill people when they had already defeated the Lon Nol regime? And then, after 1979, until 1990, a communist regime was established. Why didn't they introduce a democracy at that time when the war was already finished?[35]

> I cannot say that Nuon Chea wasn't responsible, but I think there were also other persons who were responsible, including our leaders today in Cambodia … I've attended a Case 002 hearing in Phnom Penh at the ECCC, and I saw Nuon Chea himself asking why did we cut the crocodile into pieces, and why do we only examine his body, and not his head or his tail? … When you try something in front of a Court, it has to be the full story, but I don't think that this tribunal speaks of the true story, it is not correct. Because history is A, but when the tribunal proceeds to it, it's B. It's different.[36]

The civil parties thus here side along with Nuon Chea, a former senior leader of the Khmer Rouge regime, in order to question the narrative which is told about the past at the ECCC. In mobilising Nuon Chea's metaphor of the crocodile, they debunk expectations that civil parties and the accused, i.e. two parties to the judicial

34 *Case of Nuon Chea et al*, 002/19-09-2007/ECCC/TC, Doc. E1/14.1, Transcript of Trial Proceedings, Trial Day 2, 22 November 2011, p 77.

35 Personal interview, civil party in Case 002 (male, age 57), 29 November 2014, Siem Reap, Cambodia.

36 Personal interview, civil party in Case 002 (male, age 61), 30 November 2014, Siem Reap, Cambodia.

proceedings at the ECCC which are opposed to each other in the courtroom, would not agree with one another.

This criticism of the court for not comprehensively dealing with the responsibilities for the Khmer Rouge regime, for not addressing the root causes of the conflict and producing a truncated version of history, is fuelled by allegations of political interference at the ECCC. Many civil parties which I interviewed indeed closely followed the contested Cases 003 and 004 and the refusal of high government officials to testify as witnesses in front of the ECCC. In doing so, they also scrutinise the role of the international community in the current transitional justice process and not just the Cambodian government or national ECCC officials. One Cambodian civil party lawyer indeed told me:

> Some want the witnesses working in the Cambodian government who were summoned by the court to testify and to be accused … They know that these government officials refused to do so, and so they ask why doesn't the court dare to call them? This is one of the questions which is really difficult to answer ... I then say that this is the policy related to Cambodia. But some of the civil parties cannot accept this because the court has the right and the power to summon witnesses to come to Court! But why does this Court, with the support from the UN, not dare to call and arrest them, and bring them to the court? So I say that this is the political problem in Cambodia, because this Court finds justice for you all but they don't want the Cambodian people to have problems again. Because the civil parties, they know that some or most of the high-ranking officials in the government right now are former Khmer Rouge. If this Court tried to summon them, maybe there would be problems, even if I cannot say war … But civil parties ask why did the UN, with UNTAC, come to Cambodia and dare to do everything for peace in Cambodia, and right now, when it's about finding justice for the people, why don't they dare the same way as before? I always explain that we cannot push the UN … the UN cannot bring troops of soldiers to come to Cambodia again, so the UN lets the court find justice and use their power to guarantee the proceeding of the court.[37]

In raising these political questions, I will argue below, civil parties are resisting the reduction of their role to orchestrated expressions of suffering.

Challenging the depoliticisation of victims at the ECCC

One national VSS staff noted that it was 'comfortable' for civil parties to resort to narratives of suffering under the Khmer Rouge:

> Civil parties, when they are asked to say A, they generally don't say [A], they just want to elaborate their stories … If you want to ask them: 'Please say something about your own experience in the courtroom, how do you feel?'

37 Personal interview, national civil party lawyer, 30 January 2014, Phnom Penh, Cambodia.

> Then, consistently, they just say a few words and they jump to their own story: 'When I lived under the Khmer Rouge, it was hard, it was difficult …'. … Why? Because their mentality has been fixed to the hardships, to the difficulties, to the problems […] because … That is their experience. Or maybe it is comfortable to say this, rather than [to speak of] a new experience in the court … they are too nervous to say something new, it is comfortable to say something that they know fluently … It's just easy to generate something from … you could say the store which is already in the warehouse, it's easier, they have a lot of information to produce from that.[38]

This observation shows that it is easier for civil parties to share their own experiences under the Khmer Rouge regime since they can indefinitely 'generate' public interventions on the basis of their subjective experiences. It however also alludes to the existence of standardised narratives on Democratic Kampuchea, which have been produced since the fall of the regime in 1979 and which can easily be mobilised. In her anthropological research on how survivors remember the Khmer Rouge regime, Sanders (2006) was struck by the collective aspect of their narratives. She analyses this as the standardisation of stories into 'catastrophe tales', i.e. the process of narrative construction around a few key themes (food, forced labour, the repressive regime of *Angkar*) through both remembrance and forgetting. She argues that this construction of standardised narratives serves the purpose of soothing both the audience and the narrator. It establishes safe narratives, which engage only with the narrator's '*mémoire ordinaire*', i.e. the ordinary memory which is conventionally expressed in stories related in everyday life, and thereby allows people to forget the sharpness of experiences stored in their '*mémoire profonde*' or deep memory (Sanders 2006: 10–11, 50–52).

During my fieldwork, I have also encountered the recurrence of 'meta-narratives' used by diverse respondent groups such as former Khmer Rouge cadres, government representatives and politicians, judges and rural Cambodians. The most striking example was that of the expression of 'three years, eight months and twenty days' (*bey chnam, brambey khae, maphei thngai*) used interchangeably as a synonym for the Khmer Rouge regime, notwithstanding whether this timeframe coincides or not with the actual experience of respondents who may have lived under the KR rule for longer. These expressions refer not only to the existence of psychological coping strategies in narrating the Khmer Rouge regime, as Sanders argues. They also demonstrate the salience of official discourses on the past, which can be easily and 'safely' mobilised in the context of Cambodia in order to speak of the past. Moving beyond such narratives, then, becomes an act of discursive resistance, through which civil parties of the Khmer Rouge regime resist the depoliticisation or dehistorisation of the analysis of the Khmer Rouge regime, but also the depoliticisation of their role as civil parties in the transitional justice process.

38 Personal interview, national VSS staff member, 3 February 2014, Phnom Penh, Cambodia.

Indeed, engaging with civil parties' political questions on the Khmer Rouge conflict and the analysis of the past produced at the ECCC shows that resorting to tales of suffering is not only a matter of 'comfortable' ways of speaking in public for civil parties, it also refers to what is they feel expected from them as victims participating at the ECCC. One civil party indeed told me that because he raised such questions and was not satisfied with simply narrating his experience of suffering under the Khmer Rouge regime, he was no longer invited to join regional civil party forums organised by the VSS:

> So when I participate in a [civil parties' forum], for instance the one in Kratie … I've protested and some [of the ECCC administrators] are not happy … I went to [the civil parties' forum] in Kampong Cham, I've always protested, saying that it's not the Khmers who executed the Khmers, the Khmers are intelligent too, they didn't kill the Khmer just on their own like that, it is because of external parties … But the ECCC administrators stopped me. They only want us to say who was killed amongst our family by the Khmer Rouge, that we are victims, how our life was as victims … [*Respondent shrugs his shoulders, raises his hands half-way up, his palms facing the ceiling*] They forced me not to speak of anything concerning Indochina, and so on … they only want me to speak of how I was tortured, who harmed me, that there wasn't enough food under the Khmer Rouge … [*Respondent laughs*][39]

Significantly, in two in-depth interviews with this civil party during which he shared his experience of the Khmer Rouge regime, he only referred to his biography as a background for understanding historical events and discussing the politics of the conflict. For instance, he did not once mention having been tortured, underlining herewith his interest, as a 'victim', in political discussions (who were the Khmer Rouge? what were the different factions amongst the Khmer Rouge? what was the role of foreign countries in the conflict?) rather than in sharing his biography told through the mere prism of suffering. Moreover, this respondent admitted that although he was in fact personally not interested in receiving any monetary compensation, he nonetheless had signed the petition for individual financial reparations in solidarity with the other civil parties. This suggests that notwithstanding the specific *act* of resistance – signing a petition – or its *visible aim* – claiming for individual, financial reparations – civil party resistance takes meaning in relation to the official victim subject positions that civil parties have to engage with and negotiate when participating in transitional justice processes.

Civil party resistance at the ECCC here thus becomes a form of resisting the reduction of the role of victims to the orchestrated expression of suffering under

39 Personal interview, civil party in Case 002 (male, age 57), 30 November 2014, Siem Reap, Cambodia. The selection of participants at civil parties' forums has since changed. It is co-managed by the lead co-lawyers and organised on a rotational basis.

the Khmer Rouge regime, i.e. the depoliticisation of victims in transitional justice processes through their relegation to a specific and regulated realm of pain and emotions, rather than their consideration as actors taking part in political and historically contextualised discussions of the past.

Conclusion

This chapter has engaged with civil party participation at the ECCC as a space for resistance and negotiation of the victim subject positions produced in transitional justice processes. Some civil parties participating in the state-sanctioned transitional justice process in Cambodia are indeed at the same time resisting the terms set by this process through discursive forms of resistance which may culminate in more visible forms of resistance such as public demonstrations and petitions.

This chapter has focused on two main themes of this civil parties' resistance to transitional justice in Cambodia: the exclusion of individual, financial reparations and the limited temporal jurisdiction of the ECCC. These case studies illustrate how civil parties resist from within, yet against the terms of transitional justice. Moving beyond the visibility of resisting acts and of claims of civil parties, this chapter has shown that to some civil parties, the meaning of resistance in civil party participation ultimately lies in the challenge it poses to one of the main roles reserved for victims in the transitional justice process, that of the orchestrated expression of suffering. Civil parties resist the depoliticisation of their participation in transitional justice; their resistance thus at the same time constitutes a claim for, and the enactment of, a higher degree of participation. Civil party resistance indeed creates spaces for the expression of dissent and the discussion of issues which exceed the terms set by the transitional justice process.

This analysis ultimately demonstrates the importance of allowing victims to 'speak back' to the analytical categories of transitional justice discourse and practice, and to the victim subject positions produced in transitional justice processes, as long as victims' participation remains limited to the implementation, rather than the design of transitional justice.

Bibliography

Bonacker, Thorsten. 2013. 'Global Victimhood: on the Charisma of the Victim in Transitional Justice Processes'. *World Political Science Review* 9(1): 97–129.

Brounéus, Karen. 2007. 'Truth-Telling as Talking Cure? Insecurity and Retraumatization in the Rwandan Gacaca Courts'. *Security Dialogue* 39(1): 55–76.

Brudholm, Thomas. 2008. *Resentment's Virtue: Jean Améry and the Refusal to Forgive.* Philadelphia: Temple University Press.

Ciorciari, John D, and Anne Heindel, eds. 2009. *On Trial: the Khmer Rouge Accountability Process.* Phnom Penh, Cambodia: Documentation Center of Cambodia.

———. 2014. *Hybrid Justice: The Extraordinary Chambers in the Courts of Cambodia.* Ann Arbor: The University of Michigan Press.

Appeal Judgement. Case of Kaing Guek Eav alias Duch, 001/18-07-2007/ECCC/SC. ECCC Doc No F28. ECCC [SCC].

Case 001 Judgement. Case of Kaing Guek Eav Alias Duch, 001/18-07-2007/ECCC/TC. ECCC Doc No E188. ECCC [TC].

Franzki, Hannah, and Maria Carolina Olarte. 2014. 'Understanding the Political Economy of Transitional Justice: A Critical Theory Perspective'. In *Transitional Justice Theories*, edited by Susanne Buckley-Zistel, Teresa Koloma Beck, Christian Braun, and Friederike Mieth, 201–21 73. New York: Routledge.

Hamber, Brandon, and Richard Wilson. 2002. 'Symbolic Closure Through Memory, Reparation and Revenge in Post-conflict Societies'. *Journal of Human Rights* 1(1): 35–53.

Hammarberg, Thomas. 2001. 'How the Khmer Rouge Tribunal Was Agreed'. *Searching for the Truth*, Khmer Version of the Magazine of the Documentation Center of Cambodia. www.d.dccam.org/Tribunal/Analysis/How_Khmer_Rouge_Tribunal.htm (last accessed 30 May 2017).

Heder, Steve, and Judy Ledgerwood, eds. 1996. *Propaganda, Politics, and Violence in Cambodia: Democratic Transition Under United Nations Peace-Keeping*. Armonk NY: M.E. Sharpe.

Hollander, Jocelyn A and Rachel L Einwohner. 2004. 'Conceptualizing Resistance'. *Sociological Forum* 19(4): 533–54.

Hughes, Caroline and Vanessa Pupavac. 2005. 'Framing Post-conflict Societies: An Analysis of the International Pathologisation of Cambodia and the Post-Yugoslav States'. *Third World Quarterly* 26(6): 873–99.

Jarvis, Helen and Tom Fawthrop. 2004. *Getting Away with Genocide? Elusive Justice and the Khmer Rouge Tribunal*. London: Pluto Press.

Kesselring, Rita. 2015. 'Experiences of Violence and the Formation of the Political: Embodied Memory and Victimhood in South Africa'. In *The Politics of Governance*, edited by Till Förster and Lucy Koechlin, 151–79. London: Routledge.

Kuch, Naren. 2014. 'Victims Stage Protest Outside Tribunal'. *The Cambodia Daily*, 18 October 2014. www.cambodiadaily.com/news/kr-victims-stage-protest-outside-tribunal-over-reparations-70257 (last accessed 30 March 2017).

Lambourne, Wendy. 2012. 'Outreach, Inreach and Civil Society Participation in Transitional Justice'. In *Critical Perspectives in Transitional Justice*, edited by Nicola Palmer, Phil Clark and Danielle Granville, 235–61. Cambridge: Intersentia.

Lefranc, Sandrine, Lilian Mathieu and Johanna Siméant. 2008. 'Les victimes écrivent leur Histoire'. *Raisons politiques* 30(2).

Lilja, Mona. 2013. *Resisting Gendered Norms: Civil Society, the Juridical and Political Space in Cambodia*. Farnham, UK: Ashgate Publishing.

Ly, Sok-Kheang. 2011. 'Reparation in Question'. DC-Cam's Report of Living Documents and Victim Participation Projects. www.cambodiatribunal.org/assets/pdf/reports/Reparation%20in%20Question.pdf (last accessed 30 March 2017).

MacGinty, Roger. 2012. 'Between Resistance and Compliance: Non-participation and the Liberal Peace'. *Journal of Intervention and Statebuilding* 6(2): 167–87.

Madlingozi, Tshepo. 2007. 'Good Victim, Bad Victim: Apartheid's Beneficiaries, Victims and the Struggle for Social Justice'. In *Law, Memory and the Legacy of Apartheid: Ten Years After Azapo V President of South Africa*, edited by Wessel Le Roux and Karin van Marle, 107–26. Pretoria: Pretoria University Law Press.

Mani, Rama. 2008. 'Editorial. Dilemmas of Expanding Transitional Justice, or Forging the Nexus Between Transitional Justice and Development'. *International Journal of Transitional Justice* 2(3): 253–65.

McEvoy, Kiean and Kirsten McConnachie. 2013. 'Victims and Transitional Justice: Voice, Agency and Blame'. *Social & Legal Studies* 22(4): 489–513.

Meister, Robert. 2002. 'Human Rights and the Politics of Victimhood'. *Ethics and International Affairs* 16(02): 91–108.

Mendeloff, David. 2004. 'Truth-seeking, Truth-telling, and Post-conflict Peacebuilding: Curb the Enthusiasm?' *International Studies Review* 6(3).

Miller, Zinaida. 2008. 'Effects of Invisibility: in Search of the "Economic" in Transitional Justice'. *The International Journal of Transitional Justice* 2(3): 266–91.

Mohan, Mahdev. 2009. 'The Paradox of Victim-centrism: Victim Participation at the Khmer Rouge Tribunal'. *International Criminal Law Review* 9(5): 733–75.

Moon, Claire. 2006. 'Narrating Political Reconciliation: Truth and Reconciliation in South Africa'. *Social & Legal Studies* 15(2): 257–75.

———. 2012. "Who'll Pay Reparations on My Soul? Compensation, Social Control and Social Suffering'. *Social & Legal Studies* 21(2): 187–99.

O'Toole, James. 2010. 'Reparations Remain a Key Issue'. 27 July 2010. www.phnompenhpost.com/national/reparations-remain-key-issue (last accessed 30 March 2017).

Pham, Phuong, Patrick Vinck, Mychelle Balthazard, and Sokhom Hean. 2011. 'After the First Trial: a Population-based Survey on Attitudes About Social Reconstruction and the Extraordinary Chambers in the Courts of Cambodia'. Human Rights Centre, University of California, Berkeley. http://hhi.harvard.edu/sites/default/files/publications/after-the-first-trial.pdf (last accessed 30 March 2017).

Pham, Phuong, Patrick Vinck, Mychelle Balthazard, Sokhom Hean, and Eric Stover. 2009. 'So We Will Never Forget: A Population-based Survey on Attitudes About Social Reconstruction and the ECCC'. Human Rights Centre, University of California, Berkeley. http://hhi.harvard.edu/sites/default/files/publications/so-we-will-never-forget.pdf (last accessed 30 May 2017).

Richer, Philippe. 2009. *Le Cambodge de 1945 à nos jours.* Paris: Presses de Sciences Po.

Robins, Simon. 2012. 'Transitional Justice as an Elite Discourse: Human Rights Practice Where the Global Meets the Local in Post-conflict Nepal'. *Critical Asian Studies* 44(1): 3–30.

Rubli, Sandra. 2012. 'Transitional Justice: Justice by Bureaucratic Means?' *swisspeace Working Paper* (4). www.swisspeace.ch/fileadmin/user_upload/Media/Publications/WP4_2012.pdf (last accessed 30 March 2017).

Sanders, Aafke. 2006. *The Evil Within. Genocide, Memory and Mythmaking in Cambodia: Master Thesis, Radboud University.*

Sperfeldt, Christoph. 2012. 'Collective Reparations at the Extraordinary Chambers in the Courts of Cambodia'. *International Criminal Law Review* 12(3): 457–90.

Stammel, Nadine, Sebastian Burchert, Sopheap Taing, Estelle Bockers, and Christine Knaevelsrud. 2010. 'The Survivors' Voices: Attitudes on the ECCC, the Former Khmer Rouge and Experiences with Civil Party Participation'. www.bzfo.de/images/stories/pdf/bzfo_cambodia_report_2010.pdf (last accessed 30 March 2017).

Thomas, Sarah and Terith Chy. 2009. 'Including the Survivors in the Tribunal Process'. In *On Trial: the Khmer Rouge Accountability Process*, edited by John D. Ciorciari and Anne Heindel, 214–93. Phnom Penh, Cambodia: Documentation Center of Cambodia.

White, Stuart. 2014. 'Anger Towards Khmer Rouge Tribunal'. *The Phnom Penh Post*, 18 October 2014. www.phnompenhpost.com/post-weekend/khmer-rouge-accused-pledge-boycott-trial (last accessed 30 March 2017).

Chapter 7

Multivocal resistance to transitional justice in post-genocide Cambodia

Kosal Path

Introduction

Resistance to foreign intervention in its internal affairs runs deep in the historical consciousness of the Cambodian people. After Cambodia gained independence from France in 1953, it enjoyed a brief period of peace and prosperity under Prince Sihanouk's royalist authoritarianism. After 1955, Cambodia was ruled by strong personalities and their respective visions of political order: Sihanouk (royalism), Lon Nol (republicanism), Pol Pot (ultra-socialism) and Hun Sen (authoritarianism) (Chandler 2008). Until the United Nations (UN)-sponsored general election in 1993, this nation had never experienced liberal democracy. The West expected this liberal peace experiment[1] to transition Cambodia from intra-state conflict to peace, the rule of law, democratic governance and economic development (Richmond and Franks 2008: 27–48).

However, this top-down approach overlooked the local dynamics of zero-sum power politics in the post-war period and, as a result, it fell victim to what political scientists call 'state capture', i.e. the elite hijacking of political transition and extraction of resources for power monopoly and private interests (Grzymala-Busse 2008: 638–73). How Prime Minister Hun Sen ruled Cambodia for the past 30 years, as Stéphanie Giry (2015) put it bluntly, takes a peculiar form of 'political chimera that is part vestigial communism, part crony capitalism, part neo-feudal paternalism and part divine-right monarchism' (Giry 2015: 144–59).

Such divergence from the liberal peace pathway after the 1993 UN-sponsored election cannot be fully understood without appreciating the local configurations of domestic politics and agency in this turbulent political transition. Transitional justice that officially began with the establishment of the Extraordinary Chambers in the Court of Cambodia (ECCC), commonly known as the Khmer Rouge Tribunal (KRT), in 2006, is yet another dose of UN-backed liberal peace expected to bring about genocide justice, truth recovery, reconciliation of genocide victims

1 A normative framework that foregrounds the United Nations Transitional Authority in Cambodia (UNTAC) institutional reforms in the areas of human rights, rule of law, democratization, and social rehabilitation and development in Cambodia in the early 1990s.

and the rule of law in Cambodia. However, as I will show below, the pathway and scope of transitional justice in post-genocide Cambodia was determined by the evolution of Cambodia's domestic politics in the second half of the 1990s.

To be sure, Cambodia's transitional justice model is a peculiar amalgamation of non-governmental organisations' (NGOs) initiatives at publicised documentation/ truth recovery after 1995 and genocide education after 2009, the state-sanctioned amnesty for and integration of former Khmer Rouge (KR) cadres after 1998 and the symbolic justice, i.e. the trials of a few top KR leaders by the UN-backed KRT. Just as the Hun Sen government's desire for a hybrid tribunal struck a chord with donors' funding fatigue and disappointment with rampant corruption on the Cambodian side (Brinkley 2013: 41–48), its assertive resistance to more trials in 2015 is implicitly tolerated by Western powers, leaving transnational human rights isolated in their quest for more trials beyond Case 001 and Case 002. Rather than a set of mechanisms put in motion by one dominant actor at one time, these mechanisms were borne in sequence out of a complex process of political negotiations between the Cambodian government and the UN, propelled by sustained advocacy of NGOs and civil society.

Notably, truth recovery and reconciliation in post-genocide Cambodia is largely a process driven by local civil society organisations of which the Documentation Center of Cambodia (DC-Cam), an NGO created by Yale University's Cambodian Genocide Program, has played the most outstanding role in sustaining its momentum over the past two decades. Since 1995, DC-Cam has documented, catalogued and publicised the KR atrocities, making an enormous contribution to truth recovery in the absence of an official truth commission. While DC-Cam, mostly run by Cambodian staff, have taken important initiatives to mobilise resources and funding support mostly from foreign donors, it has also worked hard to retain the necessary support of the Cambodian government, particularly the Office of the Prime Minister, the Council of Ministers, the Ministry of Interior, the Ministry of Education and the Ministry of Culture and Fine Arts, to expand its role to encompass KR history writing, genocide education, community dialogues and its grand establishment of the Sleuk Rith Institute to provide a permanent home for genocide memory, research and the study of genocide and human rights (Ciorciari and Ramji-Nogales 2012: 3; Dy 2015: 190–95). DC-Cam can function without government interference, as long as its work does not conflict with the Hun Sen government's 'win-win policy' of national reconciliation (Leang 2009),[2] which I will discuss in more detail below.

2 In reaction to DC-Cam Director Youk Chhang's remark quoted by a local newspaper as saying that 'they [the ECCC] should show motives to PM Hun Sen if they want to charge other KR leaders', Hun Sen lashed out at Youk Chhang on national television and warned him not to interfere in these additional cases. In his letter to Hun Sen on the same day, Chhang maintained that he never organized a seminar to push for additional charges on KR leaders.

Drawing on ethnographic observations, 126 interviews with former KR cadres and survivors and 30 interviews with their adult children conducted in five communes of the Anlong Veng district between April 2011 to March 2012 in the Anlong Veng region, a former KR stronghold, in combination with discourse analysis of publicly available texts and speeches by Prime Minister Hun Sen, this study demonstrates Cambodia's multilevel resistance to a Western emancipatory model of transitional justice in a broader context of liberal peace. This chapter advances a twofold argument. First, it argues that in the politics of negotiating transitional justice, Hun Sen's strategies are in accordance with the logic of hybridity – i.e. it did not amount to a direct offence against international justice promoted by the West, but rather, by emphasising the principle of state sovereignty and the sacred importance of peace, insisted on Cambodia's right to develop its own hybridised and localised version of transitional justice.

The peculiar form of transitional justice in Cambodia is the byproduct of the Hun Sen government's resistance to the Western model of transitional justice centred on a top-down, linear political transition from the culture of impunity to the rule of law and respect for human rights. At the national level, the Hun Sen government's prioritisation of the amnesty-for-peace deal with former KR cadres over genocide justice is largely driven by his conception of reconciliation and peace grounded in his own experience as a former KR cadre and Cambodia's political realities in the second half of the 1990s. The result is a minimal approach to transitional justice in the form of symbolic justice for that nation and minimum coexistence between survivors/victims and former KR cadres/perpetrators. To augment his consolidation of power against his rivals in the late 1990s, particularly the royalist party FUNCINPEC, Hun Sen's 1998 'win-win' national reconciliation policy struck an amnesty-for-peace deal with KR collaborators, and then coopted their leaders into his client–patron network by offering amnesty and full rights as citizens, material incentives and power in his government as an integral part of his peace plan. Hun Sen's resistance to the trials of Case 003 and Case 004 is illustrative of tilting toward peace at the expense of justice.

Secondly, at the local level, former KR communities' resistance manifested in the form of challenging the official narratives largely framed by the KRT temporal jurisdiction limit by discursively articulating their own narratives of 'shared victimhood' in a broader and more complex historical process dating back to the US-supported *coup* against Prince Sihanouk on 18 March 1970, followed by the US carpet bombing of Cambodia in the early 1970s. The narrative pattern that emerges for their personal and family story-telling are in accord with the state's discursive representation of 'we are all victims of the Pol Pot regime' that underlay the 1998 'win-win' policy.

Similarly, laying blame solely on the few top KR leaders for what happened during the KR regime, former KR cadres and their families produced and reproduced their personal and family narratives in the frameworks where Cambodian society today retrieves the past. Distancing themselves from the evil KR past, their narratives clearly paint a complex picture of social and historical forces that engulfed their lives before the KR revolution, one that appeals to the rehumanisation of their experiences, and lays claim to the notion that not all KR are perpetrators. In sum, their narratives are productive of the present social contexts to which they have to adapt socially for personal psychological well-being and family existence.

This chapter is divided into two sections. In the first section, I advance a post-colonial perspective on transitional justice as a theoretical and methodological alternative to delineate the friction between global transitional justice mechanisms and local realities in post-conflict societies. It demonstrates the agency and interests of the target state (Cambodia in this case) in hybridising and localising transitional justice mechanisms, and brings experiences and perspectives of local stakeholders to the centre of debate on transitional justice in the aftermath of war and genocide. The second section then turns to the ex-KR community's discursive narrative of 'victimhood' in tandem with 'heroisation' in the context of the 'win-win' policy.

Analytical framework: a post-colonial approach to transitional justice

Since the 1970s, the debates about transitional justice processes revolve around the relative efficacy of the three broad, overlapping categories: mechanisms of accountability (trials, truth commissions and lustration), victim-oriented restorative justice mechanisms (reparations, truth recovery and healing), and mechanisms of security and peace (amnesties, coexistence, integration of war factions and institutional reforms). As some transitional justice researchers attempt to develop a general theory of rebuilding state institutions in post-conflict societies (Olsen, Payne and Reiter 2010), others stress the importance of the reconstruction of social relations between communities and civil society and the incorporation of local agency and knowledge into the transitional justice process (Williams, Nagy and Ester 2012; Andrieu 2010: 537–58). There has been a growing body of scholarship showing friction/divergence between the top-down global transitional justice mechanisms and local realities, stressing the importance of rebuilding social relations at the locale (Hinton 2011a; Kent 2011: 434–55; Lundy and McGovern 2008: 265–92).

Similarly, in the case of Cambodia, researchers have increasingly explored the roles of the locale (Zucker 2013: 793–800; Ciorciari and Ramji-Nogales 2012: 1–5; McGrew 2011b; Gray 2014). Building on the insight of this critical approach to transitional justice, this study seeks to delineate a post-colonial framework for the analysis of resistance to transitional justice discourse in post-genocide Cambodia. A post-colonial approach entails three analytical tasks. First, it requires that Cambodia's transitional justice be contextualised in a broader temporal frame of Cambodia's political history, and that the experiences and perspectives of local stakeholders who are both the subjects and objects of transitional justice be the foci of its design. In doing so, it explores the origins and characteristics of Cambodia's peculiar transitional justice process from Cambodian perspectives, taking into consideration local political configurations and political elites' preferences.

Secondly, it lays claim to new sites of inquiry and fieldwork to study transitional justice at the locale. Epistemologically it requires an inquiry into bottom-up ethnographic and historical understandings of the local and, in so doing, can contribute to ontological reevaluation of key concepts, including justice, reconciliation and truth recovery, in light of different non-Western experiences. A post-colonial approach does not necessitate that we unambiguously establish the Cambodian situation at present as strictly speaking post-colonial. Rather, it can be drawn upon as an alternative approach to analyze the subjectivity and agency of local actors or stakeholders without being weighed down by the intellectual baggage of the dominant actors (Chakrabarty 2008; Chandra 2013: 479–91).

In this study, I draw on Bhabha's (2005) insight of how local natives 'hybridise and localise' the master's knowledge to deploy a range or forms of subversion and resistance. This 'guerilla type' of agency, as Kapoor (2003: 561–77) characterised it, is more effective than direct counter-hegemonic confrontation, which is more liable to cancellations and opposition by the dominant actors. Similarly, this study shows how local agents challenged dominant actors, carved out space and contested dominant narratives to advance their discourses of resistance to the Western liberal model of transitional justice at the national and communal levels.

In particular, this study demonstrates the ways in which Prime Minister Hun Sen, as a prolific master of client–patron politics throughout his political career (Gottesman 2003: 260–315, 311–15), used guerrilla-type resistance to shape the contour and processes of transitional justice in favour of his party's political interests and his vision of peace and reconciliation in post-genocide Cambodia. As his intimacy with the West increased over time, his strategies of subverting Western powers became more sophisticated, i.e. a combination of accommodation, cooption, blockage strategies and, sometimes, direct political interferences. As a result, transitional justice in actuality is neither Western nor Cambodian, but rather a practice that manifests itself in hybridisation and localisation whereby the Hun Sen government has proactive agency.

Hybridised and localised resistance to transitional justice

In 2006, the KRT, an internationalised court in Cambodia's judiciary system, is specifically intended to bring about a cluster of tangible liberal goods such as human dignity, justice, truth recovery and reconciliation, social repair and the rule of law. However, this hybrid tribunal's temporal jurisdiction is limited to the KR regime (1975–79), stripped out of Cambodia's turbulent political history and surrounding contexts of what happened before the KR regime. As the KRT is drawing to a close, the impact of this hybrid tribunal takes centre stage in the public and academic debate. Transitional justice practitioners and proponents of a hybrid trial such as the KRT are inclined to represent the KRT as a successful case in their transitional justice discourse, thus forging a sense of belonging to what Hinton (2014b, 10) called, 'transitional justice imaginary'. A much more modest outcome would be expected if we take into consideration a constellation of political factors surrounding its establishment and its justice process, including the Cambodian government's political interference in the KR trials.

Hun Sen's 1998 'win-win' policy

In retrospect, given Cambodia's domestic political circumstances in the 1990s, the transitional justice process in post-genocide Cambodia fell victim to state capture whereby the dominant political elites (Prime Minister Hun Sen and his ruling party) hybridised and localised Western liberal ideas, including peace-building, reconciliation and development, to promote their vision of transitional justice and their narrow political interests. The resultant transitional justice pathway in Cambodia is productive of the Hun Sen government's 1998 amnesty-for-peace deal with former KR cadres, which set the baseline for his negotiation with the UN and Western governments to establish the KRT. From the very beginning, the KRT was/is never purely about justice for the victims of the KR regime. Against the backdrop of mounting international criticisms of his regime's widespread human rights abuses in the aftermath of the July 1997 in-fighting and widespread chronic corruption, Hun Sen began to couple resistance with conformity, and in fact became more adept at framing his defiance in a way that resonates with the desire of the international community to see Cambodia's return to the path of liberal democracy.

In 2002–03, Hun Sen cooperated with the UN to establish the tribunal to try ageing KR leaders, hoping to shore up his regime's legitimacy (Un 2013: 783–92). McCargo (2011: 613–27) referred to the KRT as 'the play-within-a-play', which characterised the political drama between Hun Sen and the international community. There has never been any doubt that Hun Sen prioritised the hard-won peace, and therefore he will seek to control the court and its outcome (Murdoch 2014). The resistance to transitional justice, resembling Hun Sen's signaling of a return to liberal democracy after the July 1997 *coup* against his then arch-rival Prince Norodom Rannariddh, took the Western narrative of liberal peace as a reference point, yet emerged as a sophisticated subversion in the form of hybridity, a product of Hun Sen's increased intimacy with the pressure of the Western powers.

To understand the origins of Hun Sen's 'win-win' policy, one needs to closely examine Hun Sen's stratagem in his political-military struggle for domination in the years of 1995–1998 (Nem 2012). The KR desire to integrate into a newly elected royal government was cultivated long before the 1998 final integration, and its origins can be traced back to the time of implementing the Paris Peace Agreement in the early 1990s. After the first general election in 1993, while the new coalition government adopted national reconciliation and economic development, the Khmer Rouge hardliners pushed for continuous war and communist revolution, causing disillusion among the rank-and-file combatants and their families (ibid: 85). However, regional KR commanders were more aware of the war fatigue and the harsh living condition of their combatants. For instance, Yim Phanna, a former KR commander of Special Division 980 under Ta Mok and leader of the last mass defection to the government recalled the war fatigue and the aspiration for peace among his combatants (Dy and Dearing 2015: 115). By the mid-1990s, the KR suffered a series of military defeats and defections to the government, leaving Anlong Veng as the sole stronghold from which to continue its military struggle as the balance of force tilted in favour of the Royal Cambodian Armed Forces (RCAF) in 1994–95 (Nem 2012: 76–77).

By 1995, then-Second Prime Minister Hun Sen, who dominated the armed forces, succeeded in making local KR commanders realise that they could not achieve their political objectives through armed struggles as their hardline leaders believed. At the same time, Hun Sen saw the opportunity to implement his 'win-win' policy, which combined his 'divide and conquer' strategy with 'trust building' to chip one region after another from KR control (Nem 2012: 8). Central to the war termination process, Hun Sen and his military wing focused on four strategic regions, namely Oral, Malai, Samlot and Anlong Veng. In secrecy, he immediately put his policy to the test in Oral, where KR commander Keo Pung was a moderate who was tired of war. To entice Pung and to build trust, Hun Sen personally assured Pung the following: (1) physical safety (free from prosecution), (2) property, (3) full rights as citizens and jobs; and (4) government support to help all KR cadres earn their living (ibid: 104–10). The policy success dubbed as the 'win-win' policy affirmed his belief that this formula would help him to terminate the KR military and political movement (ibid: 111).

From 1995 to 1997, Anlong Veng remained the last KR stronghold. As soon as the Vietnamese withdrew their troops from Cambodia in 1989, the KR leadership viewed the Anlong Veng region as a strategic base for their military operation and its vast untapped land and timber as a supplementary source of food and revenue. In 1994, Pol Pot moved to Anlong Veng and set up his command centre on top of the Cardamom Mountain, appearing still as the figurehead of the movement (Wood 2009: 24). However, in reality, with 11 army divisions under his command, Ta Mok was the strongman who could wield power in this region. In the early 1990s, he wasted no time in turning Anlong Veng from a battleground jungle into a permanent home for his followers and a base to wage war against the government forces.[3] With huge funding from logging and trade with Thailand, Ta Mok oversaw the construction of roads, bridges, dams, water reservoirs, hospitals, schools (Dy and Dearing 2015: 48–49) and an administrative system of two districts (Trapeang Prasat and Anlong Veng), 11 communes and 60 villages in Anlong Veng; in 1996, the region was home to 5122 households with a total population of 22,466 people and covering 9200 square kilometers.[4]

3 Seng 1997.

4 Lun Seng's notebook. From 1986 to 1997, as head of Ta Mok's political school, he was entrusted to train all military officers in political ideology and military leadership.

As a leverage in future negotiation with the government, Ta Mok hoped to turn this region into an autonomous region stretching along the Thai–Cambodian border, build a self-reliance agriculture-based economy supplemented by logging money, and use the 11 KR army divisions under his command to harass the government forces. In early 1997, as the 1998 general election approached, the coalition government dominated by the Cambodian People's Party (CPP) and Front Uni National pour un Cambodge Indépendant, Neutre, Pacifique et Coopératif (FUNCINPEC) failed, and the deterioration of the relationship between First Prime Minister Norodom Rannaridh and Second Prime Minister Hun Sen became more acute. At the heart of this struggle for power between the two parties was the issue of military power.

From the CPP perspective, FUNCIPEC's strategy was to erode Hun Sen's control over the RCAF, as well as to secretly beef up its own military power to counter the CCP forces (Nem 2012: 153–62). The factional confrontation quickly worsened at all levels. In June, the CPP viewed the newly formed political-military alliance between FUNCIPEC and the Khmer Rouge hardliners as an existential threat to the CPP (ibid: 161). In late June 1997, Ta Mok struck a deal with FUNCIPEC, which sparked the 5–6 July fighting in Phnom Penh between forces loyal to First Prime Minister Prince Norodom Rannariddh and those loyal to the then Second Prime Minister Hun Sen in the coalition government. Rannaridh was ousted from power and his general Nhek Bun Chhay fled to ask for Ta Mok's help and refuge.

To the government, peace and gradual integration of former KR cadres and their families into the mainstream society is more important than truth recovery and legal justice. To end this civil war, as Hun Sen later recalled, the 'virtue of accommodation and concession' underlay his peace concept, and formed his three 'safety policies' bolstered by economic development as a cornerstone of his 'win-win' policy in 1998 (Hun Sen's Speech, 21 October 2006). His policy gave the defectors close to what they had ever dreamed of: (1) administrative autonomy; (2) land ownership; and (3) full rights as citizens and amnesty from any legal prosecution for their involvement during the KR regime. After 1998, leaders of KR defectors were given civilian and military posts in the Hun Sen government, while others were installed at the helm of local leadership to ensure local autonomy and security for a community of more than 20,000 former KR cadres.

Since 1998, the government has brought development to the region by improving infrastructure, including roads and bridges connecting to the prominent tourist city of Siem Reap, public services including schools and hospitals, and Buddhist monasteries. The Ministry of Tourism sought to create a sprawling museum complex to commemorate Hun Sen's 'win-win' policy, which ended the KR political and military movement in Anlong Veng. Since 2003, the government has asked for help from DC-Cam to develop a 'historical–tourist area or *dambon tescho pravoatesas*' in this region (Wood 2009: 15–16).

By preserving Ta Mok's legacy including bridges, dams, schools, hospitals and other infrastructure as historical sites, the government honors the spirit of the 'win-win' policy and allows the community to have a sense of belonging to the region (ibid: 14). However, as Long and Reeves (2009: 78–79) correctly observed:

> As places of interpretation and commemoration of the KR past, the sites in Anlong Veng revealed Hun Sen's strategy of 'reconciliation' and 'integration' plays out in an utter failure of interpretation and a complete surrender of moral responsibility for commemoration of the past to the exigencies of development and integration of Anlong Veng into the nation.

As a consequence of Hun Sen's 1998 'win-win' policy, coexistence without meaningful reconciliation between survivors/victims and former KR cadres/perpetrators in various communities is becoming permanent (McGrew 2011a, 514–21).

To Hun Sen and his CPP comrades, the Western powers' renewed interests after the UN-held general free and fair election in 1993 redeemed their sense of guilt for not only failing to intervene to prevent the mass killing by the KR regime, but also supporting the KR movement after the regime was toppled in 1979, and therefore their desire for retributive justice mechanisms reflects a neo-colonial attitude toward international justice in post-genocide Cambodia (Fawthrop and Jarvis 2004: 238). With his monopoly of power in the government in tact since 1979, Hun Sen and his CPP allies sought their involvement in and financial support for the KRT, and then devised guerrilla tactics including repetitive political interferences in the KRT to subvert the international justice process, and in time the Western interests in the court wore out and withdrew completely. As Gottesman (2003: 356) keenly observed: 'Cambodia's leaders have accepted a new political discourse, to be sure, but they do so only to the extent that it does not jeopardise their power. This strategic, self-serving adaptation has, in fact, been the hallmark of their rule since 1979'.

Therefore, Hun Sen's political inference in the justice process in post-genocide Cambodia is hardly surprising to anyone who has intimate knowledge of his personal investment in the 'win-win' policy from 1995 to 1998 to ensure that history would record him, not foreigners, as the terminator of the KR organisation (Nem 2012: 201–202). By design, the hybridity of the KRT entails that it is not a fixed court, but an internationalised one structured according to what Ciorciari and Heindel (2009: 72) called 'the balance of influence' between the national and international sides of the court. The involvement of the Ministry of Justice in hiring or firing the national staff of the court gives the Hun Sen government the power to shape the desired outcomes of the court by frequently directing the national side of the KRT affiliates and staff to toe the government line, thus causing the split along national/international lines.

At first, Hun Sen's proposal called for a full investigation of the three phases of Cambodia's civil wars from 1970 to 1998, beginning with the 1970–73 carpet bombings by US B-52s, which killed an estimated 500,000 people, through the KR regime 1975–79, and the overthrow of the KR in 1979–98. He said: 'The international community should not forgive and forget any periods for political gain'. However, on 22 January 1999, the UN Secretary General's special representative for human rights in Cambodia, Thomas Hammarberg, told Hun Sen that any UN-sponsored trial would exclusively cover the four years of KR rule, 1975–1979 (Billington and Paoli 1999: 50). At the donors' meeting in Japan in February when the Hun Sen government was seeking US$1.3 billion, Hun Sen, whose astute political pragmatism was notorious, accepted the temporal jurisdiction of the trials, and put forth his condition – i.e. only the top KR leaders were to be tried. Referring to the five surviving KR leaders, Nuon Chea (Brother No 2), Khieu Samphan (head of state), Kaing Guek Eav (S-21 director) and Ieng Sary (Foreign Affairs Minister) and his wife Ieng Thirith (Minister of Social Affairs), he told the public: 'Now that the fish [is] in our basket, we can decide how to cook it' (Billington and Paoli 1999: 52). To subvert the normative power of the West and their push for an international tribunal, he criticised Western governments, especially the US, for their lack of 'genuine morality' for supporting the KR movement in the 1980s while condemning the 1979 trials as show trials (ibid).

Emphasising the priority of maintaining 'peace and unity' first promoted by the 1991 Paris Peace Agreement and achieved by his 1998 'win-win' policy, Hun Sen adamantly resisted the international community's push for more trials beyond Case 001 and 002, and emphasised social rehabilitation and economic development as a way to reconnect former KR fighters and their families with the rest of the country. The Khmer concept of reconciliation, *ka phsas phsa,* literally means 'heal the wound (*phsas* as a verb) and reconnect the broken pieces (*phsa* as a verb)'. It suggests an end to political divisions, bringing former enemies back together and restoring national unity, and a process of healing, both individually and collectively as a nation. Only then can a nation heal and move on. Along this line, a renowned genocide researcher and survivor Youk Chhang (2010) referred to reconciliation as 'picking up all the little pieces and put[ting] them back together'. This implies that rebuilding a shattered society after wars and genocide requires social repair and rehabilitation at individual, community and national levels.

Hun Sen repeatedly referred to 1998 as a major turning point in Cambodia's political history because it was the first time when 'all corners of the country' were united under the control of one central government. In a meeting with the leaders of KR defectors Yim Phanna and Yim Pem, Hun Sen spoke of empathy with them because he was once a KR soldier; he remarked: 'They [the KR leaders] created war and dropped it on us. We are the ones suffering because of them. Let's work together for national reconciliation and unity' (Dy and Dearing 2015: 64). His empathy towards former KR cadres articulated in a discourse of 'We are all victims of wars created by the KR leaders', dispelled former KR cadres' fear of prosecution but, as I will discuss below, consequently became a standard narrative template for former KR cadres to construct their personal narratives, bleached of their personal responsibility.

A theory of justice, from a post-colonial perspective, must be grounded in local experiences and viewpoints of those who suffer the injustice, and account for the voices of the marginalised, the powerless and the vulnerable who cry out for recognition (Gray 2014: 85). Local understanding of justice in Cambodia is more complex than conventional transitional justice measures allow for, and greatly varies from survivors/victims to KR cadres/perpetrator groups. The Khmer term for justice is *Yuttethor*, which implies fairness, honesty and impartiality; this kind of justice is traditionally carried out by a monk or an elder in the local Wat (Buddhist temple). An important element of the Khmer conception of justice is rooted in the Buddhist concept of 'Dharma', which emphasises 'corrective action'. The punishment for transgression on Dharma would be a reincarnation into cockroaches in the next life (Diclklitch and Aditi 2010: 519). This notion of justice puts more emphasis on rebalancing 'Dharma' in life, and does not involve incarceration. In the case of perpetrators, it involves getting them back on the correct path. For survivors, 'truth telling' or 'knowing what happened to their lost loved ones' is more important than physical imprisonment of former KR leaders. It is more about personal closure than legal punishment.

For instance, in Anlong Veng where many former KR cadres were maimed during the wars, justice took the form of restoring their livelihood and integrating their families into mainstream society. Here survivors, laymen, village chiefs and civil society, with the support of the Cambodian government, have used cultural traditions, particularly Buddhism, to socialise and integrate former KR cadres and their families into society. The act of humanity here is seen not in terms of a Western notion of retributive justice, but rather through the prism of a Khmer Buddhist concept of '*pea rum ngoap duoy ka min chong pea* or vindictiveness is ended by non-vindictiveness'. Based on this Buddhist understanding, the KR vindictiveness cannot be ended by an act of vengeance, which tends to produce a cycle of revenge. At stake is the social-cultural rehabilitation of former KR cadres and their families and the reconnection of the broken pieces with the rest of the society.

Evidently, former KR cadres slowly returned to Buddhism, strangely enough through the generous acts of the survivors who moved to live in the community. Even by the KR mass defection in 1998, ex-KR cadres showed significant apathy toward Buddhism, a clear manifestation of the lingering effect of anti-Buddhism during the KR period (Harris 2013). In 1999, a year after the integration and the dissolution of the KR political and military organisation, there was only one Buddhist monastery or 'Wat', namely Wat Thlat in Anlong Veng. By 2011, there were 103 monks and 14 Buddhist monasteries, seven of which were built between 2005 and 2010. These monks provide religious services to a population of roughly 37,000 in Anlong Veng.

Over time, ex-KR and their families have returned to embrace Buddhism as part of their livelihood. As Saom Ronn, survivor and head of the Buddhist Committee in Anlong Veng put it, 'most of these monasteries are largely built by generous financial contributions from survivors who moved to live there after 1998 and monks who volunteered to provide services to former KR cadres and their families'.[5] In spite of the fact that apathy toward Buddhism and even grudges

5 Author's interview with Saom Ronn, head of the Buddhist congregation in Anlong Veng on 11 October 2011.

toward monks remain quite strong among the ex-KR population of Anlong Veng, Buddhist monasteries played an important role in integrating ex-KR community into society.[6] Monks are invited by ex-KR cadres to perform religious functions or traditional rituals such as funeral and wedding services for their children.

Phim,[7] who lost one of his legs to a landmine explosion during the civil war in the early 1990s, asserted in his narrative that he secretly worshiped Buddhism during the KR regime, which was considered reactionary.[8] On a typical rainy day during *Pchum Ben* (a Khmer tradition of paying homage to the dead) in October 2011, my research assistants and I went to the Buddhist temple in Srah Chhouk village, and we met Phim and his village chief Horm there by chance. Phim told us, 'I have rediscovered Buddhism', and opined that Buddhism would help rebuild his community and lead his people to 'do good things in life'.[9] The trend reveals that former KR cadres have slowly embraced Buddhism as an integral part of community building, and reconnecting with mainstream society.

Narratives of 'victims' and 'heroes'

In fact, truth recovery is expected to enable a process of national 'reconciliation', a term mentioned in the June 2003 agreement between the UN and the Royal Government of Cambodia to establish the KRT.[10] However, the KRT by design cannot provide the complete truths of what caused the Cambodian genocide because its temporal jurisdiction only covers the period 1975–79, and as Hinton (2014b: 7–17) pointed out, simply sheds light on 'a "truth" bleached of historical processes', skirting the factors that enabled the KR to rise to power. At the national level, two state-sanctioned discourses of narratives are at odds with each other. On the one hand, the most publicised memory of the KR genocide is actively reproduced in the genocide museums and memorial sites across the country and through the yearly celebration of the 'the Day of Liberation on January 7' and 'Anger Day' and so forth.

In sum, such commemoration demonises the KR and maintains the ruling CPP as the saviors. On the other hand, the 1998 'win-win' policy discursively recast a narrative of shared victimisation by the Pol Pot genocidal regime, which justifies collective amnesia for and empathy toward former KR cadres and their families. It is the latter, as I will show below, which becomes the frame for former KR cadres and their family to discursively represent their personal experiences and family

6 ibid.

7 Note that I use aliases to conceal the identity of interviewees in this chapter.

8 Bin Molyka's (author's research assistant) interview with Phim in Srah Chhouk village, Trapeang Prey commune, Anlong Veng district. Entry date: 31 August 2011.

9 ibid.

10 See Agreement Between the United Nations and the Royal Government of Cambodia Concerning the Prosecution Under Cambodian Law of Crimes Committed During the Period of Democratic Kampuchea, 6 June 2003.

histories, and to contest the official narratives emanating from the KRT temporal jurisdiction limited to the KR regime.

On the roles of narratives and how they are developed, Hunt (2010: 116) writes: 'As systems of personal knowledge, narratives involve the attempt to develop a coherent past, which involves over-emphasising the role of some events (memories) and under-emphasising others (memories that do not fit our current conceptions of ourselves)'. Narratives may or may not correspond to reality. It is important to stress that among the KR cadres I interviewed, some appeared to be perpetrators who intend to conceal their past wrongdoings forever. However, what is at stake here is that through their storytelling, they seek to resist the truncated narratives emanating from the KRT by traversing their personal experiences through the much broader historical contexts of the revolution, war and after the war from 1970 to 1998. KR cadres cast themselves as 'victims' not in a strict sense of the term, but rather in relation to their personal loss to the KR revolution and wars brought about by a cluster of social-political upheaval after the US supported *coup* against Prince Sihanouk, and the US carpet bombings of Cambodia in the early 1970s.

From 1979 to 1989, the war of resistance to Vietnam's occupation of Cambodia meant that another generation of the KR population, who are today between the age of 25 and 35 years old, spent their childhood in the mountain jungle. In ex-KR communities, such historical contexts are crucial in their storytelling and used as a starting point in their narration for a specific purpose of building notions of self-identity and bringing their narratives in line with Hun Sen's discourse of 'we are all victims of the Pol Pot regime' and the wars in his 1998 'win-win' policy. By reproducing 'victim' narratives modelled on the Hun Sen government's 'win-win' policy and by extension, in accordance with the government discourse of blaming just the top KR leadership for what happened, former KR cadres not only distance themselves from the public demonisation of the KR regime, in some way perpetuated by the KRT, but also implicitly demand public empathy towards their families.

Gleaned from 126 interviews with former KR cadres and survivors and 30 interviews with their adult children conducted in five communes of the Anlong Veng district between April 2011 to March 2012[11], a prevailing meta-narrative that emerges clearly resists the KRT's truncated temporal jurisdiction and the public tendency to demonise the KR as one evil group. In their story-telling, they kept pondering the apocalyptic social forces that caused the KR revolution. When asked why they joined the KR revolution in the early 1970s, responses ranged from 'I volunteered because Prince Sihanouk called on us to liberate the country from the US and its puppet regime led by [General] Lon Nol', 'the US bombings destroyed my village', to 'I had to join because all the young people had left my village to join the KR revolution'.[12] To them, these forces, including imperialism,

11 According to the Anlong Veng district census in 2012, out of a total population of 36,908, roughly 20,000 people are former KR cadres and their families. This indicates that nearly 40% of the population in this region are non-KR people who moved from the interior to settle here.

12 This is a consistent pattern of responses that emerge from all of my interviews with former KR cadres in Anlong Veng.

disruptive social upheaval and forceful revolution that dragged them into the abyss of the revolution and war after war, must be part of the collective memory.

For instance, Phim, recalled that soon after Lon Nol's *coup* against Prince Sihanouk took place in March 1970, in his village in Udong district (Kamphong Speu province), just some 20 kilometers from the capital Phnom Penh, all the young people were enthusiastic about joining the KR. Like him, most teenagers had no idea what communism meant or did to a society.[13] Pheap, who was in sixth grade at Chuon Nat junior high school, returned to his village in Kampong Siem district (Kampong Cham province) to join the KR revolution with his former teachers. In his account, he was a soldier on the front line at the Cambodian–Vietnamese border, and he was not allowed to return to his village to visit his parents. When the regime was about to fall, he returned to his village only to find that his parents had been killed for 'anti-revolutionary activities'.[14] He believes that local peasants who were oppressed before the KR regime tended to apply their power in excess during the KR regime.[15]

Si, who was a teenager in a children's mobile brigade and a daughter of a KR deputy chief of the village during the Pol Pot regime, recounted her family's fear for their lives when her father was charged with a crime against the revolution because someone reported to the village chief that her mother had stolen rice and chicken to eat at home. During the Pol Pot regime, all food belonged to the collective. She recalled:

> The KR security agents regularly checked our kitchen for any trace of rice or chicken. My father and mother were ordered to self-confess in the livelihood meeting.[16] Since then, we lived in fear of arrest because many people were arrested and transported away, and only their clothes returned to the village.[17]

Sitha, a former KR singer for her commune, spoke of her constant fear of being arrested in her line of work. She said,

> Obedience to the Angkar [KR upper echelon] authority is a must. Singing at various work sites is an important political task shrouded by dangers because

13 Bin Molyka's (research assistant) interview with Phim in Srah Chhouk village, Trapeang Prey commune, Anlong Veng district. Entry date: 31 August 2011. Phim became a KR soldier at the age of 17.

14 Bin Molyka's interview with Pheap in Srah Chhouk village, Trapeang Prey commune, Anlong Veng district. Entry date: 4 September 2011.

15 ibid.

16 During the KR regime, the regularized practice of criticism and self-criticism in the so called 'livelihood meetings' was a crucial component of the KR thought reform program to mould KR revolutionaries. Those who failed to refashion themselves in accordance with the KR ideology faced arrest and torture before their death.

17 Author's interview with Si in Thlat village, Thlat commune, Anlong Veng district. Entry date: 2 September 2011.

> it involved political ideology. I got a chill in my spine when I was once criticised for the incorrect use of words in my singing.[18]

Another female KR cadre Roeum, who became a KR chief of a sewing unit, spoke of terror and lack of food in her cooperative. In her narrative, each of the unit members including herself were given a daily quota of sewing 100 Khmer traditional skirts called *sarong*. If anyone in her unit could not complete the quota, she was heavily criticised in a criticism and self-criticism meeting held every evening.[19] 'Planting a kapok tree' or '*dam daem ko*', as Roeum recalled, became a common KR metaphor for silence of any criticism or reminding everyone to only mind their own business.[20] In summary, the former KR narrative discourse of 'I am a victim too', is deployed in accordance with the Hun Sen government's discourse of reconciliation in the 'win-win' policy.

However, in tandem with the 'victims' discourse is a common narrative of 'heroisation' within the ex-KR community and in family settings. At this level, resistance manifests itself in their denial of their individual responsibility and moral self-confrontation. Such narration serves the purpose of forging a coherent 'comradeship' collective identity for psychological health and in-group identity. In family settings, former KR cadres select and organise their personal memories along this hero–victim conundrum to build a coherent identity and family history and these memories have been transmitted to their children (Kanavou, Path and Doll 2015: 149–69). In the community, memory of comradeship, heroism and sacrifice for the country and foreign invaders, especially their 'liberation' of the country from the American imperialists and their heroic fight against their Vietnamese occupiers in the 1980s, is the most important bond that ties the entire community together. Although the lingering effects of the KR agrarian ideology of '*dam chenh choem* or agricultural farming–animal husbandry' mean that land is a crucial factor, which necessitated them to stay in Anlong Veng rather than move back to their birthplaces, the 'comradeship' collective identity in this community reproduced through narration over time serves as an important mechanism for coping with their trauma and avoiding moral self-confrontation with their individual responsibility.

The 'heroisation' narratives are widespread in intergenerational transmission of family history, during social gatherings and even at dining tables in this community. On a rare occasion, Cheng, who was a former KR commander and political commissar, invited me to a dinner at his house. As it turned out, several other former KR cadres were also invited to join that dinner. Half way through dinner,

18 Ngoeum Phally's (research assistant) interview with Sitha in Santepheap village, Anglong Veng Commune, Anlong Veng district. Entry date: 6 October 2011.

19 Author's interview with Roeum in Thlat village, That commune, Anlong Veng district. Entry date: 12 September 2011.

20 ibid.

the conversation turned from land grabbing by big private companies, a sharp price drop for their cassava, to the heroic fight during the war against the Vietnamese occupiers during the 1980s. When left sanctioned by the state, the narrative in their comfort zone, including family settings or social gatherings such as this, is filled with a strong sense of comradeship and soldierly heroism against their foreign foes, especially the Vietnamese occupiers in the 1980s, which reflects resistance to the temporal jurisdiction of the KRT, as well as the court's over-simplification of identity into the 'perpetrators–victims' dichotomy.

A small number of KR cadres did not shy away from their roles during the KR regime, but stopped short of admitting wrong doings. At the beginning of his story-telling, Chhoeun recounted his personal pride as a KR militiaman (notorious for their role in arrest and killing at the local level). When probing more into the killing, he shifted to his story of being a soldier who fought his entire life against domestic and foreign enemies.[21] In his narrative, he articulated his experience as a 'patriotic warrior'. Similarly, Sam recalled his heroic fight to liberate Phnom Penh from the Lon Nol regime on 17 April 1975, and later was appointed to lead a special force regiment in the KR navy.[22]

When asked about the contribution of the KRT to national reconciliation, Sam, who was brought by the KRT Office of Public Affairs to attend the KR trials in October 2010, opined that: 'Millions of US dollars could have been used to build roads, schools and hospitals'.[23] When asked about his experience at the Tuol Sleng Genocide Museum, he replied: 'Those bones and skulls were nothing more than the political propaganda staged by the Yuon [a derogative term for the Vietnamese]'.[24] Unlike Sam, some former KR cadres acknowledged that the mass killing took place during the KR regime, but put the blame on a small group of local officials. For instance, Rouen, who became a KR chief of a sewing unit at the age of 18, spoke of a common KR metaphor of '*dot oaykhluoch, roy oay chhao* or burning to scorch, stirring uncooked', referring to the subversion of the leadership's policy by radical local officials.[25]

Conclusion

In the politics of genocide justice, Hun Sen's resistance strategy was in accordance with the logic of hybridity – i.e. it did not amount to a direct offence against international justice promoted by the West, but rather, by emphasising the principle

21 Bin Molyka's interview with Chhoeung in Srah Chhouk village, Trapeang Prey commune, Anlong Veng district. Entry date: 1 October 2011.

22 Author's interview with Sam in Srah Chhouk village, Trapeang Prey commune, Anlong Veng district. Entry date: 2 October 2011.

23 ibid.

24 ibid.

25 Author's interview with Roeum in Thlat village, That commune, Anlong Veng district. Entry date 12 September 2011.

of state sovereignty and the sacred importance of peace modelled by the premise of the 1991 Paris Peace Agreement, insisted on Cambodia's right to develop a hybridised and localised formula of transitional justice. His discursive representation of the 1998 'win-win' policy as a 'peace building operation' modelled on the UN peace plan in the 1991 Paris Peace Agreement is indicative of the way in which post-colonial agency can subvert the normative power of the West in an indirect way.

The Hun Sen government did not openly resist nor cooperate with the West over the prosecution of the KR. He bowed to the West's demand to limit the temporal jurisdiction of the KRT to the Democratic Kampuchea period (1975–79), but used the limited subject matter scope of the KRT to subvert any attempt to expand the trial beyond Case 002 in order to safeguard his amnesty-for-peace deal with former KR cadres in his 1998 'win-win' policy. After the establishment of the KRT in 2006, the Hun Sen government's resistance to transitional justice takes the form of state capture whereby the Hun Sen government used guerrilla political tactics to shape the contour and outcomes of transitional justice in favour of his ruling party's narrow political interests. In former KR strongholds such as Anlong Veng, integrating former KR cadres/perpetrators into mainstream society through social reconstruction backed by economic development is more important than legal justice. At the community level, the narrative discourse of 'we are all victims of the Pol Pot regime' articulated in the 1998 'win-win' policy became a discursive template for former KR cadres to recast their personal narratives of 'victimhood' and 'heroisation', bleached of their individual responsibility and in denial of moral confrontation.

Bibliography

Andrieu, Kora. 2010. 'Civilizing Peacebuilding: Transitional Justice, Civil Society and the Liberal Paradigm'. *Security Dialogue* 41(5): 537–58.

Bhabha, Homi. [1994] 2005. *The Location of Culture*. London: Routledge Classics.

Billington Gail and Dino de Paoli. 1999. Interview with Samdech Hun Sen. 12 February 1999. 'Cambodian Prime Minister Seeks Reconciliation through Reconstruction'. *Executive Intelligence Review* 27(7): 50–55.

Brinkley, Joe. Sep./Oct.2013. 'Justice Squandered: Cambodia's Khmer Rouge Tribunal'. *World Affairs*. www.worldaffairsjournal.org/print/70861 (last accessed 30 March 2017).

Chakrabarty, Dipesh. 2008. *Provincializing Europe: Postcolonial Thought and Historical Difference*. Princeton, NJ: Princeton University Press.

Chandler, David. 2008. *A History of Cambodia*. 3rd Ed. London: Westview.

Chandra, Uday. 2013. 'The Case for a Postcolonial Approach to the Study of Politics'. *New Political Science* 35(3): 479–91.

Chhang Youk. 2010. Remarks at Stanford Graduate School of Business. April 22, 2010. www.gsb.stanford.edu/insights/youk-chhang-picking-pieces-cambodia (last accessed 30 March 2017).

Ciorciari, John and Jaya Ramji-Nogales. Sept. 2012. 'Lessons from the Cambodian Experience with Truth and Reconciliation'. *Buffalo Human Rights Law Review* 19: 193–216.

Ciorciari, John and Anne Heindel, eds. 2009. *On Trial: The Khmer Rouge Accountability Process*. Phnom Penh: The Documentation Center of Cambodia.

Diclklitch, Susan and Malik Aditi. 2010. 'Justice, Human Rights, and Reconciliation in Postconflict Cambodia'. *Human Rights Review* 11: 515–30.

Dy, Khamboly and Christopher Dearing. 2015. *A History of the Anlong Veng Community: The Final Stronghold of the Khmer Rouge Movement.* Phnom Penh: The Documentation Center of Cambodia, No. 22.

Dy, Khamboly. May 2015. 'Genocide Education in Cambodia: Local Initiatives, Global Connections'. PhD. diss., Rutgers University.

Fawthrop, Tom and Hem Jarvis. 2004. *Getting Away with Genocide? Elusive Justice and the Khmer Rouge Tribunal.* Ann Arbor, MI: Pluto Press.

Giry, Stéphanie. Sep./Oct. 2015. 'An Autopsy of Cambodia's election: How Hun Sen Rules'. *Foreign Affairs* 94(5): 144–59.

Gottesman, Evan. 2003. *Cambodia After the Khmer Rouge: Inside the Politics of National Building.* Chiang Mai, Thailand: Silkworm Books.

Gray, Tally. 2014. 'Justice and Transition in Cambodia, 1979–2014: Process, Meaning and Narrative'. PhD. diss., University of Westminster.

Grzymala-Busse, Anna. April–May 2008. 'Beyond Clientelism: Incumbent State Capture and State Formation'. *Comparative Political Studies* 41(4/5): 638–73.

Harris, Ian. 2013. *Buddhism in a Dark Age: Cambodian Monks under Pol Pot.* Honolulu: The University of Hawaii Press.

Hinton, Alexander, ed. 2011a. *Transitional Justice: Global Mechanisms and Local Realities after Genocide and Mass Violence.* New Brunswick, NJ: Rutgers University Press.

Hinton, Alexander. 2014b. 'Justice and Time at the Khmer Rouge Tribunal: In Memory of Vann Nath, Painter and S-21 Survivor'. *Genocide Studies and Prevention: An International Journal* 8(2): 7–17.

Hun Sen's Speech. 2006. At the Closing of Open Academic Forum Commemorating the Fifteen Anniversary of the Political Settlement on the Cambodian Conflict on 21 October 2006. www.yumpu.com/en/document/view/27526369/speech-at-the-closing-of-open-academic-forum-commemorating-/4 (last accessed 30 March 2017).

Hunt, Nigel. 2010. *Memory, War, and Trauma.* New York: Cambridge University Press.

Kanavou, Angeliki, Kosal Path, and Kathleen Doll. 2015. 'Breaking the Cycle of Repetition: The Cambodian across Generations in Anlong Veng'. Chapter 13 in *Breaking Intergenerational Cycles of Repetition: A Global Dialogue on Historical Trauma and Memory*, edited by Pumla Gobodo-Madikizela, 149–69. Leverkusen, Germany: Barbara Budrich Publishers.

Kapoor, Ian. 2003. 'Acting in a tight spot: Homi Bhabha's postcolonial politics'. *New Political Science* 25(4): 561–577.

Kent, Lia. 2011. 'Local Memory Practices in East Timor: Disrupting Transitional Justice Narratives'. *The International Journal of Transitional Justice* 5: 434–55.

Leang, Delux. 2009. 'Chhang Youk sent a clarification letter to Hun Sen'. Radio France Internationale. 8th September 2009.

Long, Colin and Keir Reeves. 2009. '"Dig a hole and bury the past in it": Reconciliation and heritage of genocide in Cambodia'. Chap. 5 in *Places of Pain and Shame: Dealing with 'Difficult Heritage',* edited by William Logan & Keir Reeves, 68–81. Abingdon UK: Routledge.

Lundy, Patricia and Mark McGovern. June 2008. 'Whose Justice? Rethinking Transitional Justice from the Bottom Up'. *Journal of Law and Society* 35(2): 265–92.

McCargo, Duncan. 2011. 'Politics by Other Means? The Virtual Trials of the Khmer Rouge Tribunal'. *International Affairs*, 87(3): 613–27.

McGrew, Laura. 2011a. 'Pathways to Reconciliation in Cambodia'. *Peace Review: A Journal of Social Justice* 23: 514–21.

McGrew, Laura. 2011b. 'Reconciliation in Cambodia: Victims and Perpetrators Living Together, Apart'. PhD diss., Coventry University.

Murdoch, Lindsay. 2014. 'Gareth Evans Slams Abbott Government's Dealings with Cambodia', Sydney Morning Herald, 1st March 2014.

Nem, Sowath. 2012. *Civil War Termination and the Source of Total Peace in Cambodia.* Phnom Penh, Cambodia: Reahoo.

Olsen, Tricia, Leigh Payne and Andrew Reiter. 2010. *Transitional Justice in Balance: Comparing Processes, Weighing Efficacy.* Washington D.C.: United States Institute of Peace Press.

Richmond, Oliver and Jason Franks. 2007. 'Liberal Hubris? Virtual Peace in Cambodia'. *Security Dialogue* 38(1): 27–48.

Un, Kheang. Nov. 2013. 'The Khmer Rouge Tribunal: A Politically Compromised Search for Justice'. *The Journal of Asian Studies* 72(4): 783–92.

Williams, Melissa, Rosmary Nagy and John Elster, eds. 2012. *Transitional Justice.* New York and London: New York University Press.

Wood, Timothy. 2009. 'Tracing the Last Breath: Movements in Anlong Veng'. PhD. diss, Rice University.

Zucker, Eve. Nov. 2013. 'Trauma and Its Aftermath: Local Configurations of Reconciliation in Cambodia and the Khmer Rouge Tribunal'. *The Journal of Asian Studies* 72(4): 793–800.

Chapter 8

Concluding reflections

Briony Jones and Julie Bernath

Studies of resistance have been characterised by a concern with struggles against inequalities, whether through organised collective action, the hidden daily choices of those who have been marginalised or proactive engagement and disruption of systems, processes and decision-making. The body of work on resistance is rich and has been developed by anthropologists, historians, geographers, political scientists and sociologists, among others. Transitional justice literature is also preoccupied with a series of questions: What counts as justice? For whom and for what do justice processes work? Who is marginalised and who empowered by such processes? What can be considered a legitimate process? Despite the clear connections between these themes there has been limited work bringing resistance and transitional justice together.

We argued in the introduction that this is a missed opportunity to understand more about the empirical unfolding of transitional justice, to look beyond the transitional justice process itself towards contexts that shape and are shaped by different perceptions of justice, and to contribute to the current debates about power and legitimacy as transitional justice processes are enacted. In addition, we have argued that a series of assumptions exist in transitional justice work about the motivations of actors considered to be 'deviant' in their behaviour vis-à-vis the goals and activities of transitional justice processes.

We have unpicked these assumptions throughout the preceding chapters and reflected on the subjective nature of resistance, the dynamic ways in which actors, contexts and histories interact, and shifted the analytical lens from 'deviancy' to 'resistance'. In this way, we have come to expect that which has previously been framed as the unexpected. Actors and actions that have been read as deviant from the starting point of transitional justice itself are in fact the expected empirical working out of a series of power relationships, contestations over legitimacy and manifestations of alternate visions of peace and justice.

Where to begin? Departing from 'the norm'

Research on transitional justice processes most often takes transitional justice itself as the starting point of the question/s being posed by the scholar, whether the purpose is to critique or to describe. In this way we have rich descriptions of processes, impact studies as well as scholarship which addresses what happens if we alter how we 'do' or 'think' transitional justice, for example if we take seriously an African transitional justice (Okello and others 2012), or a transitional justice from below (McEvoy and McGregor 2008; Shaw and Waldorf 2010). There is an impressive body of work on transitional justice, to which this book is certainly indebted. However, if transitional justice is our point of departure, this has both methodological and analytical consequences. It takes transitional justice as the norm, accepting its existence as a given, bounded and identifiable object ready for analysis, description and deconstruction. This necessarily frames the type of research which is carried out and the type of analysis which is done in terms of the relationship between whatever is being observed or examined as transitional justice itself. It restricts us in our ability to take transitional justice out of the equation, to ask whether it even exists at all beyond a set of mechanisms or actions we observe, and to wonder whether the purpose of these processes is justice at all.

This volume does not directly address these questions but it does refuse to take transitional justice as the norm and instead departs from the point of resistance. Each chapter, in a different way, is first and foremost interested in what we can learn from the acting, the framing and the denial of resistance. This is a different endeavour to one which seeks to identify a typology of resistance to transitional justice, or one which seeks to learn how transitional justice can be re-imagined and re-enacted in order to address such resistance. The assumption of each chapter is not in fact that acts of resistance are necessarily about transitional justice at all, or at least not in the ways which might be expected by those focused on deviancy from the process or taking transitional justice as the point of departure. With this approach, each chapter, and the volume as a unified whole, argues for the value of researching resistance for what it can tell us about context, power and legitimacy.

Coming back to those analytical insights later in this chapter we reflect here on the framing of the starting point in each chapter and what this means for the claims made by the authors. In the chapters on Côte d'Ivoire the two authors both aim to look beyond the transitional justice process itself in order to understand different forms of resistance. Because Fatogoma begins with the context of the country's history of violence he is able to read resistance as a manifestation of ongoing political violence and not only or even primarily as an opposition to the transitional justice process. Although such acts of resistance can be understood as directed at transitional justice, for example a boycott of the consultations of the Dialogue and Truth Commission, by starting with the acts rather than the supposed target of resistance they can be analysed in a way which places the contestations at the centre of the discussion rather than relegated to the position of by-product of a process which has not been understood or accepted by the pro-Gbagbo spoilers.

In a similar vein, Jones analyses interviews with these supposed spoilers in order to research their discursive strategies and the meaning which they give to their self-identification as resisters of transitional justice. If she were to start with the transitional justice process and work outwards, these actors would be categorised through their identities rendered relevant by the process, e.g. as pro-Gbagbo supporters. However, starting with the actors leaves open several analytical possibilities which can capture identities beyond that of spoilers.

Turning to the chapters on Burundi both authors tackle the complicated question of the participation–resistance dynamic. While literature on transitional justice might suggest that participation could be assumed to be the opposite of resistance, in fact we know from the work of resistance studies that we must go beyond such dichotomies in order to appreciate its many forms. This takes us beyond a concern with transitional justice outreach to create 'buy in' from the local population, which is what we get if we take transitional justice as the starting point, and towards questions about the boundaries around what is named as 'a transitional justice process'.

Rubli begins with the 'usual suspects' of the Burundian political elite, labelled as spoilers and seen as resisting the transitional justice process due to fears over prosecution and/or loss of political power. Through an exploration of a series of empirical 'moments' she unpicks the apparent contradictions in the simultaneous resistance and compliance of these actors. What we learn is that their actions, choices and motivations must be seen in a historical context, and similarly that a particular transitional justice process is not a singular phenomenon but rather a product of these different actions, choices and motivations. In this way, the resistance–compliance dichotomy breaks down. For Birantamije the actors selected for study are civil society actors participating in the process. Taking transitional justice as one kind of public policy rather than an exceptional point in time of a country's history he illustrates how attempts to create a new balance of power both inside and outside of this process creates resisters who mobilise inside the spaces afforded by the transitional justice process.

The chapters on Cambodia also tackle both the 'spoilers' and the 'participants' in the process. Bernath addresses victims as civil parties, the supposed beneficiaries of the process. By starting with their experiences and narratives, she is able to avoid the problems which come with starting with the process. If one takes transitional justice as a given, as the starting point, then the most pertinent questions around participation become how actors come to accept the good that is being offered to them. Lack of buy-in implies lack of understanding. However, taking the narratives and experiences of the civil parties as a starting point we learn much more about relevant context for the crimes which is not included in the transitional justice frame and we can see exposed the instrumentalisation of 'the victim' by transitional justice entrepreneurs. Read this way the question changes from being one of how beneficiaries can be convinced that they are such, to one of how the words and deeds of the beneficiaries deconstruct transitional justice processes.

Path in his chapter focuses on the Hun Sen Government and the former Khmer Rouge, analysed through the lens of post-colonialism. He examines aspects of the local Cambodian context and culture, which explain why and how multilevel forms of resistance to the transitional justice process play out. In this way, he is able to provide a foundation to his rejection of the common reading of resistance by spoilers in Cambodia, highlighting instead aspects of hybridisation and localisation which render simplistic dichotomies between the Government/population, Cambodians/Westerners meaningless.

Beginning with resistance rather than departing from the norm of transitional justice is both a methodological and analytical choice with both a methodological and analytical effect. The methodological choice is one which prioritises data co-constructed with actors most often cast as deviant who are not often the subjects of research on transitional justice. The methodological expectation is that this data will be rich and relevant to many of the pressing analytical questions being posed in the literature, or perhaps being side-stepped in the literature. In concrete terms this meant deliberately seeking out certain categories of actors to interview or observe, a purposive sampling approach with specific aims but indeed selective. This came with certain challenges which will be discussed further in the following section addressing the issue of interpretation. Analytically each author approaches the subject from the starting point of resistance and from this position looks towards transitional justice, cultural context, historical context or ongoing human rights violations among other aspects. The analysis moves outwards from this initial point on the basis that resistance constitutes a legitimate and fruitful object of enquiry, beyond being a side note in the central narrative of transitional justice. These points will be returned to as the chapter progresses.

Who interprets? The ethics of naming resistance to transitional justice

Our decision to conceptualise resistance as subjective, i.e. not to identify resistance but to ask what it means from different vantage points and in different contexts, is borne of our understanding of transitional justice as a political process in which one should in fact reasonably expect resistance. This is because the actors with which, towards which, and against which transitional justice processes work are agents able to manifest their agency (to a greater or lesser degree). The value of this approach is that we do not take a static norm/deviancy distinction for granted and we are able to start from the point of view not of the norm but of the resistance itself. As we have written this methodological and analytical choice played out in different ways in each of the case study chapters. What is common to them all is an ability to avoid the problem of seeing resistance everywhere, and to avoid the oppressed becoming trapped by the terms produced by the oppressor. If we ask what counts as resistance from a given vantage point this will produce a necessarily bounded understanding of which acts constitute resistance and which acts do not. Going beyond this, if we can incorporate the varied and perhaps contrasting subjective positions on resistance held by different actors, what becomes relevant is how they each understand resistance not how it may be defined from the position of the norm, in this case deviancy from transitional justice.

However, one of the questions which might understandably be posed by a subjective conceptualisation of resistance is how researchers can manage and give space to different interpretations of resistance, especially in contexts where the word 'resistance' may not be used at all by the interviewees. Is it still possible for the researcher to interpret the words of an actor as describing or labelling resistance without undermining the very methodological and analytical purposes of having chosen a subjective conceptualisation of resistance in the first place? The different case study chapters approach this issue in necessarily different ways, with the burden of interpretation either falling more towards the researcher or more towards the interviewee. We would characterise these differences as scholars grappling with the question of how to balance a subjective conceptualisation of resistance with a desire to say something purposeful with regard to the content of resistance in their case study examples.

In the case study chapters on Côte d'Ivoire Fatogoma and Jones write about actors labelled as 'spoilers' and understood as resisting transitional justice from many different vantage points, including self-identifying as resisters in many instances across both chapters. In this sense the relevance of the subjective conceptualisation of resistance is not so much a distinction between an act being defined as resistance or not by a given actor, but rather the meaning given to the label of resistance itself. For example, both national and international transitional justice advocates in Côte d'Ivoire label pro-Gbabgo supporters as deviant in their continued resistance towards the activities of the transitional justice process, be it boycotting the work of the Dialogue and Truth Commission or protesting outside of the International Criminal Court (ICC) and demanding the release of former President Laurent Gbagbo.

Whilst many of these actors also self-identify as resisters or claim for themselves the label of resistance for their acts they may mean something entirely different by using the term resistance than that implied by those who label them from afar. Fatogoma explores the ways in which the continuum of political violence shapes the timing and form of resistance, understanding the words of the interviewees as connecting the dots of resistance beyond the sole target of the transitional justice process. As the researcher, he did much of this interpretive work. In the case of Jones, she looks at the discursive strategies of resistance by a small sub-set of self-identified resisters, analysing their words as spoken to her and taking for granted the self-analysis of the interviewees before interpreting them as a whole collection of voices. In this way, these two chapters focus on acts agreed by different actors to be 'resistance' but analyse the meaning and content given to this term by the different actors themselves.

In the case study chapters on Burundi the burden of interpretation falls much more towards the researcher. Rubli in her work on the usual suspects of the political elite is focused on actors defined by others as resisters but who would not label themselves in this way. The interview material, unlike that of the chapter by Jones, for example, does not contain self-explanation of acts of resistance. However, this is where the interest lies in this chapter. Rubli selects particular moments in the transitional justice process, and contrasts the labelling of certain acts as resistance with the motivations ascribed by either the actors themselves or herself as a researcher. This requires in-depth researcher knowledge of the details of the political contexts in which these actors are manoeuvring.

Birantamije has a similar approach, analysing as he does civil society actors who are participating in 'making' the transitional justice process at the same time as they 'resist it'. Some of these actors identify more clearly with resistance as an idea and some are interpreted by the researcher as engaged in acts of resistance. In both chapters we can see clearly the responsibility of interpreting resistance when a subjective stance is taken. Speaking for the interviewees requires a certain level of knowledge of the context, a transparency about alternative interpretations and an acknowledgement of the limitations of what can be said about them or on their behalf.

The case study chapters on Cambodia also walk this difficult line when they analyse resistance as claimed by actors, as well as acts which are labelled resistance in ways which illuminate or obscure historical contexts or ongoing political machinations. Bernath unpicks moments of participation of civil parties and how their behaviour in the courtrooms of the ECCC may be understood as resistance, or not, linking this interplay with broader discussions over the nature of the 'good victim' and the power balance between lawyers, civil parties and what is often termed political interference. Path interviews the usual suspects of former Khmer Rouge cadres and positions their narratives of heroisation in contrast to the more prevalent discourses around 'victim victims' and spoilerism. The challenge here is to what extent their words can and should be taken at face value, and Path demonstrates that this methodological challenge can be addressed by not seeking to establish the veracity of actors' stories or claims, but in trying to understand where different actors' stories may diverge. The social, political, historical contexts in which an act comes to be defined as resistance can indeed tell us more than methods which seek to identify an act as resistance.

When operationalising research with a predetermined conceptual approach to resistance – that of a subjective act of labelling – it becomes too easy to see resistance everywhere, and to end up undermining the very purpose of such an approach by interpreting for the actors what their acts and their words mean. This is especially true when working in different language contexts, where the word 'resistance' may not be used or have a certain historical baggage which renders it problematic to use. Not all of the case study chapters focus on actors who self-identify as resisters or on contexts in which the word 'resistance' is used. This poses a dilemma for the work presented in this book. To some extent an approach which prioritises understanding what meaning is given to different acts by different actors can avoid a burden of interpretation question. However, when interviewees do not refer to resistance explicitly, a series of other aspects of researcher interpretation need to be employed. For example, proxies which allow the researcher to identify when an interviewee is engaged in a process of social labelling of resistance. They will bring to bear in-depth knowledge of context, of possible alternative interpretations and, even more importantly, will have to be open about how such an interpretation can be justified and the role that the interviewee and the researcher play in establishing a given interpretation.

A connected concern relates to the nature of the content of the research shared in this book. Each author writes about societies in which massive human rights violations of the past shape the research encounter, the identity of actors and the type of transitional justice process. Taking a subjective approach to resistance to transitional justice does raise ethical questions about the normative position researchers may or may not take on such crimes. Not being concerned in a methodological sense with the veracity of the stories of different actors, some accused of human rights abuses or other crimes, is not the same as being an apologist for these actors. This is an approach which has been taken by other scholars. In research on perpetrators of war crimes convicted by the International Criminal Tribunal for the Former Yugoslavia, Rauschenbach et al explain that: 'Our analysis does not require that we judge the perpetrators accounts as valid or invalid, true and false; we are simply interested in their subjective account of the events for which they are accused' (2016: 222).

Nonetheless, in this book a space is provided in which such opinions can be expressed and one cannot be naive about the possible implications. For example, one interviewee from Côte d'Ivoire explicitly stated a sense of relief that he was being listened to and a hope that this would lend support to his efforts to secure the release of former President Laurent Gbagbo from the ICC. It is a choice whether to continue to provide a space in which such words may be repeated or lent more credence. We have made a decision that our methodological approach, borne of our conceptual approach, seeks out, repeats and articulates varied voices, regardless of the veracity of the stories they tell us. This book is positioned clearly in terms of its assumption that there is more analytical value in understanding how such stories come to be expressed and framed and what differences between them can tell us of the politics of the empirical unfolding of transitional justice in these places at these times.

Who resists? A diversity of actors

This volume examines the resistance of a diversity of actors and illuminates the multiple standpoints from which transitional justice processes are perceived, shaped and experienced. This derives from the subjective approach of resistance which we have adopted. Asking what resistance means from different vantage points and in different contexts, we reflect upon the agency of, and the relationships between, the multiple actors involved in transitional justice processes. This collection of case study chapters analyses as actors of resistance those perceived as the 'usual suspects' of resistance in transitional justice, i.e. powerful spoilers who act in deviancy with regards to transitional justice processes, but also actors in subaltern positions who tend to dominate works in resistance studies.

In their case study chapters on Burundi and Cambodia, Rubli and Path both reflect upon the resistance of the 'usual suspects', i.e. the political elite which has secured access to state power today and has intimate connections with past or present sequences of human rights violations. Fatogoma and Jones also examine the resistance of those identified in the context of Côte d'Ivoire as the 'spoilers' of the transitional justice process, the supporters of the former President Laurent Gbagbo. Whilst they have lost access to state power, the pro-Gbagbo supporters continue to engage in wide-ranging forms of mobilisation both in Côte d'Ivoire, as Fatogoma describes, but also in the diaspora communities, such as the respondents from the Committee of Actions for Côte d'Ivoire–USA interviewed by Jones.

All of these chapters demonstrate the analytical value in studying resistance of those cast as 'spoilers' of transitional justice processes. In her case study of resistance by political decision-makers in Burundi, Rubli for instance shows how their motivations to resist transitional justice cannot be reduced to merely the attempt to avoid prosecution, but also include factors such as different understandings of justice and reconciliation and the ways in which political decisions are taken and policies implemented. In her case study of the discursive resistance of pro-Gbagbo supporters, Jones also argues that engaging with these actors allows us to understand how different grievances inform their resistance beyond that of the refusal to accept defeat and the responsibility for mass human rights violations, as is often suggested by external actors such as the UN.

In contrast to this set of actors, Birantamije and Bernath turn their analysis to actors who wield less power: civil society actors in Burundi and civil parties participating in the ECCC trials in Cambodia. Path also reflects upon the resistance of ordinary members of the former Khmer Rouge communities living in the Northwestern parts of Cambodia. The case study chapters of this book thus contribute to debunking the problematic binary of powerless resisters vs powerful oppressors, which shapes many works in resistance studies and problematically reduces and essentialises identities. They speak to recent ethnographic work which has shown that those who resist, especially when they engage in more direct and visible forms of resistance, may not necessarily feel that they are powerless or in a 'subordinate and silenced position' (Palmer 2014: 239). Birantamije for instance observes how resistance from civil society organisations in Burundi demonstrates that although these organisations do not wield enough power to directly influence the policy decisions of the government, they nonetheless act as actors invested with the legitimacy to contest these. Most importantly, through their analysis of different types of actors, these chapters together illustrate how resistance is embedded in 'multiple systems of hierarchy' whereby individuals may be 'simultaneously powerful and powerless within different systems' (Hollander and Einwohner 2004: 550; see also Bernath and Rubli 2016).

A connected assumption, which the case study chapters contribute to question, is the idea that resistance is mainly the response of 'local' actors facing international transitional justice interventions. This analytical focus on the local is central to the few studies of resistance in transitional justice scholarship (see e.g. Sriram 2012).

It also constitutes a key feature of works on hybridity in critical peace scholarship which not only perceive resistance as a necessary component in the interaction between local and international actors (Richmond 2010; Distler and Riese 2013), but attribute resistance in a static way to local actors only, in an opposition to external liberal peace agents (Jones 2016). In his model of the hybrid peace as a critique to the liberal peace for instance, MacGinty (2011: 84) defines resistance as the 'ability of *local* actors to ignore, resist and subvert the liberal peace'.

In contrast to such a local resistance vs international imposition binary, the authors propose a more complex analysis of actors. Whilst none of the chapters focuses on the potential resistance of international actors involved in transitional justice processes, as other scholars have (see Baaz and Lilja 2016), the authors nonetheless question in different ways the idea that resistance is mainly local, and merely a response to international actors and their interventions. Rubli for instance argues in the case of Burundi that the analysis that the decision-makers resist the implementation of the transitional justice provisions detailed in the Arusha Agreement because they perceive it as an international imposition is mainly one constructed by external observers to the process, rather than being held by the political elite itself.

In the case of Cambodia and the discussion on the political interference of Hun Sen's government in the ECCC, Path highlights that the role of 'Western powers' in the transitional justice process cannot be seen in disconnection from their previous involvement during the decades of conflict in Cambodia. Not only have they failed to intervene to prevent the mass atrocities committed by the Khmer Rouge regime, they have also supported the remaining Khmer Rouge factions after the regime fell in 1979. Whilst not legitimating the resistance from Hun Sen's government to a fair and transparent accountability process, Path's analysis does question simplistic assumptions on a local vs international binary, and demonstrates that in fact both international and national political actors are involved in a quest for legitimacy over whom history will record as having brought peace and justice to the Cambodian people.

The other case study chapters also propose a more detailed analysis of actors involved in resistance to transitional justice. Birantamije for instance reflects on how the resistance of one category of actors in Burundi, namely civil society organisations, targets the policies and discourses of another category of 'local' actors, the political elite in government. In her case study on Cambodia, Bernath suggests that the resistance of local actors, the civil parties at the ECCC, is directed against how they are treated not only by international but also by Cambodian transitional justice entrepreneurs. This book thus speaks to recent critical peace scholarship engaging with the notion of friction which moves beyond an international vs local dichotomy and suggests that global and local actors, or indeed a combination of both, may resist aspects of peacebuilding processes (Björkdahl and others 2016).

Finally, the case study chapters portray actors of resistance as dynamic and reflecting fluctuating positions over time, rather than constituting a homogeneous group of actors motivated by the monolithic purpose of blocking transitional justice processes. The case study chapters by Rubli and Path for instance look not only at different power configurations over time in Burundi and Cambodia respectively, but also examine the shifting discourses and positions of the political decision-makers. Rubli traces the evolving stances of members of the Burundian political elite from the adoption of transitional justice provisions in the Arusha Agreement in 2000 until the setting up of the Truth and Reconciliation Commission in 2014 and beyond. With regard to Cambodia, Path also demonstrates how the position of the Hun Sen government shifted throughout time from a clear focus on consolidating power until the finalisation of the 'win-win' policy in 1998, towards accommodating to a certain extent the demands for retributive justice from international powers in 2002–2003.

In her case study of civil parties' participation and resistance at the ECCC, Bernath then tells us how actors might use their agency very differently as some of them engage in resistance where others do not. She also highlights how actors might engage in the same forms of resistance for different purposes. Birantamije also examines in his chapter the diversity of civil society actors in Burundi, from grassroots organisations such as victim's associations to more formalised and professionalised coalitions such as the 'Group for Reflection on Transitional Justice'. He highlights how some civil society actors attempt to resist the ways in which the different ethnic communities in Burundi permeate into the sphere of civil society whilst others remain divided along these lines.

How do actors resist? Analysing multiple forms of resistance

As a whole, this collection of chapters illuminates the ways in which forms of resistance are 'shifting categories whose meanings are in constant flux' (Hoffman 1999: 680–81). Rather than attempting to outline a singular mode of resistance to transitional justice processes, the authors highlight the multiplicity of forms of resistances which take shape in relation to changing socio-political relations as well as localised aspects of the ways in which transitional justice processes constitute exercises of power. Drawing from interdisciplinary approaches to the study of resistance, the authors examine diverse forms of resistance rather than referring only to a single selection thereof. This includes collective or individual, organised or sporadic forms of resistance enacted in both public and private spaces.

Existing understandings of resistance to transitional justice often revolve around the notion of a refusal to act in ways supportive and enabling of transitional justice processes, or the explicit attempt to block these processes. In his chapter on Côte d'Ivoire, Fatogoma speaks to these approaches in locating resistance in the boycott of pro-Gbagbo supporters, as well as strategies of exclusions and withdrawal from the state-sanctioned transitional justice process. However, the authors in this collection also show that resistance cannot be understood only as a form of self-exclusion from a transitional justice process. They do so in two different ways. First, they challenge the idea that resistance to transitional justice excludes participation through different channels in these processes. Birantamije indeed unpicks the different ways in which civil society actors in Burundi resist the government-controlled transitional justice process through 'making' their own. In her case study chapter on civil party participation at the ECCC, Bernath also argues that civil parties' resistance constitutes at the same time a claim for, and the enactment of, a higher degree of participation. Rubli similarly breaks down the compliance–resistance dichotomy in demonstrating that Burundian political decision-makers do not resist transitional justice per se, but rather specific aspects of the entire process.

Secondly, when it comes to actors excluded from the state-sanctioned, formal transitional justice process, the authors show that resistance may in fact take the form of proposing concrete alternatives. Here, Fatogoma observes how Gbagbo's party and allies resist Ouattara's transitional justice model in formulating complex alternatives such as the 'Estates-General of the Republic' and even suggesting an extremely detailed structures and operational plans. With regards to Burundi, Birantamije similarly argues that an important aspect of the resistance of civil society organisations to the dominant government's approach on transitional justice consists in suggesting alternative policies on the basis of surveys and workshops that are communicated through press releases and memoranda.

Beyond resistance through participation or the proposal of alternatives, most of the authors focus on discursive forms of resistance. In her case study chapter on Côte d'Ivoire, Jones suggests that the analysis of the discursive strategies of resistance provides a particularly heuristic entry-point for accessing the 'meaning-making' and subjective positions of actors identified either by themselves or by observers as engaged in resistance. The analysis of discursive practices of resistance thus goes hand in hand with the subjective approach of resistance adopted by this book. Qualitative interviewing may then methodologically provide one of the ways to access these forms of discursive resistance. As Bernath has observed, research interviews themselves constitute spaces for the articulation of discursive forms of resistance as they both question and reproduce the dominant or more influential discourses of societies. It follows that researchers may become explicit addressees of the respondents' discursive struggles, especially when respondents themselves self-identify as resisters as in the case of Jones. As we have seen, this reinforces some of the difficult ethical questions discussed in the previous sections of this chapter.

Discursive forms of resistance revolve around the key analytical categories which participate in distributing legitimacy and resources in specific ways in transitional justice processes. Fatogoma for instance shows how the notion of the 'true victim' constitutes an important object of discursive forms of resistance across political divides in Côte d'Ivoire as each political camp attempts to promote 'their own victims' as the only legitimate ones in order to influence the direction of the transitional justice process. Discursive struggles around what constitutes a 'good victim' are also key in shaping the resistance of civil parties participating at the ECCC, as Bernath argues in her case study on Cambodia. Discursive forms of resistance will, however, always be shaped differently, according to the specific contexts in which they are deployed. This transpires from Jones' detailed analysis of the use of language by self-identified resisters in Côte d'Ivoire, which shows how previous rhetorics on resistance and revolution in the context of Côte d'Ivoire clearly shape the respondents' claims for legitimacy.

A final insight which emerges from this collection of chapters with regards to forms of resistance relates to the significance of the setting in which they take place. This is most explicit in Path's analysis of the discursive resistance of members of the former Khmer Rouge community in Cambodia. Indeed, he shows that whilst they embrace the discourse of shared victimisation in the public sphere, a discourse which is actively promoted by the Hun Sen government in accordance with its 'win-win' policy, former Khmer Rouge members share in addition to that a different discourse in the more private spheres of family settings or social gatherings in their own community. Path describes this as a discourse of 'heroisation'. A form of denial of individual responsibilities which participates in the avoidance of moral self-confrontation, this discourse mainly emerges in the 'comfort zones' of private settings. Here, Path's analysis speaks to works in resistance studies, and most prominently of Scott, who shows the importance for researchers to move beyond the 'public transcript' of formal, power-laden settings which tend to be 'inauthentic' in order to access the 'hidden transcript', i.e. the 'offstage speeches, gestures and practices that confirm, contradict or inflect what appears in the public transcript' (Scott 1990: 4–5).

This insight from resistance studies is particularly significant with regards to the study of transitional justice both because of the power-laden nature of institutionalised transitional justice mechanisms (Manning 2012: 229) and the limited spaces which are available for the public dissent and contestation of dominant discourses and practices in the contexts in which most transitional justice processes take place.

Rather than introducing a notion that there are 'separate spaces for power and resistance' (Moore 1998: 350–51), as Scott's binaries of onstage vs offstage might problematically suggest, the authors here illuminate the ways in which different forms of resistance play out in different spaces. This is indeed what we learn from Birantamije in his case study of civil society organisations in Burundi. He argues that civil society organisations, whilst producing a critique to power which 'remains hidden from the eyes of the dominant' and avoids open confrontations with authorities, gradually create the 'social spaces for a culture of dissent' through their resistance. Forms of resistance which remain hidden from the public sphere and the scrutiny of the powerful might still contribute to shaping the public space.

Concluding thoughts on what counts as resistance

The chapters in this volume have argued both individually and as a collection that if we take resistance seriously as an object of enquiry, and seek to understand its subjective dimensions, then we can learn more about the politics of the processes of transitional justice as an empirical phenomenon. This is a theme which is currently important for transitional justice scholars who are broadly seen as more critical in their approach, undertaking research on subjects such as power, agency and legitimacy.

What is clear from the case study chapters is that the process of labelling an act as resistance to transitional justice is shaped by many different factors, some more closely and others more loosely connected with the actual transitional justice process. When resistance is cast as deviancy from the norm of transitional justice – we think here of the spoilerism trope – then the assumed object of resistance is transitional justice itself and the assumed motivation is a lack of acceptance of the values contained within, and outcomes expected by, the transitional justice process. We have shown this not to be the case. In fact, a variety of different contexts, alternative understandings of justice, or ongoing human rights abuses or political violence may be more relevantly discussed than a simple 'pro' or 'anti' transitional justice stance. However, transitional justice processes cannot easily be separated from these other objects or determinants of resistance that we have identified. They are deeply embedded in them even if policy would sometimes suggest otherwise. The key point is that we should not start with transitional justice nor should we accept it explicitly or implicitly as the norm. This will always lead to the assumed good of transitional justice, with agency which falls outside of its frame cast as deviant spoilerism. This is not only a very partial way to understand the politics of how transitional justice unfolds empirically but is ethically dubious in the way it will silence certain voices and perspectives.

Following this, such a partial view will hinder transitional justice policy. It is not the purpose of this book to develop a series of policy points but it would be remiss to ignore entirely the practical ramifications of what we write here. The question of dividing between transitional justice supporters and spoilers is simplistic in analytical terms but it also has the effect of weakening the basis on which alternative options may be considered. As we have seen in the cases discussed here, policy suggestions or alternative understandings of peace and justice articulated by those who are labelled as spoilers, are only understood as a manifestation of spoiler behaviour. They are thus de facto discredited.

This may close off some alternative policy options 'tainted' by association, or blind policy-makers to the possibility of distinguishing between resistance which may be motivated and directed to the transitional justice process and resistance which may appear to be so but which is in fact shaped and informed by different contexts and factors. More nuanced knowledge of this kind could be fed into policy discussions about the possibilities and limitations of transitional justice policies, as well as a better understanding of how it is embedded in certain contexts which will necessarily affect how its work is understood by actors both within and outside of the process.

Such understanding and potential new ways of working are only possible if transitional justice advocates and processes avoid imposing a binary of power through explicitly or implicitly assuming a norm-deviancy distinction entirely informed by a transitional justice logic. The supposed beneficiaries may not consider themselves to be relatively less powerful recipients of the offerings of a specific transitional justice mechanism. They may instead understand themselves as at least equal in the dialogue over what counts as justice for them or for society as a whole. They may mobilise their agency without regard for how it will be received by transitional justice advocates or actors working to support a mechanism, but because it is theirs and they feel legitimised to do so. In the same way, the supposed spoilers may not understand themselves as actors who have definitively lost out from the process, but as actors with a stake in the future, able to offer alternative voices or to provide much needed commentary and challenge to the assumptions embedded in transitional justice as it unfolds in a given place at a given time.

Bibliography

Baaz, Mikael and Mona Lilja. 2016. 'Using International Criminal Law to Resist Transitional Justice: Legal Rupture in the Extraordinary Chambers in the Courts of Cambodia'. In *Resistance to Transitional Justice*, edited by Briony Jones and Thomas Brudholm. Special issue, *Conflict and Society: Advances in Research* 2: 142–59.

Bernath, Julie and Sandra Rubli. 2016. 'Adopting a Resistance Lens: an Exploration of Power and Legitimacy in Transitional Justice'. *Conflict and Society: Advances in Research* 2(1): 87–103.

Björkdahl, Annika, Kristine Höglund, Gearoid Millar, Jaïr van der Lijn, and Willemijn Verkoren, eds. 2016. *Peacebuilding and Friction: Global and Local Encounters in Post-conflict Societies.* London, New York: Routledge.

Distler, Werner and Sarah Riese. 2013. 'The Other Side of the Coin: Intervention and Resistance in Bosnia-Herzegovina and Kosovo'. *Zeitschrift für Friedens- und Konfliktforschung* 2: 177–208.

Hoffman, Diane. 1999. 'Turning Power Inside Out: Reflections on Resistance from the (Anthropological) Field'. *International Journal of Qualitative Studies in Education* 12(6): 671–87.

Hollander, Jocelyn A. and Rachel L. Einwohner. 2004. 'Conceptualizing Resistance'. *Sociological Forum* 19(4): 533–54.

Jones, Briony. 2016. 'Analyzing Resistance to Transitional Justice: What Can We Learn from Hybridity?' *Conflict and Society: Advances in Research* 2(1): 74–86.

MacGinty, Roger. 2011. *International Peacebuilding and Local Resistance.* Basingstoke: Palgrave Macmillan.

Manning, Peter. 2012. 'Legitimacy, Power and Memory at the ECCC'. In *Critical Perspectives in Transitional Justice*, edited by Nicola Palmer, Phil Clark and Danielle Granville, 217–33. Cambridge: Intersentia.

McEvoy, Kieran and Laura McGregor, eds. 2008. *Transitional Justice from Below: Grassroots Activism and the Struggle for Change.* Oxford, Portland: Hart Publishing.

Moore, Donald S. 1998. 'Subaltern Struggles and the Politics of Place: Remapping Resistance in Zimbabwe's Eastern Highlands'. *Cultural Anthropology* 13(3): 344–81.

Okello, Moses C., Chris Dolan, Undine Whande, Nokukhanja Mncwabe, Levis Onegi, and Stephen Oola, eds. 2012. *Where Law Meets Reality: Forging African Transitional Justice.* Cape Town: Pambazuka Press.

Palmer, Nicola. 2014. 'Re-examining Resistance in Post-genocide Rwanda'. *Journal of Eastern African Studies* 8(2): 231–45.

Rauschenbach, Mina, Christian Staerklé and Damien Scalia. 2016. 'Accused for Involvement in Collective Violence: the Discursive Reconstruction of Agency and Identity by Perpetrators of International Crimes'. *Political Psychology* 37(2): 219–35.

Richmond, Oliver. 2010. 'Resistance and the Post-liberal Peace'. *Millenium: Journal of International Studies* 38(3): 665–92.

Scott, James. 1990. *Domination and the Arts of Resistance: Hidden Transcripts.* New Haven/London: Yale University Press.

Shaw, Rosalind and Lars Waldorf, eds. 2010. *Localizing Transitional Justice: Interventions and Priorities After Mass Violence.* With the assistance of P. Hazan. Stanford, California: Stanford University Press.

Sriram, Chandra. 2012. 'Post-conflict Justice and Hybridity in Peacebuilding: Resistance or Cooptation?' In *Hybrid Forms of Peace: from Everyday Agency to Post-liberalism,* edited by Oliver Richmond and Audra Mitchell. Hampshire, England: Palgrave Macmillan.

Index

www.ingramcontent.com/pod-product-compliance
Ingram Content Group UK Ltd.
Pitfield, Milton Keynes, MK11 3LW, UK
UKHW011017180926
475701UK00004B/790

9780367232238